INSANITY

INSANITY
MURDER, MADNESS, AND THE LAW

Charles Patrick Ewing

UNIVERSITY PRESS

2008

OXFORD
UNIVERSITY PRESS

Oxford University Press, Inc., publishes works that further
Oxford University's objective of excellence
in research, scholarship, and education.

Oxford   New York
Auckland   Cape Town   Dar es Salaam   Hong Kong   Karachi
Kuala Lumpur   Madrid   Melbourne   Mexico City   Nairobi
New Delhi   Shanghai   Taipei   Toronto

With offices in
Argentina   Austria   Brazil   Chile   Czech Republic   France   Greece
Guatemala   Hungary   Italy   Japan   Poland   Portugal   Singapore
South Korea   Switzerland   Thailand   Turkey   Ukraine   Vietnam

Copyright © 2008 by Oxford University Press.

Published by Oxford University Press, Inc.
198 Madison Avenue, New York, New York 10016

www.oup.com

Oxford is a registered trademark of Oxford University Press

All rights reserved. No part of this publication may be reproduced,
stored in a retrieval system, or transmitted, in any form or by any means,
electronic, mechanical, photocopying, recording, or otherwise,
without the prior permission of Oxford University Press.

Library of Congress Cataloging-in-Publication Data

Ewing, Charles Patrick, 1949–
Insanity : murder, madness, and the law / Charles Patrick Ewing.
   p. cm.
Includes bibliographical references and index.
978-0-19-532613-0
1. Insanity (Law)—United States.   2. Insanity defense—United States   3. Mentally ill—Commitment
and detention—United States.   I. Title.
KF9242.E95 2008
345.73′04—dc22   2007051123

To My Family:
Sharon, Ben, Elaine, & Christopher

CONTENTS

Acknowledgments ix

Preface xi

Introduction xvii

1. Jacob Rubenstein 3
2. Robert Torsney 22
3. David Berkowitz 36
4. John Wayne Gacy, Jr. 51
5. Arthur Shawcross 64
6. Scott Panetti 81
7. Eric Smith 99
8. Andrew Goldstein 114
9. Eric Michael Clark 128
10. Andrea Yates 141

Epilogue 161

Notes 167

Index 185

ACKNOWLEDGMENTS

This book is the product of many minds.

Mariclaire Cloutier, executive editor at Oxford University Press, deserves special credit for reshaping my original proposal for this book. Though I wrote the book, it was largely her idea.

Andrea Ott, a law student and soon-to-be Ph.D. in philosophy, spent hundreds of hours diligently discovering, tracking down, and reading the cases, legal documents, transcripts, and other written materials that I used to write this book, and diplomatically dealing with difficult librarians and court clerks from around the country. Toward the end of the project, in order to complete her doctoral dissertation, Andrea grudgingly turned the job over to her self-selected successor, Laura Scheestel, who had a hard act to follow. Laura not only continued Andrea's research but read the manuscript and made valuable suggestions for changes.

As always, the help of Susan Martin, administrative assistant at the University at Buffalo Law School, has been invaluable. Among the many ways Sue helped with this book was gathering and supervising a team of students who spent untold hours transferring thousands of pages of court transcripts into a form I could read.

Elaine Harris Ewing also deserves my thanks (and those of the readers) for many hours spent reviewing drafts of the manuscript and suggesting important changes that significantly improved the book.

Last, but not in any way least, as always, Dr. Sharon Harris-Ewing deserves major credit for everything I do, at least anything that is good.

PREFACE

When I arrived in Buffalo in 1983 as a young forensic psychologist and law professor, I was surprised to learn from colleagues that the insanity defense was rarely, if ever, used locally. "No jury would ever acquit anyone by reason of insanity," I was told repeatedly. It took awhile, but eventually I learned why this defense was held in such low esteem in Western New York. "Fitzsimmons," I heard again and again from criminal defense attorneys, who would sigh and shake their heads as if they had just uttered the name of a recently departed friend or relative.

But George Fitzsimmons was no friend to the legal system (especially the defense bar) and really not much of a relative. After dropping out of college and undergoing on-and-off psychiatric treatment for years, in 1969 the 30-year-old Fitzsimmons karate-chopped his parents to death in the town of Amherst, the Buffalo suburb where I have lived for almost a quarter-century.

Fitzsimmons pleaded not guilty by reason of insanity, and there followed the almost inevitable battle of the experts. Three local psychiatrists testified that Fitzsimmons was insane when he killed his parents. The defense witnesses described Fitzsimmons as delusional, grandiose, and bizarre, and diagnosed him as suffering from paranoid schizophrenia. His mental illness, they testified, had "deep roots [in] his parents' tight discipline, excessive demands and high expectations."[1]

The sole psychiatrist who testified for the prosecution said Fitzsimmons had "fabricated" much of what he told the various doctors.[2] While this psychiatrist found Fitzsimmons to have a "paranoid personality," he insisted that the defendant was sane because he "perceived the act was wrong and that he would be held culpable . . . "[3]

Fitzsimmons waived a jury trial, so the evidence was weighed by a single trier of fact. On May 22, 1970, Judge Charles J. Gaughen announced his verdict. The judge found that "at the time of acts charged in the indictment [Fitzsimmons] was suffering from a mental disease and mental defect . . . so as not to be responsible for the acts alleged . . . "[4] In view of his verdict, Gaughen ordered Fitzsimmons "committed to the Commissioner of Mental Hygiene, to be placed in an appropriate institution and there to be so held until [he] has recovered sufficiently from such mental disease or defect as to be no longer a danger to himself or to others . . . "[5]

As if the verdict had not generated enough controversy, another judge added fuel to the fire of public outrage when he ruled that, despite having killed both his parents, Fitzsimmons was entitled to their entire estate, some $125,000. As the Surrogate Court judge explained, the court had no choice in the matter since because Fitzsimmons was the only heir, had been acquitted, and thus was not subject to a state law prohibiting a convicted killer from inheriting the property of his victim.

Less than 3 years after Fitzsimmons's acquittal, a third judge would enter the case and he, too, would have little if any discretion in the matter. In 1973, after Fitzsimmons had spent only 34 months at what was then the Buffalo State Hospital, psychiatrists there petitioned the court to release him. Based upon Fitzsimmons's "record of excellent behavior" and his evident ability to "readjust to the community," 4 psychiatrists testified that he was "no longer any danger to himself or others."[6]

Faced with this unanimous and uncontroverted conclusion—and a law requiring an insanity acquittee to be discharged from custody once he no longer posed a danger to self or others—Judge Joseph A. Nevins was all but obliged to order Fitzsimmons released. Nevins ordered Fitzsimmons released under supervision of the Office of Mental Hygiene for 5 years on the condition that "he maintain himself in a state without danger to himself or to others."[7]

As early as 3 months after Fitzsimmons was released from the state hospital, he began to demonstrate signs of dangerousness. Fitzsimmons became romantically involved with a fellow patient who had also been released from Buffalo State Hospital, struck her in an act of domestic violence, and "inflicted a small wound on [her] head."[8] Hospital officials were made aware of the assault but dismissed it. Soon thereafter, when Fitzsimmons "talked of moving away," his supervising psychiatrist wrote, "There was nothing I could do to interfere."[9]

In July 1973, Fitzsimmons married his hospital sweetheart. While the newlyweds pondered buying a mobile home, Fitzsimmons's aunt and uncle, DeAlton and Euphresia Nichols, both 80-year-olds, offered the couple a place to stay in their Northern Pennsylvania home. Fitzsimmons and his bride accepted the Nichols's offer and moved in, but just 8 weeks into the marriage Fitzsimmons again assaulted his wife—this time seriously.

During an argument, Fitzsimmons choked his wife until she nearly blacked out, and then beat her about the face, head, ear, and arm. Mrs. Fitzsimmons suffered numerous facial injuries including a broken nose and was taken via ambulance to a nearby hospital emergency room. Although Fitzsimmons disputed his wife's account of the incident, he was arrested and arraigned on charges of aggravated assault and battery. Euphresia Nichols posted bail in the amount of $3500 and secured her nephew's release, but Fitzsimmons's freedom was short-lived. When a local mental health official expressed concern that Fitzsimmons might do further harm to his wife, police arrested him again, he was taken before another judge, and bail was increased to $20,000. Unable to make bail in that amount, Fitzsimmons was jailed to await trial.

When trial commenced about 2 months after the assault, Fitzsimmons's wife refused to testify and, under Pennsylvania law, could not be forced to do so. The jury heard testimony from medical personnel and witnesses who had heard the assault, but in the end the evidence fell short. The jury acquitted Fitzsimmons of felony assault, finding him guilty of only misdemeanor assault. When the judge lowered the bail back to $3500, Mr. and Mrs. Nichols again posted the required funds and Fitzsimmons was released to the community to await sentencing. Officials at Buffalo State Hospital were notified of Fitzsimmons's legal status, but declined to take any action:

> Dr. Stanley Plattman responded on behalf of the institution. He said Buffalo State could do nothing because it was the court's responsibility to revoke conditional releases from mental hospitals. Plattman added that Fitzsimmons was untouchable under New York State law anyhow, since he had left the state and taken up residence in Pennsylvania.[10]

Fitzsimmons's minor assault conviction became largely moot when, as he was awaiting sentencing, he killed his aunt and uncle. On November 13, 1973, Fitzsimmons stabbed Euphresia Nichols 11 times and DeAlton Nichols 23 times in an argument over a television program. Following the homicides, Fitzsimmons fled to New York, where he was taken into custody end and eventually extradited to Pennsylvania. Using money in a trust fund from his parents' estate, Fitzsimmons hired the nationally known criminal defense attorney, F. Lee Bailey.

Bailey served as co-counsel with Herbert Siegel, a top-flight Buffalo trial lawyer who had defended Fitzsimmons in his first murder trial. Fitzsimmons's second murder trial would last roughly a year and a half, delayed at times by concerns that he was not competent to stand trial—in other words was, by reason of mental illness, unable to understand the nature of the charges against him or to assist in his own defense. Bailey and Siegel had little choice but to present an insanity defense, despite Pennsylvania's strict adherence to an insanity standard first articulated in England in 1843 in *M'Naghten's Case:*

> In order for insanity to be a legal defense to the commission of a crime there must be such a perverted and deranged condition of the moral faculties that the defendant, at the time of the commission of the crime, was deprived of his memory and understanding and was unable to comprehend the nature of his action, and to distinguish between moral good and evil, or, as is more often stated, "to distinguish between right and wrong" in reference to the particular act in question.[11]

Not surprisingly, psychiatrists testifying for the defense said Fitzsimmons was insane while whereas those testifying for the prosecution disagreed. In the final analysis, the jury was unconvinced by Fitzsimmons's defense. They found him guilty of 2 counts of murder and the court sentenced him to serve the rest of his natural life in a state penitentiary. Although Fitzsimmons was the sole heir named in the wills of DeAlton and Euphresia Nichols, this time he was unable to inherit from those he had killed. Pennsylvania's Slayer's Act prohibited a convicted killer from inheriting the estate of his victim.

As might be expected even in the 1970s, before round-the-clock cable news coverage, the media in Western New York, Northern Pennsylvania, and nationally had a field day with the Fitzsimmons case and probably did more than any other entity involved to shape the public's negative opinion of the case and people's growing revulsion toward the insanity defense. One newspaper article, headlined "George Fitzsimmons: Buffalo's Ripper" was typical and helps explain the bias against the insanity defense that exists in Buffalo to this day:

> Just drop George Fitzsimmons' name in Buffalo.
>
> The reaction is akin to mentioning the Strangler case in Boston, or that Ripper fellow in London.
>
> George Fitzsimmons is a household word.
>
> A Buffalo cabbie suggested he ought to be executed in a manner defying detailed explanation in [a] family newspaper.
>
> "I'm glad Pennsylvania has him this time," said the elevator operator in the Erie County, N.Y., courthouse.[12]

Unfortunately, many people believed and apparently still believe that the Fitzsimmons case is typical of what happens when a mentally ill offender commits a serious crime such as murder. In Buffalo, as in many other communities, the insanity defense is treated with great skepticism if not distrust, and when it is offered it rarely succeeds. Not long ago, the Erie County district attorney, Buffalo's Frank J. Clark, put it this way: "Snowstorms in August will occur more frequently than the insanity defense is successful."[13] And, asked if the insanity defense was dead in Buffalo, John R. Nuchereno, one of the area's premier trial attorneys who has presented many insanity defenses, said, "It's not dead, but its heart beats very weakly."[14]

Though there have been a small number of successful insanity defenses in the Buffalo area since the Fitzsimmons debacle, almost all of them have been the result of a stipulation between the prosecutor and the defense attorney; both lawyers and their psychological experts agree that the defendant is insane, a jury trial is waived, and the case is placed before a judge who "finds" the defendant insane and orders him or her committed to a state forensic mental hospital. Interestingly, but perhaps not surprisingly, most if not all of these stipulated insanity verdicts have involved intrafamilial homicides—cases in which the mentally ill killer is a close relative of the victim.

But it is not just bias in the media and among the public that keeps the insanity defense from rarely succeeding here or elsewhere. The legal standards for judging insanity are, as they ought to be, extremely strict and demanding. Over the course of 30 years as a forensic psychologist, I have examined criminal defendants for possible insanity defenses not only in Buffalo but nationally, from New Hampshire to Hawaii. Out of the many hundreds of defendants I have examined for this purpose, I can count on 2 hands, give or take, the number I found actually met the legal standard for insanity.

Then there are the legal consequences of a successful insanity plea. For almost 25 years I have taught fledgling lawyers about the insanity defense and have told them all, only half-jokingly, that "You have to be crazy to plead insanity."

Why? First, because the legal standard in every state requires that the defendant be mentally disabled or mentally ill. But, second, and often forgotten by zealous attorneys, is what happens to a defendant who is actually found insane. George Fitzsimmons walked away, almost completely free, after less than 3 years of inpatient psychiatric treatment. Contrary to popular view, that result was so rare as to be almost unheard of, both here in Buffalo and across the United States.

For more than 2 decades I have conducted the vast majority of the court-ordered independent forensic examinations of patients who were acquitted by reason of insanity and hospitalized in Western New York. In every one of several hundred cases, the state has argued strenuously that the insanity acquittee needs more treatment or more limitations on his or her freedom, no matter what the patient's current mental condition, degree of dangerousness, or the length of time since his or her crime was committed. Most of the time I agree with the state's position, but even when I strongly disagree and say so in writing and in courtroom testimony, it makes little difference. People who kill others and successfully plead insanity are rarely if ever released from confinement. And, in those few cases in which they are given their freedom, it comes hedged with multiple conditions—strict limitations with which they will be saddled for the rest of their lives.

In this book, I examine 10 high-profile cases in which people charged with murder have pleaded insanity. These are not my own cases, but, except for the notoriety they have generated, most of them are not unlike the cases I and my forensic psychological colleagues throughout the country handle on a routine basis. My hope is to educate not only students and interested lay readers but also the mental health experts, lawyers, judges, and other professionals who work on these sorts of cases—in part, to dispel some of the myths about the insanity defense that have been engendered by cases like that of George Fitzsimmons.

INTRODUCTION

Anglo-American jurisprudence, in nearly all jurisdictions, includes what is commonly referred to as the insanity defense. The insanity defense is probably the most controversial doctrine in criminal law. When used successfully—a rare occurrence in American law—a defendant who has clearly committed a criminal act, even one as heinous as murder, is deemed not guilty and may not be punished. To be sure, such defendants are almost invariably required to undergo mental heath treatment and deprived of their freedom during such treatment. Indeed, defendants found not guilty by reason of insanity are frequently confined by the state for periods much longer than the sentences they might have received had they been found guilty of the crime charged.

Defenders of the insanity defense note, correctly, that this doctrine is fundamental to our system of justice as it prevents the punishment of individuals who, by reason of mental illness, cannot fairly be held responsible for their criminal acts. Perhaps that is why, although the insanity defense has been the subject of much judicial and legislative tinkering for centuries, and especially in recent decades, to this day it remains an honored, if sometimes tarnished, fixture in Anglo-American law.

Critics of the insanity defense, however, frequently note that although the moral theory underlying the insanity defense may be laudable, in practice the defense is subject to many abuses and rarely lives up to the lofty ideals it is intended to advance. They observe, for example, that the legal result of an insanity defense is unpredictable, often appears arbitrary and capricious, and frequently seems not to turn upon the mental status and criminal responsibility of the defendant but rather upon who he is, what his crime was, what lawyer represented him, what expert witnesses testified for or against him, and what jury judged him.

Evolution of Legal Standards

The question of how criminal law should deal with mentally ill offenders has provoked controversy for centuries. As early as the 14th century, English law recognized that it was morally improper to punish a person whose mentality did not allow him to understand the difference between "good and evil."[1] By 1724, the courts had developed a standard of "insanity" that forbade criminal punishment of "a mad man . . . a man that is totally deprived of his understanding and memory, and doth not know what he is doing, no more than a brute or a wild beast."[2]

Modern insanity law, however, dates most directly to *M'Naghten's Case,* an 1843 English decision of the Supreme Court of Judicature. Daniel M'Naghten had shot and killed Edward Drummond, mistakenly believing that Drummond was Prime Minister Robert Peel. M'Naghten was found not guilty by reason of insanity, the queen was infuriated, and the House of Lords asked the court to clarify the law. In what has come to be known as the *M'Naghten* standard or test of insanity, the court directed that "the jurors ought to be told in all cases that every man is to be presumed to be sane, and to possess a sufficient degree of reason to be responsible for his crimes, until the contrary be proved to their satisfaction; and that to establish a defence on the ground of insanity, it must be clearly proved that, at the time of the committing of the act, the party accused was labouring under such a defect of reason, from disease of the mind, as not to know the nature and quality of the act he was doing; or, if he did know it, that he did not know he was doing what was wrong."[3] The two "prongs" of the *M'Naghten* standard—(1) inability to know the nature and quality of the act and (2) inability to know that the act was wrong—respectively deal with what have been referred to as cognitive incapacity and moral incapacity.

The *M'Naghten* standard, like the insanity defense more generally, has proven controversial but enduring. More than 165 years later, this test (or some variation of it) is still the law in the majority of American jurisdictions.

American reform of the insanity defense resulted in several alternatives to *M'Naghten,* including the "irresistible impulse" and "product" tests. Numerous 19th-century courts, including the U.S. Supreme Court, recognized that insanity included the inability to control one's actions, despite knowing that such actions were wrong. Thus, under the "irresistible impulse" standard an accused was insane if found, by reason of mental illness, "unable to adhere to the right even though he knew the act was wrong." A handful of other courts adopted a test asking simply whether the defendant's criminal act was the "product" of a mental disease or defect.[5] The "irresistible impulse" and "product" standards both reflected a concern for the defendant's volitional capacity. Both these standards have largely been abandoned or incorporated into other insanity tests.

In 1962, the American Law Institute (ALI), an influential group of judges, lawyers, and law professors, posited a new insanity test, which was made part of the ALI's Model Penal Code, a draft of recommended criminal laws. The ALI standard, which has become the major rival of *M'Naghten*, drew upon *M'Naghten* and the "irresistible impulse" standard. Under the ALI's Model Penal Code, "a person is not responsible for criminal conduct if at the time of such conduct as a result of mental disease or defect he lacks substantial capacity either to appreciate the criminality of his conduct or to conform his conduct to the requirements of the law."[6] The ALI definition of insanity also includes the caveat that "the terms 'mental disease or defect' do not include an abnormality manifested only by repeated criminal or otherwise antisocial conduct."[7]

Under the ALI formulation, a defendant may be found not guilty by reason of insanity if lacking *either* cognitive or volitional capacity. The ALI standard also liberalized the *M'Naghten* and irresistible impulse tests by substituting the broader and more psychologically nuanced term "appreciate" for "know" and by including the term "lacks substantial capacity," thereby making the requirements for insanity more flexible and less absolute.

The next round of major changes to the law of insanity occurred in the United States after the trial of John W. Hinckley, Jr., in 1982, probably the most highly publicized insanity trial in history. In 1981, Hinckley, an apparently mentally ill drifter and son of wealthy parents, shot and nearly killed Ronald Reagan, the president of the United States. The shooting was videotaped by news media and viewed throughout the nation and much of the world. Charged with attempted murder, Hinckley pleaded insanity.

Hinckley's defense was tried under then-existing federal law, which essentially paralleled the ALI insanity standard. At the time, the prosecution had the burden of proving beyond a reasonable doubt that the would-be presidential assassin was sane.

After a 7-week trial, featuring expert testimony from six psychologists and psychiatrists, who had spent hundreds of hours examining and testing Hinckley at a cost to the government and Hinckley's family of about $450,000, a jury deliberated only 3 days before finding Hinckley not guilty by reason of insanity.

The jury's verdict, though not unreasonable given the law, the burden of proof, and the testimony presented by the defense experts in the case, touched off a firestorm of controversy that reverberated through the halls of Congress and state legislatures across the land.

In the wake of the Hinckley verdict, Congress narrowed the substantive federal insanity defense by deleting reference to volitional incapacity and by qualifying the nature of the required mental disease or defect. Under the Federal Insanity Defense Reform Act of 1984, "It is an affirmative defense to a prosecution under any Federal statute that, at the time of the commission of the acts constituting the offense, the defendant as a result of serious mental disease or defect, was unable to appreciate the nature and quality or wrongfulness of his acts. Mental disease or defect does not otherwise constitute a defense."[8] The amended federal insanity law also provided that "[t]he *defendant* has the burden of proving the defense of insanity by clear and convincing evidence."[9]

As part of the same legislation, Congress also amended the Federal Rules of Evidence in an obvious effort to limit the perceived influence of psychologists and psychiatrists on the outcome of insanity trials. The following language was added to Federal Rule of Evidence 704: "No expert witness testifying with respect to the mental state or condition of a defendant in a criminal case may state an opinion or inference as to whether the defendant did or did not have the mental state or condition constituting an element of the crime charged or of a defense thereto. Such ultimate issues are matters for the trier of fact alone."[10]

Although the Federal Insanity Reform Act was the most visible symbolic response to the Hinckley verdict and its critics, numerous state legislatures also responded to the controversial judgment. A dozen states supplemented their insanity laws by adopting a separate standard of "guilty but mentally ill," under which a mentally ill defendant could be convicted and provided treatment while still subject to criminal punishment. Sixteen states shifted the burden of proof on insanity from the prosecution to the defendant. Seven states narrowed their substantive insanity standards, whereas three enacted legislation abolishing the insanity defense. Finally, half the states responded to the Hinckley verdict by making it more difficult for those acquitted by reason of insanity to be released from confinement following treatment.[11]

These federal and state reforms quieted much of the uproar created by the Hinckley verdict. Today, the insanity defense remains on the books in some form in all but five American jurisdictions. Recently the U.S. Supreme Court summarized the state of American insanity law as follows: "Seventeen States and the Federal Government have adopted a recognizable version of the *M'Naghten* test with both its cognitive incapacity and moral incapacity components. One State has adopted only *M'Naghten*'s cognitive incapacity test, and 10 [States] have adopted the moral incapacity test alone. Fourteen jurisdictions, inspired by the Model Penal Code, have in place an amalgam of the volitional incapacity test and some variant of the moral incapacity test, satisfaction of either (generally by showing a defendant's substantial lack of capacity) being enough to excuse. Three States combine a full *M'Naghten* test with a volitional incapacity formula. And New Hampshire alone stands by the product-of-mental-illness test."[12]

Psychological and Psychiatric Expertise

Contrary to popular belief, insanity is and always has been a legal rather than psychological or psychiatric concept. Indeed, the insanity defense clearly predates the inception of psychology and psychiatry as professional disciplines. By the 19th century, however, medical "alienists" and other forerunners of today's mental health professionals began to play a significant role in the application of the insanity defense. For instance, as early as the 1840s, in *M'Naghten's Case,* nine medical experts testified that the murder defendant had been delusional and insane at the time of the killing.

Today, although the law does not require it, expert psychological and/or psychiatric testimony is a staple in virtually all insanity trials. Indeed, even in those insanity cases that do not go to trial, virtually all defendants contemplating an insanity defense will be examined by one or more mental health professionals whose input will help determine whether the plea will be offered and, if it is, whether it will be opposed by the prosecution.

Psychological and psychiatric experts have an almost guaranteed role in the administration of the insanity defense because all insanity laws, whether rooted in *M'Naghten* or the ALI standard, require first and foremost that the defendant have been suffering from a mental disease or defect.

Ironically, mental disease and mental defect are terms that often have not been defined by the law. For example, the terms are undefined in federal law, even after the Hinckley reforms, and a number of federal courts have held that "[t]he definition of mental disease or defect is essentially a factual, medical question, not a legal issue. The court should not encroach upon the jury's function of resolving possibly competing psychiatric views of this definition."[13]

Thus, for better or worse, although in the final analysis the determination of insanity is generally left to the jury, in many, if not most, cases, mental health experts are free to utilize their own definitions of what constitutes a mental disease or defect. Although there is sometimes great controversy on this issue, usually when mental health experts speak of mental disease they equate that term with mental illness, whereas when they speak of mental defect they mean mental retardation or some other disabling developmental disorder. Moreover, today, although no law requires it, most mental health experts rely upon a single standard text, the *Diagnostic and Statistical Manual of Mental Disorders,* published by the American Psychiatric Association, to specify the criteria for mental illnesses and mental retardation.[14]

Interestingly, and contrary to the assumption of many, there is generally agreement among mental health experts who examine a defendant and are asked to opine as to his or her sanity. The level of agreement among experts is, however, is far from perfect, and many cases go to trial and are decided by juries primarily because the experts do not agree as to whether the defendant suffers from a mental disease or defect and/or meets the other criteria for insanity. In many states, contrary to revised Federal Rule of Evidence 704, mental health experts are allowed to offer opinions not only about the presence or absence of mental disease or defect but also regarding the ultimate issue of insanity.

The Practical Effect of the Insanity Defense

Although the insanity defense is purportedly designed to prevent the punishment of defendants who, because of mental illness or mental retardation, cannot fairly be held responsible for their criminal acts, there is no way to tell whether the defense actually accomplishes that purpose. There are, however, plenty of reasons to question whether, as a general matter, the insanity defense actually achieves that worthy moral aspiration.

To begin with, and apparently contrary to public opinion, the insanity defense is rarely used and rarely succeeds when it is. A variety of studies spanning a number of jurisdictions have all concluded that the insanity defense is used in less than 1 percent of all criminal cases. Moreover, these and other studies have found that the defense succeeds in less than a quarter of the cases in which it is invoked.

The general public appears to regard the insanity defense with great skepticism and to see it as a legal "loophole" by which criminals avoid or minimize punishment:

> Almost every study of the public's perception of the insanity defense reports consistent support for the notion that the insanity defense is considered a loophole. The term *loophole,* in this context, reflects the public's perception that persons acquitted by reason of insanity are not dealt with as severely, in terms of length of confinement and level of security of placement, as persons found guilty of the same crimes . . . The image of the insanity acquittee who "gets off scot free" is undoubtedly the most frequent image associated with the insanity defense put forth by the media.[15]

The fact is that, contrary to this public and media stereotype of the insanity defense as "loophole," even those relatively few defendants who are found not guilty by reason of insanity almost invariably have their liberty severely curtailed, in many instances for longer than they would have if they had pleaded guilty or been convicted. In all jurisdictions, the law provides for at least some form of detention for defendants acquitted by reason of insanity; that detention is usually mandatory and, in most jurisdictions, indefinite; release hinges upon proof that the acquitted defendant is no longer dangerous.

Although the detention of defendants acquitted by reason of insanity is said to be for purposes of treatment rather than punishment, these individuals (all of whom have been found "not guilty" of the crime charged) are generally confined against their will in locked, highly secure forensic psychiatric facilities where they have little freedom.

Moreover, data indicate that the length of time these acquitted defendants are confined in such institutions is often, if not generally, greater than the amount of time served in prison by defendants convicted of the same offense. For example, studies of confinement periods in 10 states showed that in 4 states insanity acquittees spent more time confined than those convicted, in 4 states the average confinement period was about the same for both groups, and in 2 states convicted offenders were confined for longer periods than those who had been found insane.

Data from 7 of these states also indicate that, even though an insanity acquittee has been found not guilty of the charge(s) against him, the length of his confinement will be strongly associated with the seriousness of his offense. As one member of the research group that gathered many of these data has explained,

> Persons acquitted by reason of insanity are typically confined to mental hospitals until such time as they are no longer dangerous to themselves or others . . . [P]rior research has shown that determinations of dangerousness are often based primarily upon the seriousness of the offense for which an insanity acquittee has been found to be not responsible. Therefore, to the extent that assessments of dangerousness associated with decisions about releasing insanity acquittees . . . reflect the seriousness of the offense for which the insanity defendant was acquitted, they function as a mechanism for sentencing. Dangerousness can thus be seen as a mechanism for punishing insanity acquittees, despite procedural and ethical restrictions derived from insanity acquittees having been cleared of all criminal charges.[16]

Murder and the Insanity Defense

The insanity defense is most often associated in the public eye with serious crimes such as violent felonies. However, the defense is available to defendants charged with virtually any crime and seems to be raised most often by defendants charged with less serious crimes, perhaps because both experience and conventional wisdom in the legal profession suggest that these defendants will have greater success with the defense. For example, when an obviously mentally ill defendant is charged with a relatively minor crime that would result in at most a light sentence of incarceration, prosecutors may stipulate to the defendant's insanity and allow the court to find the defendant not guilty by reason of insanity without a trial.

Such is not the case, however, with criminal defendants charged with violent felonies, especially murder, the single crime which accounts for about one-third of all insanity pleas. Not surprisingly, with rare exceptions, when defendants charged with murder or other violent felonies plead insanity, and do not ultimately plead guilty, their pleas are met with the utmost resistance from the prosecution, and their cases usually go to a full trial unless they abandon the defense and/or plead guilty.

The focus of this book is on the use of the insanity defense in murder prosecutions. As a general matter, murder cases involving insanity pleas were selected for attention here not only because they more often go to full trial, thus providing a more complete and public record for scrutiny and analysis, but also because they are among the most fascinating and controversial cases in which defendants raise the insanity defense. Quite literally, homicide defendants who raise the insanity defense are often viewed by the public, the media, and even the legal system as trying to get away with murder.

From the thousands of murder cases in which defendants have claimed insanity, the 10 considered at length in this book were chosen for a number of reasons. Although only a few of them are nationally known and involve defendants whose names have become household words, all were extremely controversial, all but one went to a full trial, and each had extensive public records available for review. All involved lengthy testimony by expert psychologists and psychiatrists, thus providing excellent and detailed examples of how such expertise is used and misused by the courts in insanity trials. Finally, several of these cases resulted in appellate review, in which higher courts (including the United States Supreme Court) clarified or changed the law applicable in insanity cases.

The 10 cases examined here are presented in roughly chronological order, based upon the dates on which the alleged crimes were committed:

> Jacob Rubenstein (also known as Jack Ruby) who, in 1963, shot and killed Lee Harvey Oswald, who had just assassinated President John F. Kennedy;

- Robert Torsney, a New York City police officer who, in 1976, inexplicably shot and killed an unarmed teenager while responding to a domestic violence call;
- David Berkowitz (also known as the "Son of Sam"), a New York City man who in 1976 and 1977 killed six people and wounded several others;
- John Wayne Gacy who, from 1972 to 1978, killed at least 30 boys and young men, most of whom he then buried in a 30-inch crawl space beneath his Chicago home;
- Arthur Shawcross, a paroled child sex abuser and killer who, from 1988 to 1990, raped and strangled at least 11 women in the Rochester, New York, area;
- Scott Panetti, a Texas man, who in 1992 shot and killed his mother-in-law and father-in-law in front of his wife and young daughter and defended himself at trial despite suffering from serious and obvious mental illness;
- Eric Smith, a 13-year-old boy from rural upstate New York, who in 1993 fatally beat a four year old boy and then sodomized the child with a large stick;
- Andrew Goldstein who, in 1999, shoved a stranger to her death in front of an oncoming subway train in New York City;
- Eric Michael Clark, a rural Texas teenager, who in 2000 shot and killed a police officer who had stopped the vehicle Clark was driving in an erratic manner; and
- Andrea Yates, a mentally ill Texas mother, who in 2001 drowned her five children in a household bathtub.

INSANITY

1

Jacob Rubenstein

Born in Chicago in 1911, the son of impoverished and uneducated Polish immigrants, Jacob Rubenstein was, in retrospect, not an unlikely candidate to become the subject of one of the most notorious insanity trials in modern American history.

Rubenstein's father was a violent alcoholic who abused his wife, had a long record of arrests (mainly for assault and battery), and spent some 30 years unemployed. Rubenstein's mother, a battered, inadequate, illiterate, delusional, and ill-tempered woman, was mentally ill and spent a number of months as a civilly committed patient in a state psychiatric hospital.

Throughout much of their childhoods, Rubenstein and his seven siblings were neglected, mistreated, and uncontrolled by their parents. By the time Rubenstein was 11 years old, his parents had separated, and he was declared "incorrigible" by the Jewish Social Service Bureau and referred to the Institute for Juvenile Research for psychiatric examination and possible out-of-home placement.[1]

Though the report of this evaluation made reference to Rubenstein's egocentricity and attention-seeking behavior as well as his "sex experiences," for the most part it was directed at the boy's mother and then-custodial parent.[2] "From a superficial examination of his mother who was here with him," the report indicated, "it is apparent that she has no insight into his problem, and she is thoroughly inadequate in the further training of this boy."[3] According to the psychiatric report, the Rubenstein home was "unstable and disorganized [and] could not provide [Jacob] with the necessary controls and discipline."[4]

Within a year of this evaluation, the Chicago juvenile court concluded that Rubenstein and his siblings were "not receiving proper parental care."[5] The court directed the Jewish Home Finding Society to place the children in foster care, where they spent several years in a succession of homes.

When the Rubenstein children were reunited with their mother, she was still separated from their father. According to the children, Mrs. Rubenstein never took much interest in their welfare, was selfish, jealous, and hard to get along with, was unable to manage the home or the children, and "never cared to do anything in the home but lie around and sleep."[6] A cousin of the children said Mrs. Rubenstein ran "an irregular household" and seemed "a rather disturbed person of poor personal appearance with no incentive for cleaning or cooking."[7]

Rubenstein was frequently a truant, repeated the third grade, and never got past the eighth grade before dropping out of school at age sixteen. The consensus among his classmates and peers was that although Rubenstein was likable and not a troublemaker or one to start fights, he had a quick and volatile temper that earned him the nickname "Sparky."[8] Those who knew him as a youth said he was "willing to accept any challenge without regard to the odds against him [and] had the reputation of being a good street brawler."[9]

Rubenstein also appeared to be an ambitious youngster with a strong desire to make money. He began contributing to his own support and that of his family at an early age. By the time he was 8 or 9 years old, he was on the street selling shopping bags and fireworks. Later in his childhood and adolescence, he earned money by scalping tickets to sporting events, selling pennants and other novelty items from a pushcart, and parking cars.

As a young adult, Rubenstein left Chicago for California, and embarked upon a roughly 10-year stint in which he drifted from one poorly paid job to another. He sold tip sheets at a race track, hawked newspaper subscriptions door-to-door, scalped tickets, bought and resold watches and other small items, worked briefly as a union organizer, and sold gambling devices known as punchboards.

This rootless period of Rubenstein's life was brought to a close by the beginning of World War II. Rubenstein was classified "1-A" by the Selective Service Board, declared eligible for the draft, and soon drafted into the U.S. Army Air Force. Never progressing beyond the rank of Private First Class, Rubenstein spent his 3-year obligation working as an aircraft mechanic on various military bases in the United States and supplementing his income through petty gambling and various small-time sales ventures.

After receiving an honorable discharge in 1946, Rubenstein, then 35 years old, returned to his native Chicago and resumed his career as an itinerant salesmen, this time peddling small cedar chests, salt and pepper shakers, key chains, bottle openers, screwdrivers, and hammers manufactured by his brothers.

Within a year or so, this chapter in Rubenstein's life came to an end. He parted ways with his business partners, his brothers, and settled in Dallas, where he legally changed his name to Jack Ruby and began managing various nightclubs. Ruby, whose brothers had bought out his share of the family's small business in Chicago, used his stake to buy one Dallas club. He also borrowed heavily to purchase another. Thereafter, Ruby held stakes in a variety of bars, strip joints, and other night spots, none of which were successful financially. As a result, Ruby was constantly borrowing money from and indebted to family members, friends, and business associates. Though he also sought money from banks, he had little other use for them, conducting his business in cash and carrying whatever money he had in his pockets or the trunk of his car. His accounts, such as they were, were often in a state of disarray, and he was frequently in trouble with the Internal Revenue Service and state tax authorities for late and unpaid taxes, at one point falling 6 years behind in his payments to the IRS.

To help make ends meet, Ruby supplemented his meager business income by selling costume jewelry, sewing machine attachments, pizza crusts, vitamins and patent medicines, and razor blades. He also briefly managed the career of a child entertainer and helped produce a state fair carnival show, "How Hollywood Makes Movies."[10]

Perhaps as a result of his business failings, Ruby was a domineering, sometimes violent employer who often failed to pay his employees on time, sometimes cheated them out of their wages, and occasionally assaulted them. Surprisingly, however, until 1963, Ruby was never arrested for committing any crime of violence. Although he was arrested eight times in Dallas between 1949 and 1963, the charges included only relatively minor offenses such as disturbing the peace, carrying a concealed weapon, selling liquor after hours, permitting dancing after hours, simple assault, and failure to respond to traffic citations. From 1950 to 1963, Ruby received 20 traffic tickets. During roughly the same time period, he also had his liquor license suspended numerous times for allowing obscene performances and permitting "drunkards" on his premises.

Ruby's personal life was something of a mystery to those who knew him. Most of the people in his life were employees, business associates, or family members. Ruby spoke with a lisp, was somewhat effeminate in his demeanor, and at times spoke in a high-pitched voice. Although some who knew him believed that he was a homosexual, there is no evidence of that. On the contrary, while in Dallas, Ruby was involved in an 11-year relationships with a female divorcée, a secretary who was 4 years younger than Ruby. The two discussed marriage but did not follow through on it, and Ruby never married.

Though Ruby was well known in some circles in Dallas, and he fancied himself a friend of local police, celebrities, reporters, and mobsters, it was not until November 1963 that Jack Ruby really made a name for himself. On Friday November 22, 1963, President John F. Kennedy was assassinated as his motorcade drove through Dallas. Within 2 hours of the killing, 24-year-old Lee Harvey Oswald, a drifter and erstwhile Marxist, was arrested and charged with murdering Kennedy and a Dallas patrolman he shot in an effort to avoid arrest. Two days later, on Sunday, November 24, while in the process of being moved from the Dallas Police Department to the local jail, Oswald himself was shot dead in front of countless police officers, members of the media and a television audience estimated to be in the millions. The shooter, who would immediately become a household name, was Jack Ruby.

As Oswald was being led from police headquarters in handcuffs and paraded before a throng of reporters and photographers, Ruby (dressed in a business suit and felt hat) had walked without challenge through what passed as police security, lunged at the manacled assassin, shouted "You son of a bitch,"[11] and fired a single shot from a range close enough to leave a 2-inch powder burn at the site of the wound to Oswald's side. Despite heroic efforts by physicians in the same emergency room in which President Kennedy had been treated just 2 days earlier, within 2 hours of the shooting, Lee Harvey Oswald lay dead, Jack Ruby's single bullet having all but destroyed the assassin's spleen, pancreas, liver, and right kidney.

Arrested and charged with murder with malice, a crime that carried the possibility of the death penalty, Ruby had many strikes against him, even though his victim had just assassinated the president. His crime had more witnesses than any before it in the history of the world; he had an unsavory reputation, numerous prior arrests, and ran a striptease club; he had gunned down a man who was in police custody, handcuffed, and utterly defenseless; he had made fools of the police charged with protecting Oswald; he had further embarrassed a city already scorned as the place where a popular young president was murdered; and, perhaps most significantly, he had sealed the lips of the one man who might have answered the questions about the Kennedy assassination that exist to this day.

Even without those obvious liabilities, Jack Ruby would be a difficult man to defend given the law that governed his prosecution. Even if a jury found that he acted in the heat of passion—in other words, "under the immediate influence of a sudden passion arising from an adequate cause"—when he killed Oswald, Ruby would still be guilty of murder, albeit murder without malice.[12] The only available defense that might result in an outright acquittal in his case was insanity.

Ruby's first lawyer was Tom Howard, who had previously tried 25 capital murder cases without losing a single client to the death penalty. Howard decided to eschew an insanity defense but use the testimony of psychiatric experts, lay witnesses, and the defendant himself to establish that Ruby was a mentally unstable man who cracked under the strain of the assassination of his beloved president and the round-the-clock media coverage that ensued. If the jury responded sympathetically to this evidence, as Howard's experience told him they would, Ruby would not only escape the death penalty but serve no more than 5 years in state prison.

Howard never had the opportunity to test his intuition, however, because, early on in the proceedings, Ruby's family decided to seek a defense attorney with a much higher profile. Ultimately they settled on Melvin Belli, the nation's premier personal injury and medical malpractice litigator. Though known as the "King of Torts" for his uncanny ability to persuade juries to award huge money verdicts to his injured clients, Belli had also tried many criminal cases and was perhaps equally well regarded as an attorney with a mastery of medicine as thorough as that of many physicians.

It was Belli's fascination with, study of, and knack for medicine that provided the lens through which he ultimately saw his new client's case. In his first meeting with Ruby, Belli conducted his own admittedly amateur assessment of his client's mental status and was convinced that insanity was a possible defense. As Belli later wrote,

> He was a strange little man, this man who had assassinated the assassin of President Kennedy, and I could not even begin to guess how strange when I watched him so closely in that first 3-hour jail meeting. My own knowledge of medicine and psychology is not professional, yet I was able, through my layman's version of a psychological examination, to see that there was something grossly wrong there. As defense attorney, I was hoping for a medical diagnosis of a functional psychosis, which might be comparatively easy to prove.[13]

Based upon his knowledge of the case and his own "psychological examination" of Ruby, Belli assembled a team of psychiatrists and psychologists who would professionally assess his client. Although these professionals all agreed that there was "something grossly wrong"[14] with Ruby's mental functioning, their diagnoses did not prove to be what the defense attorney–armchair psychologist expected.

Psychologist Dr. Roy Schafer of Yale University conducted extensive tests of Ruby and ruled out psychotic disorders such as schizophrenia, manic-depressive illness, and paranoid disorder. Instead, Schafer's tests pointed to an organic mental illness. As he reported to Belli,

> On the whole, the test results indicate the presence of brain dysfunction on a physical basis. It is quite possible that Mr. Ruby has some form of convulsive disorder: his test responses are very similar in many respects to those obtained from patients who have psychomotor seizures. His religious preoccupation and his pietistic expressions, his explosive emotionality, and his disordered body image fit well the classical picture of persons with convulsive disorders.[15]

Based upon the results of the psychological testing, Schafer recommended that Ruby undergo an electroencephalogram (EEG) and a neurological examination.

Psychiatrist Dr. Walter Bromberg examined Ruby and also found evidence of a likely organic brain dysfunction. As Bromberg reported to the defense attorney,

> [T]he shooting was automatic and instinctive. This condition is well known among individuals of the Epileptic Constitution or the Aggressive Psychopathic type. It amounts to a fugue state where the consciousness is impaired and physical acts consummated in the patient's usual manner of behavior occur without conscious thought. One sees this among boxers who fight on automatically after being knocked out on their feet. One sees it in head injuries. One sees it in unstable persons where irritable brain tissue allows the emergence of aggressive impulses.[16]

By the time the third defense expert, Dr. Manfred Guttmacher, one of the pioneers of forensic psychiatry, weighed in on the defendant's condition, Ruby had undergone an EEG, the results of which were abnormal and suggestive of an organic brain dysfunction. In a memorandum to Belli, Guttmacher wrote the following:

> What we have to develop is that Jack has a definitely abnormal and damaged brain. For this we have two types of objective data, entirely independent of each other; the psychological tests of Dr. Schafer, which could not have been faked, and the definitely abnormal brain waves ... There is abundant evidence in the medical literature that people with brain waves like Jack's, showing a disturbance in the temporal lobes, in most instances, behave abnormally and are given to psychopathic-like behavior, particularly to irrational outburst of aggression, often when under stress ... [17]

Belli saw these three reports as presenting "a consistent and self-supporting scientific pattern, the most perfect psychiatric defense backed by diagnostic reports I have ever seen."[18] The problem was how he could adapt these findings to Texas insanity law and convince a jury to acquit his client.

Texas law on insanity was essentially the ancient and strict M'Naghten rule. To garner an acquittal by reason of insanity, Belli would have to prove by a preponderance of the evidence that Ruby was not only mentally ill but, as a result of that illness, had been unable to distinguish right from wrong when he killed Oswald.

The reports of Drs. Schafer, Bromberg, and Guttmacher could just as easily, perhaps more easily, have supported a mitigating defense that the troubled Ruby had acted without malice. The stakes were high for Ruby. If his defense was lack of malice and it succeeded, he faced no more than 5 years of incarceration; if he successfully pled insanity, he faced years, if not a lifetime, in a secure mental institution. Whichever defense was raised, if it failed, Ruby faced a possible death sentence.

Belli was well aware of the risks of the defense but confident in the evidence, in his experts, and in his own ability to convince the jury that Ruby was insane. He may have also realized that a full-blown insanity defense, even if it failed, would make it less likely that the jury would impose a sentence of death. But, as he explained it, his decision to pursue an insanity defense for Jack Ruby was based on concerns that went well beyond legal strategy, the nature of the evidence or the interests of his client. As Belli later recounted,

> Our obligations in the case were multiple. To Jack Ruby, we owed a defense case waged sincerely and strongly. To the community . . . we owed a disciplined, sober, complete presentation, to bare the facts, lay to rest the rumors and, not incidentally, to show the watching world how a defendant's rights were protected under the American legal system. For the medical and legal professions, we gained the opportunity to chart new ground in a case ideally adapted for groundbreaking. The obscure and episodic nature of the mental troubles that afflicted Ruby was ideally suited to expose incongruities in the law's understanding of mental illness. And the dramatic fashion in which test after test meshed to put together a picture of this man's mind would demonstrate how science can aid the law, how a soberly constructed, scientific case would unfold before a jury's eyes and let them, in the most perfect fulfillment of the juror's role, discover with the doctor witnesses what went on in the mind of this defendant, Jack Ruby.[19]

Although Belli was deeply impressed with the "consistent and self-supporting scientific pattern" of his expert's findings and thought they supported "the most perfect psychiatric defense backed by diagnostic reports" he had ever seen, both the prosecutors and a team of several other medical experts strongly disagreed.[20] Dallas District Attorney Henry Wade and Assistant District Attorney Bill Alexander had reports from other experts indicating that Jack Ruby was not mentally ill, not suffering from organic brain dysfunction, and not insane. Thus, the *State of Texas v. Jack Ruby*, like many insanity trials, would ultimately turn into a battle of the experts and the attorneys.

At trial, the prosecution fairly quickly and convincingly made its case for premeditated murder. Using film clips of the actual shooting, the state established beyond any doubt that Ruby had shot and killed Oswald. The state's proof also established that prior to the shooting of Oswald, Ruby had been calm and collected and had been managing his business competently and had not appeared unusual to people who knew him. Witnesses reported that during a press conference conducted by District Attorney Wade on the night of the Kennedy assassination, Ruby had infiltrated the crowd of reporters covering the case and, showing a pad and pencil, had announced that he was a reporter. Still other testimony revealed that the next day, when it was thought that Oswald would be transferred to the county jail at 4 P.M., Ruby had been seen at that location at about 3 P.M. Finally, prosecution testimony indicated that, after Ruby shot Oswald, Ruby said, "I hope I killed the son of a bitch," and when a police detective told Ruby that he probably had killed the presidential assassin, Ruby replied, "I intended to shoot him three times."[21]

Once the prosecution rested, Belli wasted no time in outlining the defense he intended to present, telling the jury in his short opening statement, "[W]e will show you that Jack Ruby has organic brain damage. By that I mean that this damage is discernible, that it can be found not only by the psychological testing, but by the electroencephalograms. They will show that Jack Ruby has the damage that is called psychomotor variant epilepsy."[22]

Dr. Roy Schafer, whose psychological testing had first revealed evidence of Ruby's purported brain damage, was the first expert to testify. After establishing his impressive credentials, Schafer testified that he had reached his diagnosis of Ruby based upon psychological testing alone, prior to seeing Ruby's EEG results and without taking any history from Ruby: "Essentially I had only my own records of psychological tests I had administered to him. I had seen some things in the newspapers, of course, and really nothing substantial before that . . . I came to the conclusion that he did have organic brain damage, and that the most likely specific nature of it was psychomotor epilepsy."[23]

Having gotten Schafer's diagnosis of Ruby before the jury, Belli launched into lengthy questioning about the tests Schafer had administered and how their results were linked to the diagnosis. When prosecutors Wade and Alexander objected to this testimony, ostensibly on the grounds that it was irrelevant because Schafer had not yet offered any opinion regarding Ruby's sanity under the M'Naghten standard, Belli's response was telling. The defense attorney likened the psychologist's role to that of a simple data gatherer who provided information upon which a physician could render a diagnosis, thereby demeaning all that Schafer had already told the jury. "Judge," Belli replied to the objection, "this man hasn't even taken a case history from [Ruby]. You can't ask the nurse who has taken a temperature, or a bowel specimen, whether she thinks a man has smallpox."[24]

After numerous objections and arguments, during which it was becoming increasingly clear that Schafer had formed no opinion on Ruby's sanity, the judge ordered Schafer off the witness stand, telling the defense attorney, "I'm going to exclude his testimony. I sustain the objection to it, Mr. Belli."[25] When a stunned Belli then asked, "Your honor is going to tell this jury in 1964 not to take the testimony of this great man from Yale University, in Dallas?" the judge replied, "Yes."[26]

Finally, after receiving Belli's assurances that Schafer's testimony would provide a basis for the later testimony of other experts, the prosecution and the judge relented, and Schafer was allowed to go into the details of the Wechsler Adult Intelligence Scale, Rorschach Inkblot Test, Thematic Apperception Test, word-association test, story-recall test, object-sorting test, and a host of other measures applied to Ruby.

Through no fault on his part, Schafer's direct testimony proved to be disorganized and difficult to follow. It was on cross-examination, however, that the results of the psychologist's test were rendered essentially meaningless by a single question. Wade, the district attorney, put it bluntly to Schafer: "Let me ask you, from all these ink blots and pictures and all these questions, did you form an opinion as to whether or not Jack Ruby knew right from wrong?"[27] The psychologist answered as anticipated: "No."[28]

The second expert witness for the defense was not a mental health professional but a neurologist, Dr. Martin Towler. Towler had taken a detailed history from Ruby and performed Ruby's EEG—one of approximately 4000 such tests he had performed each year since 1944. Towler told the jury that Ruby had described infrequent "spells" that had begun 15 to 20 years earlier.[29] According to Towler, Ruby's "spells" included "prickling sensations in the head" and feeling that his head "was cracking up."[30] Based upon the history of these "spells" and Ruby's abnormal EEG, Towler testified that in his opinion "the subject is suffering from a seizure disorder."[31] "This type of seizure disorder," Towler further related, "falls into the category of a psychomotor variant" of the sort that had first been described in the medical literature just a year earlier by another neurologist, Dr. Frederic Gibbs.[32]

Belli tried to have Towler testify that he had corroborated his analysis of Ruby's EEG with Gibbs, but the court sustained the prosecutor's hearsay objection to the question. Belli did, however, succeed in getting Towler to testify that during "spells" or "psychomotor variant" seizures, an individual is "behaving as an automaton."[33]

On cross-examination, Wade got Towler to concede that aside from the EEG there was no physical evidence that Ruby was anything other than a normal 51-year-old man. The district attorney also got the neurologist to acknowledge that a very small percentage of people with EEG tracings similar to those of Ruby did "not have any seizure manifestation."[34] But the district attorney's biggest score on the cross-examination occurred when Towler admitted that he had no opinion as to whether Ruby had been having a seizure at the time he shot Oswald. "I have not attempted to establish that," Towler said.[35]

On redirect examination, Belli took one last shot at getting Towler to tell the jury that his findings had been corroborated by Dr. Gibbs, but the prosecution's objection to the question was again sustained.

The third expert to testify for Jack Ruby was Dr. Manfred Guttmacher, who was then and still is, years after his death, probably America's preeminent forensic psychiatrist. Since 1972, the American Psychiatric Association has awarded annually a prize named for Guttmacher, honoring the most outstanding contribution to the literature on forensic psychiatry.

Guttmacher was the first witness to tell the jury that Ruby was insane when he killed Oswald. As he testified, "I don't think he was capable of distinguishing right from wrong and realizing the nature and consequences of his act at the time of the alleged homicide."[36] Belli did not reveal it until after the trial, but on the literal eve of the trial, Guttmacher had declined to testify that Ruby had been in a seizure state at the time he shot Oswald. Thus when the eminent psychiatrist addressed the jury, he gave short shrift to that notion and instead reported that Ruby "had a weak ego structure," had been "under tremendous emotional impact for a period of a couple of days," and "was struggling to keep his sanity" when "all of his defenses crumbled, and the deep, heavy, hostile, aggressive part of his makeup, which is very strong, became focused on this one individual, and the homicide was the result of it."[37] Only under Belli's persistent questioning did Guttmacher acknowledge the potential significance of a seizure disorder in the case. Even then, however, he did so in general terms rather than by specific reference to Jack Ruby. Choosing his words carefully, Guttmacher responded to Belli's question, saying, "I think that it's been well established in psychiatric literature that people who have psychomotor epilepsy are not infrequently subject to triggering of the attack by strong emotional stimuli."[38]

Surprisingly, on cross-examination, Alexander couldn't leave well enough alone. Thus far, Guttmacher had not testified that Ruby was in a psychomotor seizure at the time of the shooting. Apparently wanting to hammer the point home, the assistant district attorney got Guttmacher to acknowledge that he did not believe Ruby was in a seizure when he shot Oswald. But then Alexander took the questioning one step too far, violating the maxim that a lawyer should never ask a question to which he does not already know the answer:

> *Alexander:* If you say he wasn't in a psychomotor seizure at the time he committed the act, what is your diagnosis? What was he suffering from?
>
> *Guttmacher:* I think he had a rupture of the ego, and a period of episodic dyscontrol ... I don't think we have data on which we can tell whether this man was in a psychomotor epileptic attack at the time, but it could have occurred in a person of his makeup under that degree of stress ... [39]

Alexander then pressed his attack even further, sarcastically asking Guttmacher to state his "best guess" as to Ruby's condition when he shot Oswald.[40] Guttmacher replied, "My best diagnosis is that this man is a mental cripple and was carrying on his shoulders an insufferable emotional load, he cracked under it momentarily ... "[41]

Unfortunately for Guttmacher, Alexander was better prepared than he appeared from his questions. In response to Guttmacher's "diagnosis," the prosecutor produced and read from a book written by Guttmacher, *Psychiatry and the Law*. In the book, Guttmacher had written that "[a] form of disorder frequently encountered in the courtroom, though not elsewhere, is temporary insanity."[42]

As Alexander further pointed out, the book also contained the following paragraph, which the prosecutor read in open court:

> There are, of course, disorders characterized by brief periods of derangement or lapse of consciousness. In epilepsy, for example, seizures are often followed or replaced by an automatic state. But such manifestations, while transitory, are recurrent; epilepsy is anything but a temporary affliction. The temporary insanity dear to the hearts of defense lawyers, however, is wholly a thing of the moment; a man without any history of mental abnormality prior to the act, and exhibiting no symptom upon examination afterward, is

alleged to have been temporarily insane and without understanding of the nature of his act or its wrongfulness at the moment of the killing. (This particular malady seems to occur only in homicide cases.) To medical men this is about as likely as a momentary uremia in a man with a perfectly normal kidney function.[43]

"You're leaving out the very important ingredient," Guttmacher shot back.[44] To which Alexander replied, "I'm not leaving out anything, Doctor. I'm reading from your book."[45]

Guttmacher's testimony was followed by Belli's attempts to get the psychiatric records of Ruby's mother and two of his siblings admitted into evidence. When the judge refused to admit these records, Belli rested the defense case. Next came the prosecution's rebuttal case, the state's chance to present its own expert witnesses.

The first of these witnesses was Dr. Shef Olinger, a neurologist who had examined Ruby's EEG tracings and concluded that Dr. Towler had been wrong. Ruby's EEG, Olinger told the jury, showed "occasional serial discharges" that were "somewhat slower" than would be expected but "did not positively indicate any particular clinical disease."[46] Moreover, Olinger testified, even considering all of the available medical data on Ruby, he would not diagnose psychomotor epilepsy.

On cross-examination, Belli tried unsuccessfully to get Olinger to acknowledge Dr. Frederic Gibbs as having "done the definitive work on electroencephalography in the United States."[47] Belli did, however, succeed in getting the relatively inexperienced physician to concede that he was not certified in any medical specialty, that Ruby's EEG was "unusual," and that it might indicate psychomotor epilepsy.[48]

Next on the witness stand for the prosecution came Dr. Robert Stubblefield, a psychiatrist who had initially examined Ruby at the request of the court regarding the question of bail. The gist of the direct examination consisted of a hypothetical in which Stubblefield was asked to "assume" a laundry list of "facts" about Jack and his crime.[49] When asked if, assuming these "facts" to be true, he would have an opinion as to Ruby's sanity, Stubblefield replied, "If I assume the facts as you state them, in my opinion he would know the difference between right and wrong, and would know the nature and quality of his act."[50]

On cross-examination, Belli used the obvious approach to a witness who has just testified in response to a hypothetical question. He chipped away at the assumptions, particularly the assumption that Ruby had been in a full state of consciousness. But Belli was most effective when he got Stubblefield to admit that Ruby was an "unstable person" who "in the face of certain kinds of stresses" had a "lower breaking point" than others.[51]

The prosecution's next rebuttal expert was Dr. John Holbrook. Holbrook had originally evaluated Ruby in the county jail the day after he shot Oswald. Holbrook had been brought to Ruby's cell by Jim Alexander, the assistant district attorney who would later prosecute Ruby and conduct the direct examination of Dr. Holbrook. Alexander had known Ruby prior to the Oswald killing and convinced Ruby to allow Holbrook to examine him. When Ruby initially balked at the examination, worrying that it might be a "trap," Alexander had reassured him: "I've known you too long for that. I wouldn't let any friendship go down the drain just to mess you around."[52] Ruby relented and cooperated with the examination. A day later, after the prosecutor conferred with Holbrook, he announced that Ruby would be charged with capital murder and that the district attorney would seek the death penalty.

Under today's rules, as promulgated by the American Psychiatric Association and the U.S. Supreme Court, such a jailhouse examination, conducted before a defendant is represented by counsel, would not only violate medical ethics but result in the exclusion of the examining doctor as a witness against the defendant.

Even under the rules as they stood at that time, this examination and the apparently cozy relationship between Holbrook and the prosecutor should have raised red flags. Perhaps they did, but Holbrook was later appointed by the court to examine Ruby in connection with his bail application and was allowed to testify in rebuttal at Ruby's trial.

Holbrook testified that his examinations of Ruby had ruled out not only all functional psychoses but any form of epilepsy. Incredibly, although Holbrook had never discussed the crime with Ruby, Holbrook also testified that Ruby knew right from wrong at the time he shot Oswald. When asked on direct examination why he hadn't discussed the crime with Ruby, the psychiatrist said, "In the first place, a physician's job is not to determine whether someone has committed a crime or not, and in the second place it would be painful sometimes for a man who is being charged with this sort of thing to go into it, and in addition to that, very often, answers that you get from a person who is charged with a crime are highly unreliable . . . "[53]

Holbrook's testimony was followed by two additional rebuttal witnesses for the prosecution, Dr. Pere Kellaway, a neurologist, and Dr. Earl Walker, a neurosurgeon, both of whom were well-qualified electroencephalographers. Kellaway agreed that Ruby's EEG was abnormal but told the jury that there was no way of knowing why. Walker testified that Ruby's EEG results were not normal but did not necessarily indicate any brain abnormality. The EEG findings, he told the jury, could be the result an overactive thyroid, arteriosclerosis, or even past use of certain drugs.

When the prosecution rested for the second time, Belli felt the need to continue the battle of the experts by presenting the testimony of two more expert witnesses. The first was Dr. Walter Bromberg, who should have testified as part of the defense case-in-chief but was saved for surrebuttal for strategic purposes—probably to get in the last word on the subject of insanity. Bromberg told the jury that Ruby was "extremely emotionally unstable," had an "epileptoid personality," and was acting in a "state of suspended consciousness" when he shot Oswald.[54] As a result, Bromberg opined, Ruby "did not know the nature and quality of his acts" at the time of the offense.[55] On a lengthy cross-examination, much of which focused on Bromberg's career and compensation, the district attorney managed to score a few points with the jury by reading to Bromberg a passage from one of his own writings: "[N]either epilepsy or organic brain diseases, or subclinical forms of these disorders . . . is a contributing factor in major crime, including murder."[56]

When Belli rested for the second time, the prosecution was not to be outdone. In surrebuttal, the prosecutors called Dr. Robert Schwab, a neurologist, to the witness stand. Schwab told the jury that he saw only a "mild unspecific abnormality" in Ruby's EEG that could have had a number of causes including drug use, sleep deprivation, and "other mild conditions."[57] "Psychomotor variant," he testified further, was a "wave pattern" described by Dr. Frederic Gibbs, "not a disease."[58]

The tit-for-tat exchange of expert opinions could easily have ended there, but when word of Schwab's testimony reached Gibbs, who had until then steadfastly refused to testify, Gibbs changed his mind. Now, he would not only testify, but would pay his own expenses and charge no fee. Soon the Chicago neurologist who had first described the "psychomotor variant" was on the stand in Dallas.

On a direct examination that lasted less than half an hour, Gibbs testified that he reviewed Ruby's EEG and clearly saw a pattern that existed in "one-half percent of epileptics." Ruby, Gibbs said, suffered from "a very rare form of epilepsy"—psychomotor variant epilepsy—that could be detected only through an EEG.[59]

As had often been the case throughout the trial, the cross-examination of Gibbs was more eventful than the direct. Alexander asked Gibbs if he had an opinion regarding whether Ruby knew right from wrong and understood the nature and consequences of his act when he killed Oswald. As expected, Gibbs replied, "I have no opinion."[60] Alexander also forced Gibbs to acknowledge that he—like the prosecution's expert Dr. Olinger—was not board certified in any branch of medicine, and indeed had not even become licensed as a physician until 28 years after he graduated from medical school.

Even more significantly, however, Alexander confronted Gibbs with his resignation from the American EEG Society. Gibbs agreed that he had resigned from the medical association because of differences of opinion with his colleagues. Alexander then asked if Gibbs regarded himself as a heretic in the field of electroencephalography. Gibbs replied, "Possibly. I'd rather use another word."[61]

Gibbs was the trial's last witness. After hearing closing arguments and the judge's instructions, the jury took just 2 hours and 19 minutes to reach a verdict, guilty of murder with malice, and to decide on a sentence, death. The verdict and sentence were read in open court and, as the jurors filed out of the courtroom, Belli shouted, "May I thank the jury for a victory for bigotry and injustice! Don't worry, Jack, we'll appeal this to a court outside Dallas where there is justice and due process of law! I hope the people of Dallas are proud of this jury!"[62]

Belli's protests to the contrary, it appears that the Ruby jury actually did perform its duty conscientiously. Though Melvin Belli described Jack Ruby's case as presenting "the most perfect psychiatric defense"[63] he had ever seen, in fact the defense was far from perfect in either theory or execution. The case that Jack Ruby was insane was extraordinarily weak, the expert testimony for the defense was poorly presented, and a conscientious jury would have been forced to nullify the law in order to acquit Oswald's killer.

The jury foreman, Max Causey, a well-educated engineer, kept a contemporaneous journal of his experience as a juror in the case. That journal and later interviews with four other jurors explained how the jury responded to Ruby's insanity defense and why they so readily convicted him.

Causey's journal made it clear that the jurors felt that the insanity case was so weak that they did not even deliberate before unanimously rejecting it. The only thing close to deliberation that occurred was when the jury considered the penalty for Ruby. With little discussion, the vote for a death sentence quickly went from nine to three to unanimous.

Speaking only for himself, Causey made it clear that he had kept an open mind right to the end of the trial, indeed right up through the testimony of Dr. Gibbs, the last witness. Causey's journal entry for the last day of testimony, Friday, March 13, speaks eloquently of his patience and frustration with the defense offered on Ruby's behalf:

> I again awoke early and, as I had done many times during the past few days, I began going over the testimony in my mind. I wondered how significant Dr. Gibbs' testimony would be. Despite all the well

qualified and eminent professional medical experts we had heard testify, the actual conclusion was going to be our own . . . How I wished that either one side or the other would make the final decision easier. Up to this point, Friday morning, the defense had not actually convinced me that Ruby was insane to the point that he didn't know the difference between right and wrong at the time he shot Oswald. The defense never argued that Ruby didn't shoot Oswald, only that he didn't know what he was doing at the time because he was in a fugue state, or in a form of psychomotor epilepsy at the time. Granted, there had been good evidence that such a phenomenon was possible, but on the other hand it had been challenged just as effectively that it was highly improbable that this was the case . . . I wondered if the other members of the jury were weighing the evidence day-to-day as I had been . . . Were they, as I was, praying for the big break to come in the case that would make our decision a little easier? Maybe we would get that big break, at least from what we had been led to expect, from Dr. Gibbs . . .

At last we heard from Dr. Gibbs . . . He very strongly substantiated the defense's case that Ruby's brain wave tracings did very certainly indicate psychomotor variant patterns and that, in his opinion, Ruby's pattern suggested a very rare form of epilepsy . . .

Then Mr. Alexander dropped the bomb on Dr. Gibbs. He asked him if he had an opinion as to whether Ruby knew the difference between right and wrong and the nature and consequences of his act at the time that he shot Oswald. Dr. Gibbs' answer absolutely floored me, because I felt certain that he would offer his opinion to support the defense. He stated, without hesitation, "I have no opinion." I asked myself, what had been the point? Why had this eminent professional man traveled all this distance just to state that he had no opinion as to Ruby's sanity at the time of the shooting? The mere fact that he had added his weight to the defense that the EEG tracings indicated psychomotor variant, a rare type of epilepsy, was existent in Ruby did not seem worth the trip. Needless to say, I had expected more from this great man. Perhaps I had expected too much.[64]

Causey's journal also provided the foreman's assessment of what he thought Belli could have done to save Ruby from a conviction for murder with malice and a sentence of death:

In my layman's opinion, any good lawyer could have gotten Ruby off with something less than a death sentence if he had thrown

Ruby on the mercy of the court and pleaded plain old "temporary insanity" brought on by emotional stress over the loss of his beloved president . . .

If I had been Mr. Belli, and had been convinced that I could win the case with psychomotor epileptic insanity, I would have paraded additional medical witnesses to the stand who would have been wiling to testify that they had a positive opinion that Ruby did not know the difference between right and wrong and the nature and consequences of his act . . .

As it turned out, the defense counsel was numerically defeated in the medical experts willing to testify pertaining to an opinion on Ruby's sanity . . . Had the famous Dr. Gibbs ventured an opinion regarding Ruby's insanity, this would have weighed heavily in Ruby's favor . . . Mr. Belli had objected to Dr. Gibbs being asked his opinion on this question, and further stated that Dr. Gibbs was not qualified to answer such a question . . . Perhaps, technically, Mr. Belli was right, but if so, how could twelve medically unqualified jurors be asked to reach such an opinion? If Dr. Gibbs was not qualified to offer such an opinion, for whatever weight it might carry, then certainly neither were we. So, therefore, failure to have an opinion as to the sanity of a man leaves his condition status quo or sane. We the jury felt that Ruby was sane.[65]

Causey's sentiments were expanded on in later interviews with four other jurors. For example, J. Walter Rose said the jury did not accept the argument advanced by the "so-called expert witnesses" that Ruby suffered from the psychomotor variant form of epilepsy.[66] As he saw it, the evidence showed that "he actually had another form of epilepsy that would . . . cause him to lose control of himself . . . "[67] Asked how he would have handled Ruby's defense, Rose said, "I would have pleaded . . . no contest and fallen on the mercy of the court. It was pitiful. You know, the man [Ruby] sat there day in and day out, and he didn't have a chance. I wanted him to get up and say, 'Hey, I'm sorry. I did the wrong thing, I made a mistake.' But he never did that."[68]

Douglas J. Sowell, another juror, criticized the defense experts and the lack of evidence that others besides Ruby suffered from the purported mental illness:

> I found that they weren't very good witnesses. They seemed to me to believe that we, the jurors, were believing all the things they were telling us. You know, just like we weren't bright enough to figure out all this stuff—just listen to them and just vote their

way . . . If they'd have brought someone else in that had this problem and went into seizures and walked half a mile or whatever, or twenty or thirty feet . . .[69]

Asked how he would have handled Ruby's defense, Sowell said, "I would have stuck with the fact that Ruby felt that he was doing the country a favor—patriotism . . . I think I would not have even had the psychiatrists around. I think he could have built a pretty good case. A lot of people were saying that he [Ruby] did the right thing, and they should have played on that. But they didn't bring anything else with this psychomotor epilepsy thing, that's for sure. That fell on its face."[70]

Yet another juror, Robert J. Flechner, said that the defense witnesses were not convincing because "they were saying that he [Ruby] went nuts for 30 seconds and killed a guy. I mean it was like he was crazy for maybe an hour or so, and then he was all right."[71] Asked how he would have defended Ruby, Flechner said,

> Oh, I think I probably would have thrown myself on the mercy of the court . . . If they would have said he got caught up in the moment and was sorry for John Kennedy, little John, and his wife, and he [Ruby] did wrong, I think probably it would have been better. But they were saying, well, he did this and so what he needs to do is go to a shrink for a few months, and put him back out in society . . . [W]e didn't have much choice. It was either let him go to the shrink for a little bit, and turn him loose, or give him the death penalty.[72]

Finally, juror J. G. Holton, Jr. said, "Well, that [psycho]motor epilepsy stuff didn't make much sense. It was weak. I didn't latch on to a lot of it . . . I just kind of figured ol' Ruby just went off his rocker and got mad and wanted to shoot somebody."[73] Asked what his defense for Ruby would have been, Holton replied, "Yeah, well, that happened so long ago. But, I would have kind of thrown a little more mercy on the jury . . . He had all this psychiatrists' stuff and so forth, and hardly anybody swallowed it, too much. It seemed like to me that he didn't put it on the mercy of the jury."[74]

Although these five jurors all had somewhat different views of Ruby's insanity defense, all agreed that it was a mistake. To a man, they all said Ruby should have thrown himself on the mercy of the court. Indeed, all five used almost those exact words. Whether that strategy would have worked is obviously unknown and unknowable, but it is fascinating to note that it was essentially the strategy that Tom Howard, Ruby's first attorney, had planned when—before Melvin Belli took the case from him—he decided to forgo an insanity defense and try to prove that Ruby had simply cracked under the strain of the Kennedy assassination. From what these jurors had to say, it appears that Howard's plan might well have resulted in a conviction of murder without malice and a much lighter sentence for Ruby.

In the final analysis, the result of the Ruby trial may not have mattered much anyway. Two years after the trial, an appeals court overturned both the verdict of guilt and the sentence of death. Finding that the trial court should have granted Ruby's request for a change of venue from Dallas to another part of the state, the Texas Court of Criminal Appeals ordered a new trial for Ruby. Ruby remained jailed pending that trial, but died in custody before it took place.

2

Robert Torsney

On Thanksgiving Day in 1976, 15-year-old Randolph Evans could never have suspected that his life was about to end or that his death would trigger one of the most bizarre and controversial cases in the history of the insanity defense. Evans, an African-American youth, had just walked his grandmother to a bus stop near his home in the Cyprus Houses, a public housing project in Brooklyn. As he approached his building, Evans observed several police officers leaving the premises. The teen asked one of the officers what was happening. "Did you just come from apartment 7-D?" Evans inquired.[1] The officer, who had been to another apartment, replied, "You're damn right I did."[2] He then pulled his gun and shot Evans in the head from a distance of about 2 feet. Evans died several hours later.

Though Randolph Evans was killed on the evening of November 25, 1976, the seeds of his death and the uproar it caused had been brewing for years, perhaps decades. Robert Torsney, the white New York City police officer who shot and killed the African-American teenager, had been born 31 years earlier in Brooklyn and raised in the Coney Island area. Torsney had grown up in a family ruled harshly by a brutally abusive, alcoholic father who was eventually diagnosed as a schizophrenic and hospitalized for the rest of his life. As a child, Torsney was in generally good health but seemed to have more than his share of physical trauma. When he was just 2 years old, he was doused with boiling water by a sibling. At 12, he fell on his head, briefly losing consciousness; he also underwent surgery to rectify an undescended testicle.

After graduating from a vocational high school, Torsney had worked briefly as a printer before joining the U.S. Marine Corps. Torsney joined the Marines, he would later say, because his brother was a Marine and "I didn't want to be any less of a man than my brother, so I had to go in."[3] Though apparently joining the Marine Corps to prove his manhood, Torsney spent his entire 3-year tour of duty working as a printer.

Upon discharge from the military, Torsney again worked in the printing industry. A year later he joined the New York Police Department as a patrolman, the rank he held 8 years later when he shot and killed Randolph Evans.

Until Thanksgiving 1976, Torsney's career as a police officer had been uneventful but perhaps ominous. Much of the time he worked in a unit covering parades and other special events. Later, however, he volunteered for regular street duty in the city's 75th precinct, a largely black, poor, and racially tense neighborhood. Initially Torsney walked a beat in the 75th but later was assigned to a squad car. Though he had pulled his firearm many times in the line of duty, he had never fired the weapon prior to November 25, 1976.

Though Torsney's law enforcement career may have been routine prior to the killing, his personal life had not. His family and physical problems did not end when he became an adult. When discharged from the Marine Corps, Torsney returned home to find that his father had become infantile, incontinent, confused, and in need of round-the-clock nursing care. Although he denied being an alcoholic like his father, Torsney drank a six-pack of beer daily. He suffered a "nervous stomach" that required treatment with tranquilizers.[4] And, in the 4 years immediately preceding the killing, Torsney had been involved in three motor vehicle accidents, two while driving a car and one while riding a motorcycle. In the motorcycle accident, he struck the back of his head, lost consciousness, and was hospitalized for tests.

On November 25, 1976, Torsney had Thanksgiving dinner with his family at the home of his in-laws, watched a football game on television, drank several beers, reluctantly reported for duty on the 3:30 P.M. to midnight shift, and wrote in his officer's log book, "Happy Day. Felony day. Thanksgiving work day."[5] During that shift, Torsney shared a squad car with a veteran police officer. The shift was uneventful until it was nearly over. At about 11:20 P.M., Torsney and his partner received a radio call reporting a "man with a gun" and directing them to an apartment in the Cyprus Houses complex.[6] Joining several other officers who had already arrived at the scene, Torsney observed an injured woman but no man and no gun. Apparently the assailant had absconded before the officers arrived.

One by one the officers left the building and headed back to their patrol cars. With two fellow officers 50 to 75 feet in front of him, Torsney's right hand was already resting on his gun when he encountered Randolph Evans. After shooting Evans, Torsney made no effort to check on the boy's condition but instead walked to his patrol car, got in, removed the spent cartridge from his weapon, and calmly replaced it with another bullet. Torsney's partner, Officer Matthew Williams, who was already in the vehicle when Torsney shot

Evans, asked, "What did you do?"[7] Torsney responded, "I don't know, Matty. What did I do?"[8]

While other officers attended to Evans, who was still alive though mortally wounded, Williams drove Torsney to the 75th precinct, where Torsney tried to explain himself. Under questioning, Torsney admitted the obvious—that he had shot Evans—but claimed he had done so in self-defense. According to Torsney's version of the shooting, "I was confronted by this guy as I was 20 to 30 feet from the door. I was walking, and he was walking towards me. As he was walking towards me, he was reaching into his belt. We were walking towards each other. He wasn't on the path. He said, 'Hey, what happened up there?' or words to that effect. He came out with what appeared to be a chrome gun barrel. As he was talking and taking that gun out, I thought I was gonna be shot. I fired the gun as he was pulling it out."[9] The shooting, Torsney further explained, was a "reflex action."[10] Torsney recalled that he shot from his side, was "not positive" he heard the gun go off, and could remember little that happened thereafter.[11]

Neither the police nor the district attorney believed Torsney's self-serving account of the killing. None of the witnesses, including other police officers, had seen Randolph Evans reach for or draw a gun. Moreover, no gun was found anywhere near the scene. Faced with evidence that the killing was unprovoked and unjustified, a grand jury indicted Torsney for intentional murder.

Many members of New York's African-American community, including a number of black police officers, not only did not believe Torsney but were outraged by the way the case was initially handled. Three days after the killing, 150 people from the predominantly black neighborhood converged on the 75th precinct house to protest. Rocks and bottles were hurled at police officers, four of whom were injured. Three protestors were arrested. The protests continued the next day, this time peacefully, with some 75 protestors picketing the police station. Leading the protestors were members of the International Committee Against Racism and the Progressive Labor Party.

Many of these protestors were upset because the death of Randolph Evans was the third time in 3 years that a white New York City police officer had been charged with killing a black youth. The officer in one of those cases was awaiting trial at the time of Evans's death. In the other case, in 1974, 10-year-old Clifford Glover had been shot and killed by an NYPD officer searching for two grown men who had allegedly robbed a taxicab. Seeing Glover, who was black, walking down the street with his stepfather and carrying a toy gun, the officer, a white man who was not wearing a uniform and did not identify himself as a police officer, shot and killed the boy. Though dismissed from the police force, the officer was acquitted of all criminal charges.

Among the African-Americans most deeply troubled by the Torsney case were police officers who comprised the Guardians Association, a 1700-member fraternal group of black NYPD officers. At Torsney's arraignment on the murder charge, a judge allowed his release on a $40,000 bail bond paid for by New York City's police union, the Police Benevolent Association (PBA). Some 100 members of the Guardians convened within days of the bail decision and urged the group's larger membership to withdraw from the PBA. Several Guardians denounced the police and the PBA as "racist" and "insensitive,"[12] but the PBA's president defended posting Torsney's bail: "If the circumstances were reversed and it was a black cop who shot a white youth, the P.B.A. would have done exactly the same thing."[13]

Though the bail issue was controversial, it proved to be short-lived. Once Torsney was formally indicted, his bail was revoked by the judge after the prosecutor argued in court that "[f]rom the facts and circumstances it appears to have been a totally unprovoked, unjustifiable and intentional killing. The facts of this case indicate that a man—a police officer and a human being—pulls a gun and fires into the head of another human being and then walks away without breaking stride and later on he is not able to account for himself."[14]

Despite the facts, Torsney's defense attorney, who was at the time a member of the New York City Council, insisted that Torsney would plead self-defense. Brushing aside any suggestion that Torsney might raise a psychiatric defense, the defense attorney dismissed the significance of the odd "Happy Day. Felony day. Thanksgiving work day" notation in Torsney's log book, saying, "The D.A. may argue that my client is not responsible [i.e., insane] but many police officers write funny things in their memo books and this alone should not indicate a mental defect."[15]

Though Torsney always insisted that he had done nothing wrong and that the killing occurred in self-defense, his legal claim of justification was derailed by the facts and the reports of the psychiatrist and psychologist his attorney hired to examine him.

Dr. Daniel Schwartz, then director of the forensic psychiatry service at the county hospital in Brooklyn, interviewed Torsney, reviewed Torsney's history and his account of the alleged crime, and concluded that, "as a result of a mental defect, the defendant did not know or appreciate the nature, consequence and wrongfulness of his act."[16]

Schwartz's conclusion that Torsney was insane when he shot Randolph Evans was surprising in that Torsney had never suffered any known mental illness prior to or after the killing, nor had he ever been known to demonstrate any symptoms of mental illness, before or after the shooting. In essence, Schwartz was claiming that Torsney's mental illness manifested itself only at the time he shot and killed the 15-year-old youth.

As a legal matter, such a conclusion is perfectly plausible. The insanity defense requires only that, at the moment of the alleged crime, the defendant met the legal criteria—in this case, lacked the substantial capacity to know or appreciate either the nature and consequences of his conduct or that such conduct was wrong.

Clinically, however, it would be an exceedingly rare mental illness that manifested itself only precisely at the moment of a criminal act. Schwartz, however, believed that Torsney suffered from exactly such an illness: "psychosis associated with epilepsy."[17] As the psychiatrist explained,

> The defendant believes that he acted in self-defense, convinced that he saw the victim pulling something metallic out of his belt. Even if he were correct (no such object was ever found) his behavior was irrational and totally inconsistent with such an occurrence, factual or delusional. Instead of remaining on the scene (or taking cover) with his gun drawn until he was assured that the situation was under control, he reloaded his gun in an automatic way and continued walking as though nothing had happened . . .
>
> In our professional opinion the defendant's irrational behavior is best explained on a neurological basis. It actually began as he was leaving the apartment house, when he placed his hand on his gun, before the victim ever appeared. This was the beginning of an epileptic seizure, a twilight state or automatism (as described, for instance, by Straus) "during which the patient is not prostrate but acts more or less automatically." Such a state may start "without any premonitory symptoms or signs" and may show no EEG [electroencephalogram] abnormalities. Such a patient may be "only partially aware of his surroundings" and may unintentionally commit an act which would otherwise be criminal.[18]

When Schwartz used the term "our professional opinion," he may have been using the royal pronoun but more likely was referring to the report of Dr. Joy B. Roy, a psychologist who examined and tested Torsney for the defense about a month before Schwartz tendered his conclusions. Dr. Roy painted Torsney with a much broader, more psychoanalytic brush:

> In terms of the crime in question, I see many possible factors operating. The day was a holiday, when Mr. Torsney had been drinking more than usual. This may have relaxed his usual censoring ability.

The holiday, Thanksgiving day, may have also activated deep family feelings, yearnings and conflicts. The crime had involved a hurt woman and an abandoning man, which could have been reminiscent of his abused mother and his absenting father. In killing the boy Mr. Torsney may have been avenging his mother, seeking her approval, and perhaps even destroying the unacceptable aggressive parts of his own personality. At the time of his crime Mr. Torsney's partner, an older man, was some distance away, talking with another patrolman-friend. Perhaps Mr. Torsney felt his relationship with this father-person was being threatened.[19]

As for a "diagnostic impression," Joy was less certain than Schwartz but supported his conclusion:

This is a man with schizoid and depressive features. More important is the explosive quality in his personality, which may be organic or functional. The killing, followed by a dazed reaction, is consonant with the anxiety and bewilderment we may expect to see in an epileptic equivalent, where there is an episode of excitement and violence instead of a seizure, followed by confusion.[20]

Dr. Florence Schumer and Dr. Herbert Speigel, a psychologist and psychiatrist who examined and tested Torsney for the prosecution, saw no evidence that Torsney was suffering from an epileptic seizure when he killed Evans. Based upon psychological testing, Schumer reported that "[t]his individual shows poor controls over impulsiveness. This is a shallow, dependent, immature personality with chronic depression, deep fears (possibly with regard to his own angers, distrust of what will happen, concern over impulsiveness), and interpersonal guardedness and constriction. There is great stress on proving manliness, power, and assertiveness in a poorly integrated personality."[21]

Additionally, Schumer's testing led her to conclude that "there is little in the record, despite the deep problems noted above, to indicate cognitive pathology, psychoses, or bizarre or disorganized intellective or emotional processes."[22] As for the shooting, Schumer reported that the test findings "do indeed indicate that [Torsney] might well have responded in an impulsive volatile manner to anticipated threat."[23]

Spiegel, a clinical psychiatrist and medical school professor, relied heavily upon Schumer's findings, quoting them verbatim and at length in his own report. Spiegel concluded that Torsney suffered from a "neurotic character disorder" and demonstrated "a proneness to dissociate under stress with hysterical dyscontrol and transient panic" but was not psychotic and was not insane at the time of the crime.[24]

Torsney's trial, a 13-day proceeding, featured testimony from the defendant, fellow police officers, his wife and sister, and the experts for both sides. Torsney testified that he had acted in self-defense and told the jury, "Obviously, I didn't do anything wrong."[25] Two fellow police officers disagreed, testifying that Torsney "acted without apparent provocation and seemed calm during and after the shooting."[26]

Torsney's sister testified to violent beatings inflicted upon Torsney as a child by his father. Both Torsney's sister and wife told the jury that his behavior had changed following his motorcycle accident; he had become "edgy," and his marriage had almost ended as a result.[27]

Dr. Schwartz testified that Torsney suffered from a rare form of epilepsy that caused a psychomotor seizure, during which Torsney killed Randolph Evans. Confronted with Torsney's normal EEG results, Schwartz maintained that the officer's epilepsy "would probably show up in the [EEG] tracing only during an actual attack."[28] On cross-examination, Schwartz also acknowledged that his diagnosis of Torsney "was an uncertain one to make without actually having observed the defendant suffering a seizure."[29]

Dr. Roy, the defense psychologist, testified that Torsney was anxious, overcontrolled, afraid of his feelings, and prone to explosive outbursts. His lack of emotion in describing the shooting, she told the jury, suggested the possibility of an organic disorder.

In rebuttal for the prosecution, Dr. Spiegel testified that Torsney may have suffered "hysterical dissociation" but no mental disease or defect.[30] Torsney, the psychiatrist opined, mistakenly thought he saw a gun, panicked, and shot Evans.

Had Torsney ever suffered an actual attack—in other words, one of those rare psychomotor seizures hypothesized by Schwartz? The only proof that he had was Schwartz's assertion that such a seizure was "the only thing that could account for the shooting."[31] However, as far as he or any other professionals were able to ascertain, if Torsney had suffered such a seizure at the time of the killing, it was both the first and last one he ever suffered.

Torsney's attorney appeared to realize the shakiness of Schwartz's diagnosis when, in his closing argument, he tried to equate a lack of "normalcy" with "insanity," telling the jury, "Whether you accept the Spiegel finding of hysterical dissociation or you accept the concept of psychomotor seizure is really unimportant. The fact is there was not normalcy at the time of the shooting."[32] Moreover, in what appeared to be a non sequitur, the defense attorney dismissed the evidence that Evans never reached for or pulled a gun, telling the jurors, "That's what this case is all about. If there was no gun, this man is sick."[33]

These arguments, though lacking in both reason and weight, apparently appealed to the jury or at least offered them a rationale for acquitting the disgraced police officer. After only 5 hours of deliberations, the all-white panel found Robert Torsney not guilty by reason of insanity.

Was Torsney acquitted because the jury really believed the far-fetched expert testimony that the killing he committed occurred during the one and only seizure he ever suffered? Was his acquittal, as some believed, the product of racism, an all-white jury siding with a white police officer who killed a black teenager? Or was the verdict simply a product of its time, an era in which New York City was plagued by violence and the public was willing to give wide latitude to police officers, such as Torsney, in responding to the perceived epidemic of crime?

Whatever its basis, the Torsney verdict, though extremely controversial, would likely have faded from the public consciousness fairly quickly had it not been for what followed. Even critics of the verdict must have taken some solace in New York State's requirement that an insanity acquittee such as Torsney be committed to the custody of the state department of mental health until it could be judicially determined that he was no longer a danger to others. Indeed, at the time of the verdict, offenders found not guilty by reason of insanity in New York were generally committed to secure mental hospitals for rather long periods of time; in many cases these acquitted offenders spent more time locked up than did those who were convicted of the same offenses.

Torsney, however, was not only acquitted by reason of insanity but was released from state confinement in just a year and a half.

Almost immediately following his acquittal by reason of insanity, pursuant to New York law, Torsney was committed to the Mid-Hudson Psychiatric Center, a high security inpatient mental health facility with most of the trappings of a state prison. A day later, Torsney was examined by a psychologist and a psychiatrist at Mid-Hudson. Both doctors concluded that Torsney suffered from no mental illness or organic disorder and had no need of inpatient treatment. The psychologist, however, found that Torsney was a "somewhat rigid, impulsive individual" who was "subconsciously racially prejudiced and [had] deficient emotional control insofar as minimal stress would result in behavioral impulsivity."[34] The psychologist opined that Torsney "not fit for duty as a beat police officer."[35]

A month after his admission to the psychiatric center, Torsney was reexamined. This time, the same psychiatrist concluded that Torsney had "made an excellent adjustment to his present hospitalization" and observed that Torsney "neither before or [sic] after the offense [had] shown any signs of epilepsy."[36] The psychiatrist pronounced Torsney free of any symptoms of mental disorder. Indeed, as this psychiatrist would later testify, he would have recommended Torsney's immediate release, except for his belief that no New York court would ever grant release to an insanity acquittee after such a short period of confinement.

After 2 months at Mid-Hudson, Torsney was evaluated by three members of the hospital staff, including the psychiatrist who had already concluded that he suffered from no mental illness. The panel concluded that Torsney had "been cooperative with no evidence of any symptoms or signs during his stay [at Mid-Hudson] which point towards any potential for dangerous behavior."[37] As a result, Torsney was informed that he would be transferred to the Creedmoor Psychiatric Center, a less secure facility. When Torsney learned that he would be sent to Creedmoor and not released to the community, according to the doctor who gave him the news, "Torsney responded by throwing a temper tantrum like a child."[38]

Upon admission to Creedmoor, Torsney was evaluated by another panel of hospital staff members. These doctors unanimously concluded that "Torsney was not suffering from a psychosis, psychopathic disorder or organic damage and that he was not dangerous to himself or others and should be released."[39] The panel also recommended, however, that Torsney not be allowed to resume his duties as a beat police officer.

Faced with this unequivocal conclusion and the records from Mid-Hudson and Creedmoor documenting that Torsney was neither mentally ill nor dangerous, the state commissioner of mental hygiene must have still had some concerns about seeking Torsney's release. Instead of immediately petitioning the court for such release, the commissioner convened an independent review panel to examine Torsney. This panel, consisting of two psychiatrists and a social worker, examined Torsney and reported that he "can safely be released from the hospital, without danger to himself or others. His history reveals no dangerous behavior other than the instant offense, nor has he subsequently shown any inability to control impulses, any inappropriate display of hostility, nor any behavior which might be considered threatening or dangerous. He voices no intentions to do harm to anyone and is not now mentally ill, having fully recovered from the entity which led to his [acquittal] by reason of mental disease or defect."[40]

With that finding in hand, the commissioner then applied to the court for Torsney's release. At the request of the district attorney who had prosecuted Torsney, the court appointed two independent forensic psychiatrists to examine Torsney. The first of these psychiatrists concluded that Torsney was not psychotic or dangerous to himself or others and that there was no justification for "continued incarceration on psychiatric grounds."[41] The second court-appointed psychiatrist concluded that "Mr. Torsney is neither a lunatic or [sic] a psychopath and is not a menace to others or to himself. In my opinion, there is nothing about his present mental condition which warrants his continued incarceration, and he appears to be capable of returning to a productive and useful place in society."[42] This doctor added, however, that, in view of what he termed Torsney's "questionable impulse control and inability to deal with stress," Torsney should be "gradually discharged over several weeks to ensure his satisfactory return to the community."[43]

Faced with these reports and the uncontroverted and unanimous testimony of more than a dozen witnesses (including psychologists, psychiatrists, neurologists, and a forensic nurse) over 9 days that Torsney was neither psychotic nor dangerous, the court ordered the former police officer released from state custody on the conditions that he not be permitted to carry a gun, no longer work as a police officer, and continue outpatient psychiatric treatment for 5 years.

The third of these conditions, of course, appeared unusual in light of repeated statements by doctors at both Mid-Hudson and Creedmoor that Torsney suffered no mental illness. Moreover, the court's written decision to release Torsney seemed somewhat odd, if not foreboding, as the judge acknowledged Torsney's impulsivity but appeared more concerned about the lack of gun control in American society. In concluding his opinion, the judge wrote,

> Witnesses have testified that this patient is emotional and impulsive which is to be considered a personality disability and not a mental illness. These experts tell us he should not have a gun. How many others are there in a similar incapacity presently authorized to carry such a weapon?
>
> When will we awaken to the realization that society is a party to the slaughter—it has happened before; unfortunately it will happen again until we control the possession of handguns and/or at the least provide a mechanism for continued evaluation of the mental condition of any and all persons authorized to carry such weapons.[44]

Though ordered released, Torsney was not immediately freed. The court's release order was appealed by the district attorney, and the Appellate Division, New York's intermediate appeals court, concluded that Torsney continued to suffer from a "dangerous personality disorder," reversed the judge's order, and voided Torsney's conditional discharge.[45] The appellate court noted "the glaring failure of the State Department of Mental Hygiene . . . to fully investigate and treat, if necessary, Torsney's condition (diagnosed at his criminal trial to be either psychomotor epilepsy or hysterical neurosis, dissociative state)."[46] Castigating the Department of Mental Hygiene for merely "warehousing" Torsney, the appeals court further observed that

> Dr. M. Vandenbergh, a psychiatrist at Mid-Hudson, testified that Torsney was suffering from an impulsive and explosive personality disorder but was not dangerous. As Dr. Vandenbergh did not believe that Torsney ever suffered from psychomotor epilepsy, no neurological examinations or electroencephalographic tests were ever conducted. Although he believed Torsney should be released, he did not think the court would be amenable to releasing Torsney after only two months of confinement. Accordingly, he did not recommend individual treatment for Torsney or his release. He merely warehoused him . . .
>
> It is clear that Torsney was at least suffering from a personality disorder which contributed to his actions on November 25, 1976. More importantly, he still suffers from that same condition today. Indeed, the presentation of the petitioner did not rebut the presumption of dangerousness; it only buttressed it. Regrettably the Department of Mental Hygiene never treated Torsney's condition properly or equipped him to deal with his "impulsive dyscontrols." The department never administered individual care but only provided Torsney with a structured environment"—little more than a "warehouse."[47]

Torsney appealed the Appellate Division's decision to the Court of Appeals, New York's highest court, which had the final say in the matter, ordering Torsney released just 19 months after he was first committed to Mid-Hudson. The four-judge majority of the seven-member Court of Appeals explained its decision on constitutional grounds:

> An individual's liberty cannot be deprived by "warehousing" him in a mental institution when he is not suffering from a mental illness or defect and in no need of in-patient care and treatment on a ground which amounts to a presumption of a dangerous propensity flowing from, as in this case, an isolated, albeit tragic, incident occurring years ago. Were this the standard for involuntary institutionalization, logical extension would require that anyone convicted

of a violent crime should upon completion of his sentence similarly be required to demonstrate that he or she is not dangerous before his release into the community. Whatever its label, confinement on a showing of mere propensity amounts to nothing more than preventive detention, a concept foreign to our constitutional order.[48]

Writing in dissent for himself and two other judges, Chief Judge Sol Wachtler found evidence in the record to indicate that Torsney was mentally ill and dangerous. Judge Wachtler reminded the court of the expert's opinions at Torsney's insanity trial: "Dr. Herbert Spiegel concluded that Torsney is 'prone to hysterical dissociation under stress,' and Dr. Florence Schumer found Torsney to be 'volatile' and 'impulsive.' According to Dr. Daniel Schwartz, Torsney was suffering from psychomotor epilepsy. Dr. Joy Roy's examination of Torsney revealed that '[when] he feels attacked and threatened the aggression escapes the censor and may erupt in impulsive behavior.'"[49]

The chief judge also noted that both of the court-appointed psychiatrists who testified at Torsney's release hearing found Torsney to be volatile, impulsive, and explosive, that one opined that Torsney suffered from an "impulsive or explosive personality disorder" and that the other feared that "under stressful circumstances Torsney might erupt again."[50] Combining the psychological and psychiatric evidence from both trials, Wachtler concluded that "it becomes all too apparent that Torsney's condition has never changed substantially and that he remains as dangerous today as he was on the day he shot Randolph Evans."[51] As for the majority's concern "that we not transform the hospital into a penitentiary where one could be held indefinitely," Wachtler replied, "I agree, of course, that hospital confinement should never be abused to deprive someone of his liberty unfairly. However, when a person, driven by an explosive personality disorder, has proven by an act of senseless violence that he is a menace to others, so long as the psychological condition persists it is our obligation to protect the public from further acts of violence that he may commit."[52]

Altogether, 13 judges (including the release trial judge) reviewed the psychiatric and psychological evidence regarding Torsney's mental illness and dangerousness. Eight of those 13 judges (5 from the Appellate Division and 3 from the Court of Appeals) concluded that Torsney was mentally ill, dangerous, and in need of further confinement to prevent him from harming the public. In July of 1979, Robert Torsney was released from Creedmoor Psychiatric Center because 4 of the 13 reviewing judges happened to be members of the state's highest court.

The results in the Torsney case were extraordinary, to say the least. Torsney managed to beat the odds twice, once when he was found not guilty by reason of insanity and again when he managed to dodge the bullet of long-term confinement that ordinarily follows an insanity acquittal in a murder case. In the minds of some, the judgments of the jury and courts in this case gave the insanity defense not one but two black eyes. The case was widely reported and interpreted as one in which the insanity defense was manipulated in order to exculpate a guilty defendant and allow him to almost literally get away with murder.

Certainly one could reasonably view the case in that fashion, but another explanation might be simply that this case was a fluke, one of those rare instances in which the unusual circumstances of the case lead to legal consequences that, though deeply troubling, turn out to be correct.

The results in Torsney's case may be an indictment not of the insanity defense, but of the limitations inherent in the professions of those charged with administering it. To begin with, there seems little doubt that Robert Torsney did not suffer from any major mental illness when he shot Randolph Evans. The explanation given in his defense, that he suffered from a psychomotor seizure at the time of the killing, made little sense clinically and was likely offered because mental health professionals retained by the defense found it to be the only remotely plausible explanation for an otherwise unexplainable killing. Even the experts for the prosecution were forced to resort to diagnostic labels rarely ever used and of questionable validity. Asked to explain the inexplicable, as forensic psychologists and psychiatrist so often are, the experts on both sides of the Torsney matter did the best job they could.

The same may be said of the psychologists and psychiatrists who pronounced Torsney neither mentally ill nor dangerous after he was acquitted by reason of insanity. They were asked to explain not why Torsney killed Randolph Evans but rather his mental state long after the killing. Because Torsney likely never suffered from any major mental illness, these posttrial experts appear to have gotten the right answer, at least on the issue of mental illness: Torsney, like millions of other Americans, suffered from a personality disorder.

But the posttrial experts also had to decide whether Torsney was dangerous. Though psychological and psychiatric predictions of future dangerousness have improved a great deal since 1979, they have never been very accurate. Indeed, in 1983, not long after the Torsney case was resolved, the American Psychiatric Association informed the U.S. Supreme Court that two out of three such predictions proved to be wrong. The court responded by affirming the use of such predictions in legal proceedings, noting, "Neither petitioner nor the Association suggests that psychiatrists are always wrong with respect to future dangerousness, only most of the time."[53]

The psychologists and psychiatrists who opined that Robert Torsney was not dangerous were, despite the limited state of the art at that time, probably correct. There is no indication that, after being released from Creedmoor, Robert Torsney ever again committed a serious act of violence, or at least one that became known to the public.

3

David Berkowitz

Shortly after 1 A.M. on July 29, 1976, 18-year-old Donna Lauria and 19-year-old Jody Valente sat in Valente's car, which was double-parked outside Lauria's home in the Bronx, one of the boroughs of New York City. The teens had met earlier in the evening, Valente had driven Lauria home, and the two were chatting.

Lauria's parents approached the car and asked her to come in. Lauria promised to come inside shortly but by the time her parents had gone into the house, the young women were suddenly approached by a man with a gun. Without saying a word, the man aimed his firearm at the women and shot one in the head and the other in the thigh.

Donna Lauria, with a gunshot to the head, was dead on arrival at a nearby hospital. Jody Valente survived and was able to give the police a description of the assailant—5 feet, 8 inches tall, about 175 pounds—and say the gun he fired five times was a long-barreled pistol. An analysis of the shooting scene revealed little of use except that the bullets recovered were extremely large slugs that had been fired from a .44-caliber revolver, an unusual weapon associated more with old western gunslingers than modern urban street killers. Based upon this limited evidence, and given the nature of other nearby shootings around the same time, detectives hypothesized that the killing was likely the work of an organized crime hit man who had accidentally shot the wrong person.

Three months after the killing of Donna Lauria, 20-year-old Carl Denaro was shot as he sat in a parked car with 22-year-old Rosemary Keenan in Queens, New York, not far from the spot where Lauria was shot dead while sitting in a parked car with Jody Valente. Denaro who, like Lauria and Valente, had shoulder-length dark brown hair styled like that of a woman, was shot in the head from behind. Though he survived, portions of his skull were shattered and had to be replaced with a metal plate. Initially, police recovered only a bullet fragment too deformed to allow identification. But, a few days later,

Keenan found the rest of the bullet in her car, and police were able to identify it as a .44 caliber.

About 6 weeks after the Denaro shooting, two other young New York City women were shot. On November 29, 1976, the day after Thanksgiving, 18-year-old Joanne Lomino and 16-year-old Donna DeMasi were walking home from a restaurant that served as a teen hangout in their "virtually crime-free middle-class neighborhood of neat, detached one-family homes."[1] Reaching Joanne's home at about 12:30 A.M., the girls sat on the stoop to talk. After chatting for about 10 minutes, Joanne headed up the stairs toward the front door while Donna made her way down the steps to the sidewalk. Suddenly a man appeared on the street, turned, and began walking toward the teenagers. When he was close enough to be heard, he started to ask, "Say, can you tell me how to get to . . . ?"[2] But before he finished the question, he pulled a gun from beneath his three-quarter length army coat and began firing at Lomino and DeMasi.

Donna was shot in the neck and collarbone; Joanne was struck in the back. Although both girls survived, Joanne was left paralyzed from the waist down as a result of the bullet lodged in her spine. Ballistics testing revealed that the bullets fired at the two teens were .44 caliber. Other than the ballistics finding, a vague description of the assailant provided by Donna (i.e., about 5 feet, 10 inches tall and weighing perhaps 150 pounds or more), and a composite drawing by a police sketch artist, the authorities had little to go on.

Two months after Joanne Lomino and Donna DeMasi were shot, another New York City woman was shot and killed in an affluent neighborhood. On January 30, 1977, Christine Freund was sitting in a car at 12:30 A.M. with John Diel. The couple was planning to announce their engagement 2 weeks later, on Valentine's Day. Diel, who was driving, was about to pull away from the curb when seemingly out of nowhere came gunshots. Christine was struck in the shoulder and head and died at a nearby hospital before emergency surgery could be performed.

The bullets that killed Christine Freund, like those fired at Donna Lauria, Jody Valente, Carl Denaro, Joanne Lomino, and Donna DeMasi, were .44 caliber. Finally, the police put the four cases together and considered that a single perpetrator might be responsible for all of them. One of the NYPD detectives investigating the cases told the media, "I'll admit that evidence tying the four similar shootings together is scarce. But if I had to guess I'd say there's a nut running around."[3]

It would not be long after that statement was made that the police had solid physical evidence that a single perpetrator—or at least a single gun—was involved in all of the shootings. On March 8, 1977, at about 7:30 P.M., less than a block from the site of Christine Freund's killing, Virginia Voskerichian, a 19-year-old Columbia University student with long dark-brown hair, was gunned down as she walked from a bus stop to the home she shared with her parents.

Virginia died instantly, but a witness saw a man running from the scene; he was described as being in his late teens or early twenties, standing 5 feet 8 inches tall, weighing about 160 pounds, and wearing a waist-length coat and a stocking cap. Any doubt that this killing was tied to the four earlier shootings was put to rest when ballistics tests finally demonstrated not only that Virginia Voskerichian was slain with a .44 caliber bullet but that the bullet was fired from the same gun used to shoot Donna Lauria, Jody Valente, Carl Denaro, Joanne Lomino, Donna DeMasi, and Christine Freund.

Following the ballistics match, the police were almost certain that they were seeking a serial killer. New York City Mayor Abraham Beame, however, did not wait for proof certain. He announced, "We have a savage killer on the loose. He is singling out women with shoulder length dark brown hair. We don't know why . . . "[4]

If Beame had been premature in concluding and announcing that the shootings were definitely the work of a single perpetrator, there would soon be little doubt that the mayor was correct. On April 17, 1977, just 6 weeks after Virginia Voskerichian was killed, 19-year-old Valerie Suriani and 20-year-old Alexander Esau were parked on a street of two-story, single-family homes in the Bronx when both were shot in the head through the car's windshield.

When police arrived at the scene, they found Valerie already dead. Alexander was mortally wounded but still breathing. On the seat of the car, officers found an envelope addressed to Capt. Joseph Borrelli, a detective who had been identified in the media as one of the lead investigators on the previous shootings. Inside the envelope was a note:

> I am deeply hurt by your calling me a wemon [sic] hater. I am not. But I am a monster.
> I am the "Son of Sam." I am a little "brat."
> When father Sam gets drunk he gets mean. He beats his family. Sometimes he ties me up to the back of the garage. Other times he locks me in the garage. Sam loves to drink blood.
> "Go out and kill" commands father Sam . . .
> I feel like an outsider. I am on a different wavelength then [sic] everybody else—programmed too [sic] kill.
> However, to stop me you must kill me. Attention all police: Shoot me first—shoot to kill or else keep out of my way or you will die!

. . .

Mr. Boreli [sic], sir, I don't want to kill anymore. No sir, no more, but I must "honour thy father."

. . .

POLICE: Let me haunt you with these words:
I'll be back!
I'll be back!
To be interpreted as—bang, bang, bang, bank [sic], bang—ugh!
Yours in murder,
Mr. Monster[5]

Focused on this self-named "Mr. Monster"—a serial killer the media had dubbed the ".44 caliber killer"—a police task force conducted one of the most extensive manhunts in the city's history. Leaving no stone unturned, detectives turned to criminal profilers in an effort to get a psychological picture of the killer that went beyond his crude note to Capt. Borrelli. Dr. Harvey Schlossberg, a psychologist and New York City police officer, saw "Mr. Monster" as a depressed, friendless, and enraged loner who had been rejected by a woman and was "very sick and really needs help."[6] The police psychologist viewed him as "psychologically disturbed" but not "stupid."[7] The .44-caliber killer, Schlossberg opined, no longer needed to kill because he was now engaged in a cat-and-mouse game with the police: "He can leave evidence, taunt us with it, but now he doesn't have to kill . . . "[8]

After Schlossberg profiled the killer, so did a group of 45 psychiatrists who met with police detectives for 3 hours at a nearby state psychiatric hospital. Perhaps the most memorable opinion came from one doctor who opined that "[e]very time he shoots, he's ejaculating."[9] Not surprisingly, the detectives were unimpressed.

Two other psychiatrists, both with considerable forensic experience, joined the chorus of mental health experts offering their views to the police and the public. Although many experts' opinions were no doubt taken with a grain of salt by skeptical detectives, those of Dr. Martin Lubin and Dr. James Brussel had to be given serious consideration. Lubin, who told police that the killer was psychotic, was the former chief of forensic psychiatry at Bellevue Hospital. Brussel had, 2 decades earlier, personally developed the field of criminal profiling while preparing a police-requested psychological portrait of New York City's "Mad Bomber." Brussel's profile of George Meteskey, the unknown suspect who had terrorized the city with homemade bombs since the 1930s, had been almost a perfect match. Amazingly, Brussel had even accurately predicted what clothing the "Mad Bomber" would be wearing when he was arrested.

Brussel agreed with Schlossberg that the .44-caliber killer was mentally ill, "a classical paranoid," had been rejected by a woman he loved, and was likely taking great pleasure in toying with the police.[10] "This fellow," the psychiatrist concluded, "is burning that he's got the police licked."[11] Unlike Schlossberg, however, Brussel was convinced that "Mr. Monster" would kill again before turning himself in or making any further efforts to communicate with the police.

Putting all of the psychological and psychiatric input together with the scant evidence they had, New York police publicly issued a psychological profile of the killer, describing him as a "neurotic, schizophrenic and paranoid" individual who might believe that he was suffering from a kind of demonic possession.[12] The profile also described the killer as "probably shy and odd, a loner inept in establishing personal relationships, especially with women."[13]

As it turned out, Dr. Brussel was technically correct. The ".44 caliber killer" made his next contact not with the police but with a newspaper columnist who had written about him. In late May 1977, Jimmy Breslin of the *New York Daily News* received a letter signed "Son of Sam." Among other things, the writer told Breslin, "I appreciate your interest in those recent and horrendous .44 killings" and cautioned that more homicides could be anticipated: "[Y]ou must not forget Donna Lauria and you cannot let people forget her, either. She was a very sweet girl but Sam's a thirsty lad and he won't let me stop killing until he gets his fill of blood."[14]

Breslin responded with an appeal in the newspaper to "Son of Sam" to give up, much like the appeal that was made to George Meteskey decades earlier after the "Mad Bomber" communicated with reporters at another New York City newspaper.[15] The killer ignored Breslin's plea.

Meanwhile, as the manhunt continued, unknown to New York City police, residents of nearby Yonkers were also receiving some strange letters. Sam Carr received two letters complaining about his dog, a black Labrador retriever. One letter told Carr, "Our lives are being torn apart because of this dog."[16] A second letter (signed "A Citizen"), in handwriting that appeared to match the first, was more detailed and ominous:

> I have asked you kindly to stop that dog from howling all day long, yet he continues to do so. I pleaded with you. I told you how this is destroying my family. We have no peace, no rest.
>
> Now I know what kind of a person you are and what kind of a family you are. You are cruel and inconsiderate. You have no love for any other human beings. Your [sic] selfish, Mr. Carr. My life is destroyed now. I have nothing to lose anymore. I can see that there

shall be no peace in my life, or my families [sic] life until I end yours.[17]

Carr and his family called the Yonkers police, who took the complaint but did little else to investigate it. Even when, 2 weeks later, someone shot the Carr's dog, the lack of evidence meant that little could be done to bring the perpetrator to justice.

Harassment of the Carrs did not end with the letters and the shooting of their dog. Soon, they were contacted by Jack Cassara, another Yonkers resident, who also had received some unusual mail. The top left-hand corner of the envelope bore the name Carr along with the Carr family's address. Inside was a get-well card and a letter expressing concern over an accident in which Cassara had supposedly fallen off a roof and been injured; it was signed "Sincerely, Sam and Francis."[18] Because Cassara had never experienced any such accident, he was curious and contacted the Carrs. The two families met and compared notes, literally and figuratively. The Cassaras' son suggested that perhaps the writer was a young man who had briefly rented a room over the family's garage, complained about their dog, and then moved abruptly without even asking for the return of his security deposit. When police looked into the man identified by the Cassaras' son, they learned that one of the man's neighbors, Craig Glassman, had also recently received some odd anonymous letters.

The first letter Glassman received mentioned Sam Carr and the Cassaras, accusing them of being part of a "demon group."[19] The letter went on to say, "I know that the Cassaras and Carr are out to get me and they put you here."[20] A second letter was peppered with references to Satan, demons, and "streets running red with blood at the judgment" and accused Glassman of being "the master [who] drove me into the night to do your bidding."[21]

Lacking anything more than circumstantial evidence to identify the alleged writer, and believing that at worst this was a case of harassment and firing a gun within city limits (assuming that the letter writer and dog shooter were the same person), Yonkers police placed the Carr–Cassara complaint on the back burner, where it would simmer for quite some time.

Although New York City police continued their manhunt and hoped for a breakthrough in the "Son of Sam" investigation, they did not get one. Instead, on June 26, 1977, their elusive quarry struck again. At about 3:00 A.M., 17-year-old Judith Placido and 20-year-old Sal Lupo left a Queens discotheque, sat in Lupo's car, smoked, and talked for about 10 minutes before each was shot by a stranger with what ballistics testing would later identify as a .44-caliber revolver—the same one "Son of Sam" had used in all of his earlier shootings. Lupo was struck once in the arm, whereas Placido was hit three times in the head, but both survived. Two eyewitnesses described the shooter as a man about 5 feet, 10 inches tall, weighing around 170 pounds and wearing a beige three-quarter-length coat. Significantly, both witnesses saw the man drive away from his crime in a yellow car.

Increasingly desperate for meaningful leads in the investigation, the police issued yet another profile of the "Son of Sam." In addition to painting him as a sexually frustrated schizophrenic loner who had been rejected by a woman, they suggested that he was polite, very intelligent, probably college educated, worked days at a white collar job, and was likely a Catholic or Episcopalian. The police also made a public plea for his surrender, acknowledging that he had "problems," was "suffering pain and anguish," and "not in control of [him]self."[22] If he would just communicate with the police, they assured him, they would do their best to alleviate his problems.

Again, the "Son of Sam" chose to communicate with the police not with words but with actions. Just over a month after shooting Sal Lupo and Judith Placido, the serial killer struck again. On July 31, 1977, exactly 1 year and 2 days after his reign of terror had begun, he changed his venue to Brooklyn but used the same .44-caliber revolver to shoot another couple, Robert Violante and Stacy Moskowitz, both 20-year-olds. Robert survived but was blinded; Stacy died from gunshot wounds to the brain.

Robert and Stacy would be "Son of Sam's" last victims. Before the serial killer could strike again, detectives got the break they had sought for months. A witness to the Moskowitz killing told detectives that police officers had been ticketing illegally parked cars in the area around the time of the shooting. Tracing the parking tickets, officers quickly learned that one of the vehicles parked nearby that night belonged to David Berkowitz. Berkowitz, the police soon realized, was a former neighbor of Sam Carr, was the former tenant of the Cassaras who had complained about their dog before abruptly moving out, and was now living in an apartment directly above Craig Glassman, who had received odd anonymous letters complaining of a "demon group" conspiracy including the Carrs and Cassaras. Unknown to the New York City police, detectives in Yonkers had already been investigating Berkowitz's possible role in the letters sent to the Carrs and the shooting of their dog.

Berkowitz was soon arrested and confessed to the yearlong shooting spree. He was a 35-year-old Army veteran and postal worker with a checkered employment history. Born out of wedlock, he was given up by his mother as an infant and adopted by Nathan and Pearl Berkowitz, who raised him together until Pearl died when he was 16 years old. Berkowitz lived alone, had no friends, and had never had a meaningful relationship with a woman.

Though Berkowitz had no formal history of psychological or psychiatric treatment, there were plenty of reasons, other than his killing spree, to suggest that he was mentally ill. Growing up, he was regarded as an odd, difficult, erratic, and hyperactive child who was taunted by his peers because he was Jewish and adopted. After dropping out of school to join the Army, he had become heavily involved in drugs but then quickly became a born-again Christian who preached the Gospel to his fellow soldiers at Fort Knox.

Upon discharge from the military, Berkowitz had returned to New York City and worked at numerous jobs, including one as a security guard. He was fascinated with uniforms and fires. He joined the local police auxiliary, hung around firehouses, and kept a meticulous journal that included notes on roughly 1500 fires he started and/or reported.

When police entered Berkowitz's squalid apartment, they found sheets covering the windows. The walls, into which holes had been punched or pounded, were covered with various forms of graffiti. For example, on one wall was written,

Hi.
My name is Mr. Williams
And I live in this hole[23]

On another, Berkowitz had scrawled the following:

I have several children
who I'm Turning
INTO killers. WAIT
Til they grow up.[24]

Still another wall contained a message penned in block letters:

My neighbors
I have no respect
For and I treat them
Like shit.
Sincerely
Williams[25]

Police also found extensive notes in a folder captioned "the official file for the killings of the chosen executioner—David Berkowitz."[26] Included among Berkowitz's "file" was a paper marked "quota remaining as of 4/20/77" listing 19 towns and neighborhoods in the New York City area and the number of killings planned for each.[27] Also found among his papers were numerous handwritten pages stating, for example, the following: "Today is Friday, blood day. Today I spill blood for the people."[28] "I, like dogs, are [sic] trained to kill. I kill on command."[29] "Oh, Sam, give us peace let us live like humans Sam please my ears hurt my head hurts."[30]

But beyond Berkowitz's crimes, his background, the state of his home, and his writings, his explanation for the shootings also smacked of serious psychopathology. He told police who interviewed him and mental health experts who examined him that he had been directed to kill by "Sam." "I had a sign and I followed it. Sam told me what to do and I did it...," Berkowitz said.[31] "His commands," he added, "come to me through his dog. They told me to kill. Sam is the devil."[32] Asked if "Sam" was Sam Carr, the man whose dog had been shot and who had been threatened, Berkowitz smiled as he replied, "What do you think?"[33]

Faced with a client who had confessed to killing six people and wounding eight others because he had been commanded to do so by a devil or demon communicating with him through a dog, Berkowitz's attorneys had little option but to question both his sanity and his competence to stand trial. Convinced that Berkowitz was neither sane nor competent, the defense attorneys asked the court to appoint two mental health experts to consider the threshold question of competence—if Berkowitz was in fact not competent to stand trial, he could not be tried and thus could not raise any defense, including insanity.

Both court-appointed psychiatric experts, Drs. Daniel Schwartz and Richard Weidenbacher, joined in a report to the court that Berkowitz was not competent to stand trial: "It is the opinion of each of us that the defendant is an incapacitated person, [who] as a result of mental disease or defect, lacks capacity to understand the proceeding against him or to assist in his own defense."[34]

Because Berkowitz was found to have an IQ of 118, it was clear that his lack of competence was not due to any mental defect. The psychiatrists, who had examined Berkowitz for a total of about 11 hours, diagnosed the serial killer as suffering from paranoia and found his prognosis to be guarded. They told the court that

> [d]espite the presence of a rather elaborate paranoid delusional system, the question of this defendant's fitness to proceed is not that simple. He is well aware of the charges against him, understands that by society's standards his acts were criminal and has the intellectual capacity to learn whatever there is about the legal proceedings that he does not already know ... The problem is that his psychosis prevents him from assisting in his own defense. [H]e is so

emotionally dead that the outcome of the case is totally immaterial to him.[35]

The opinion of Drs. Schwartz and Weidenbacher that Berkowitz cared little if anything about what happened to him was buttressed by portions of an audiotape of Schwartz's interview of Berkowitz, which was played for the judge. In the taped psychiatric interview, Berkowitz told Schwartz,

> I'm not a bad person. I know I'm not a bad person. They'll put me away for a long time. I'm ready to go . . . If I go to court I'll say "If you lock the door and throw away the key, I'd like that very much. I'd have peace of mind." If I don't fight a maximum sentence, they'll say "he's not trying to get out of it," so maybe they'll believe me.[36]

In the same taped interview, Berkowitz told the examining psychiatrist that "evil demons commanded" him to shoot his victims.[37] "It was Sam," Berkowitz told Schwartz, referring to Sam Carr, "I'm the son of Sam."[38] Berkowitz added that he wanted to go to trial in order "to tell the world about the demons."[39]

Ordinarily in New York the opinions of two independent, court-appointed mental health experts (by statute, two psychiatrists or one psychiatrist and one psychologist) regarding a criminal defendant's competence to stand trial are routinely accepted by the prosecutors, defense counsel, and the courts. But this was no ordinary case. The prosecutor made a motion to require Berkowitz to submit to a third competency examination conducted by the state's hand-picked psychiatrist, Dr. David Abrahamsen. Not surprisingly, Abrahamsen, a psychoanalyst who would later publish a magazine article, book chapter, and book about his interviews with Berkowitz, concluded that the defendant was competent to stand trial.

Interestingly, the prosecutor's expert agreed with the independent, court-appointed doctors that, although competent to be tried, Berkowitz was paranoid and delusional: "David feels that his distorted beliefs are of such importance that all other topics should be relegated to the sidelines. Thus the defendant's main excuse for committing the crimes is his delusions . . . While the defendant shows paranoid traits, they do not interfere with his fitness to stand trial."[40]

The trial judge agreed with Abrahamsen and found Berkowitz competent to stand trial:

> I've listened to the testimony of three experts. It's a very inexact sphere, the science of psychiatry. The question is can he perceive, recall and relate? Yes. Does he have a rudimental understanding of

the trial process? Yes. Can he establish a working relationship with his attorneys? Yes. Is he sufficiently intelligent to listen and evaluate? Yes. Is he able to stand trial? Yes. Therefore I find we are able to proceed.[41]

Berkowitz's trial was expected to begin less than 2 weeks after this finding of competency, but the proceedings were further delayed when the judge was forced to recuse himself after making a number of inappropriate public pronouncements about the case. First he told the media that Berkowitz was "virtually certain to spend most, if not all of his life in a maximum-security mental institution—whether he was found guilty of murder or innocent by reason of insanity."[42] Then in an interview with a reporter from the *New York Post*, the judge appeared to want to make sure any member of the jury pool would realize that Berkowitz would be locked up indefinitely regardless of the verdict:

> *Judge:* Well, it's an archaic principle of law that the jury must have no concern with sentencing. And so, if Berkowitz goes to trial, and takes an insanity defense, I cannot let them know he won't walk.
> *Interviewer:* If they don't know that, why would Berkowitz bother with an insanity defense?
> *Judge:* They'll know.
> *Interviewer:* How?
> *Judge:* You're going to tell them.[43]

Once this judge was recused, another jurist was assigned the case but it languished for so long that another competency hearing had to be held because a defendant must be competent at all stages of the proceedings against him. By the time the second hearing took place, about 6 months after the first, even Dr. Schwartz believed that Berkowitz was competent to stand trial, in part because Berkowitz had by then returned to the born-again Christian beliefs he first adopted while in the Army. As Schwartz explained his about-face, "The most important changes in my opinion are that whereas in August 1977 [Berkowitz] believed in a certain group of demons . . . his belief now is in a very widely and very commonly shared belief, namely Jesus Christ . . . What he says is that he wants to devote his life to goodness, to Jesus . . . "[44]

Based upon the testimony and reports of Schwartz and three other mental health experts, the new judge found Berkowitz competent to stand trial. In his ruling the judge stressed that "the defendant has given full consideration, pro and con, to the legal alternatives available to him and understands them."[45] He also noted that Berkowitz had "a complete understanding of the process of trial and the roles of the judge, jury, prosecutor, and defense attorneys," demonstrated a "working relationship with his attorneys" and showed "no emotional outbursts, disruptive behavior, or bizarre conduct."[46]

About 2 weeks after being found competent to stand trial, Berkowitz rejected his attorneys' advice to go to trial with an insanity plea. Instead, Berkowitz pleaded guilty to all charges and admitted that he had set over 2000 fires in New York City between 1974 and 1977. "We kept trying to get him to change his mind, right up to the last minute, but he won't do it," one of his attorneys said, adding, "We go on record stating that the defendant has a mental disease or defect which makes it impossible for him to fully understand the charges against him."[47]

Berkowitz's guilty pleas went smoothly, despite his attorneys' fears. One by one, the judge went through the charges in each of the six murders, and Berkowitz unemotionally acknowledged that he shot the victims and intended to kill them. For example, with regard to the killing of Stacy Moskowitz, the last in the string of six homicides, the judge asked Berkowitz why he had gone to the Brooklyn neighborhood that night. Berkowitz replied, "To kill somebody."[48] Asked "Did you have any particular person in mind?" Berkowitz said, "No."[49] Asked whom he had shot first, Stacy Moskowitz or her date, Robert Violante, Berkowitz indicated that the first shot was fired at Moskowitz. When the judge asked where he had aimed the gun, Berkowitz replied, "At her head."[50] Asked by the judge "what consequences [he] expect[ed] when [he] pulled the trigger," Berkowitz responded, "To me or to them? That I'd be arrested and put in jail. They would die. They would die."[51]

Two weeks after entering his guilty pleas, Berkowitz was back in court for sentencing. Though he had earlier been found competent to stand trial and had been allowed to plead guilty, those involved in the case were mindful that his competence was a matter that had to be considered at all stages of the proceedings, even sentencing. Thus, the judges and the prosecutors (one each from the three boroughs in which Berkowitz had killed) could not have been pleased when, while being led into the courtroom, Berkowitz tried to jump through the courtroom's seventh story window and, when subdued, began chanting "Stacy was a whore" and yelling "That's right. That's right. I'd kill her again. I'd kill them all again."[52] Over the objection of one prosecutor, the court delayed sentencing for a month and ordered yet another round of psychiatric evaluations for Berkowitz.

Again found competent, Berkowitz was brought before the court for sentencing. Still, the court remained concerned about Berkowitz's mental status, perhaps fearing that he or his attorneys would find yet another way to place his competence in doubt. In questioning Berkowitz before pronouncing sentence, the judge, himself, seemed to do exactly that.

After reminding Berkowitz of his earlier claim that his crimes were committed in response to the voices of demons, the judge asked, "Did you make the plea or did the demons?"[53] When Berkowitz responded, "I took the plea," the judge pressed on, asking, "It was your decision?" To which Berkowitz replied, "They had some influence."[54] When the judge finally attempted to get Berkowitz to say that he had decided on his own to waive an insanity defense, all Berkowitz would say was that he made the decision but had not done so alone.

Apparently satisfied that Berkowitz, who was sedated with a powerful psychotropic medication, was competent and had made a knowing, voluntary, and intelligent waiver of his right to go to trial with a defense of insanity, the judge sentenced Berkowitz to 25 years to life in prison, telling those assembled in the courtroom, "It is this court's fervent wish that this defendant be imprisoned until the day of his death."[55]

Less than a month after being sentenced, Berkowitz was transferred from the custody of New York City to that of the New York State Department of Correctional Services (DOCS). Upon arrival at state prison, Berkowitz was examined by two psychiatrists who found him mentally ill and recommended that he be transferred from DOCS to the state Department of Mental Hygiene. Berkowitz raised no objection, and a local judge ordered the transfer after concluding that Berkowitz was "insane."[56] One of Berkowitz's longtime defense attorneys applauded the transfer, saying that the determination made by the two state psychiatrists was "a foregone conclusion."[57] As the lawyer added, "It confirms what we've been saying since the inception of this case. The man is mentally ill and was always mentally ill . . . He should have been civilly committed in the first place . . . There were many times when even the most unknowledgeable layman could see he was off the wall."[58]

Though Berkowitz's transfer to a secure mental institution may have reinforced his defense lawyers' conviction that their client was incompetent, insane, and should never have pleaded guilty, it was short-lived. Within a couple of months, Berkowitz was back in state prison, where he has remained since, serving what will most likely be a life sentence with no parole.

Was he mentally ill, incompetent, or even insane? Certainly many people, including many mental health experts and legal authorities thought so. After Berkowitz was adjudicated competent for the final time, Professor Sanford Kadish, a renowned criminal law expert and then-dean of the law school at University of California at Berkeley, said, "From everything I've heard, Berkowitz is a perfect example of an obviously insane person being persecuted because of popular pressure."[59] However, years later, Berkowitz would tell a different tale to Dr. David Abrahamsen, who never believed that Berkowitz was mentally ill, incompetent, or insane, but rather was a malingering psychopath who loved to be the center of attention and manipulated those who examined and represented him. In a letter from the New York State Correctional Facility at Attica, Berkowitz wrote,

> I vividly recall the talks I had with Dr. Daniel Schwartz, for they were, to me, ecstasy. They were the talks that produced the feedback I wanted. What a pleasure it was back then to hear this man exonerate me of all blame for my six murders. Oh, the pleasure of hearing this man telling his colleagues how sick I was—how ill—how insane.
>
> I knew that all I had to do was slide "Sam Carr" and the "demons" into the conversation and I'd have him bending over his chair in my direction. Why he'd practically be wiping the tears from my eyes and comforting me, saying, in a sense, "don't fret, don't cry, you're a sick, sick boy."
>
> Goodness, what a nice man he was—always telling me what I wanted to hear—always helping me push my rising guilt feelings back down into my mind. And thank God he listened to it for it was all I had. Had someone taken it away, then I'd have been standing there stark naked, guilty as ever, and nothing to hide behind, no safe ground, nothing but my own self.
>
> However, I think that you, Dr. Abrahamsen, would be missing an important clue unless I told you this. That Dr. Schwartz was me! So were the police officers who caught me and so was my defense counsel. They, too, were me.
>
> All the others were my little puppets. People to be manipulated. They bent forward when I wanted them to, they talked about the subjects that I wanted to speak of, and they told me just what I demanded to hear—that I was not guilty!
>
> So, in a sense, they were extensions of me, to be picked up and placed back down on the ground when I was finished with them.[60]

Berkowitz has adjusted well to prison, become a self-proclaimed born-again Christian, and served enough time to qualify for parole, in the unlikely event the parole board would ever grant it. Although Berkowitz insists that he suffers no mental disorder and that he poses no danger to society, he has repeatedly asked the state parole board not to release him. Indeed, prior to one recent parole hearing, he wrote to the governor, explaining why he should not be paroled:

> Dear Governor Pataki,
>
> I can give you no good reason why I should be considered for parole. I can, however, give you many reasons why I should not be. The loss of six lives and the wounding of even more are reasons enough . . .
>
> In all honesty, I believe I deserve to be in prison for the rest of my life. I have, with God's help, long ago come to terms with my situation and I have accepted my punishment.
>
> [I]f and when I go to this (parole) hearing, it will only be to show respect to the parole board, to apologize and take responsibility for my criminal actions, and to basically tell them what I am now telling you—that I do not deserve parole.
>
> Respectfully,
> David Berkowitz[61]

4
John Wayne Gacy, Jr.

In 1966, John Wayne Gacy, Jr., his wife, and their infant son moved to Waterloo, Iowa, a small working-class city known for meatpacking and manufacturing. Gacy, then 24 years old, came to Waterloo to manage three Kentucky Fried Chicken franchises owned by his father-in-law. For Gacy, who had bounced from one job to another since dropping out of high school, the position offered a lifestyle he could not have otherwise imagined. Even though his father-in-law disliked Gacy, he offered the young man a salary of $15,000 a year plus a 20 percent commission on the net income of the stores he managed.

Although Gacy had lied about his education, falsely claiming degrees in accounting and management, he not only managed to run the businesses but soon became a bit of a local celebrity. Ingratiating himself with the leadership of the local chapter of the "Jaycees" (Junior Chamber of Commerce), Gacy quickly became a leader of the civic group. Elected chaplain, he led ecumenical prayer breakfasts and was widely regarded as the likely next president of the organization. Meanwhile, Gacy also played a prominent role in the local Merchants' Patrol, a volunteer security organization that protected the business places of its members. Being part of that organization gave Gacy the chance to patrol the streets at night, allowed him to attach a flashing red light to his car, and provided him with an excuse to carry a handgun.

Despite his growing reputation as a community leader, Gacy had a dark side few people knew about: a sexual attraction to teenage boys. While patrolling the streets, ostensibly to protect his fellow businessmen, Gacy and several teenage accomplices stole auto parts. Gacy also provided alcohol to his underage male employees and allowed them to drink in his basement. Much worse, Gacy approached a number of these boys for sex, attempted to sexually assault one of them, and repeatedly coerced or forced another to give him oral sex.

While running for the presidency of the local Jaycee chapter in 1968, just 2 years after arriving in Waterloo, Gacy was indicted for sodomy. Despite the indictment, many in the community remained loyal to Gacy and accepted his claim that he was being framed by another Jaycee in an effort to discredit him and undermine his presidential candidacy. Even though Gacy failed two polygraph tests regarding the charges, authorities reportedly were contemplating backing off from the indictment.

Gacy, however, made that impossible when he hired one of his 18-year-old employees to assault one of the boys who had accused Gacy of multiple acts of sodomy. The hired attacker did his job, was arrested, and confessed to police that the assault had been orchestrated by Gacy. As a result, several more charges were added to the sodomy counts Gacy was already facing. Gacy was jailed pending trial and ordered to undergo an examination at a state psychiatric institution.

Seventeen days of observation, interviews, and testing resulted in a comprehensive psychological profile of Gacy. Gacy's full-scale IQ of 118 placed him in bright normal range, and the intellectual testing revealed that he had "a high degree of social intelligence or awareness of the proper way to behave in order to influence people."[1] Personality testing failed to "provide any support for the presence of unusual thought processes" and pointed to "a diagnosis of sociopathic personality disturbance, antisocial reaction"—essentially what is today labeled antisocial personality disorder.[2]

The psychologist who tested Gacy also found him to be a "smooth talker" who demonstrated a "total denial of responsibility for anything that has happened to him," lacked remorse, was "unsocialized," failed to learn from experience, and tried to "outwit the other fellow and take advantage of him before being taken advantage of himself."[3]

Two psychiatrists who also examined Gacy concurred. They reported that "Mr. Gacy [is] an antisocial personality, a diagnostic term for individuals who are basically unsocialized and whose behavior pattern brings them repeatedly into conflict with society. Persons with this personality structure do not learn from experience and are unlikely to benefit from known medical treatment."[4] The psychiatrist also reported, however, that Gacy appeared to be bisexual, that his sexual contact with boys was experimental or curiosity-based. The instances of sodomy, they wrote, were more "thrill seeking" than a reflection of any "absolute fixation on abnormal sex objects."[5]

Asserting that the oral sex he received from the boys in question were acts of prostitution and that he had merely been experimenting with homosexuality, Gacy pled guilty, apparently hoping that his status in the community would save him from prison. His plea may well have been influenced by the report of the probation department, which presented Gacy's explanation to the court and recommended probation with no jail time based upon Gacy's age (26), lack of a prior criminal record, solid work ethic, community service, and willingness to leave Iowa and return to his former home state of Illinois.

The sentencing judge, however, was not swayed by the mental health evaluations, Gacy's standing, or the presentence report. On December 3, 1968, he ordered Gacy imprisoned for 10 years, citing "the particular pattern you have chosen ... to seek out teenage boys and get them involved in sexual misbehavior."[6]

Though the sentence cost him his marriage and livelihood, Gacy thrived in prison, using the same intellect and social skills that fueled his business and civic success in Waterloo. Behind bars, Gacy was a model inmate, completed his high school education and began taking college courses, continued his work with the Jaycees, and was voted the top member of the prison chapter by his fellow inmates. So successful was Gacy in adapting to life in prison that less than a year and a half into his sentence, a prison psychiatrist examined him, diagnosed him as presenting a passive-aggressive personality, and recommended that he be paroled, offering the opinion that "[t]he likelihood of his again being charged with and being convicted of antisocial conduct appears to be small."[7]

Three months later, in June 1970, after serving only 21 months of a 10-year sentence, Gacy was paroled to his former home in Chicago. In less than a year, Gacy was back to his criminal pursuits, picking up, beating, and sexually abusing teenage boys and young men. Only one of these incidents resulted in his arrest, but the charges were dropped when Gacy filed a complaint against his alleged victim—a 19-year-old boy who claimed Gacy tried to force him to engage in sex—and, not surprisingly, the boy failed to appear in court.

Though Gacy had returned to his former life as a sex abuser, few people were aware of it. In October 1971, the Iowa Board of Parole, having never been informed of the recent sex charge against Gacy, discharged him from any further supervision.

In June 1972, Gacy married a recently divorced mother of two children. Shortly after his wedding, Gacy came to the attention of the police again when he was arrested that same month for assaulting a 24-year-old man and forcing him to perform fellatio. According to this man, Gacy had approached him on the street, flashed a badge, identified himself as a police officer, forced him to give oral sex, and then beaten him with a club. Gacy claimed that the man was a prostitute who tried to extort money from him in exchange for dropping the charges. After reviewing the records and accounts of both men, police dropped all charges.

Not long after that, Gacy began his own painting, decorating, and maintenance business and embarked on a career as a part-time clown and small-time politician. His business, PDM Contractors, was relatively successful and profitable because of Gacy's work ethic and his reliance upon cheap labor from teenage boys. As a self-developed clown, Gacy spent many hours entertaining children at hospitals and various community events. As in Waterloo, Gacy also committed himself to numerous civic projects, eventually coming to the attention of a local political leader who appointed him to the municipal street lights commission, of which he soon became secretary-treasurer. As part of his political involvement with the Democratic Party in Chicago, Gacy once had his photograph taken with First Lady Rosalind Carter.

Although on the surface it appeared that the ex-convict had turned his life around, in fact Gacy was using his business as a means to gain sexual access to teenage boys. His sex life with his wife came to a halt not long after they married. When she found him perusing magazines depicting naked men and boys, Gacy openly acknowledged that boys, not women, were his preferred sexual partners. Not surprisingly, his wife filed for divorce. The decree was granted in 1976.

Though Gacy's wife and a few others knew of his predilection for sex with teenage boys, they had no idea of the lengths to which he had gone to satisfy his deviant sexual urges.

No one would even begin to understand the full extent of Gacy's depravity until 1978. In December of that year, 2 weeks before Christmas, Robert Piest, a 15-year-old high school sophomore from suburban Chicago, disappeared one night after leaving his part-time job at a local pharmacy. Earlier that evening, Gacy had been in the pharmacy to consult with the owner, Piest's boss, about work on some shelving. Gacy had returned to the drugstore just before closing to retrieve an appointment book he had inadvertently left behind. According to another store employee, Piest had left the store at closing time to talk with Gacy about a job with PDM Contractors.

When Piest never returned to the store or his home, the police were contacted and turned their attention to Gacy. It did not take them long to learn of Gacy's Iowa convictions and the time he had spent in prison there. Nor was it difficult for them to discover the details of Gacy's more recent arrests in the Chicago area for sexually abusing young men, neither of which had resulted in any further action against Gacy. Quickly, police suspected that Piest had met with foul play and that John Wayne Gacy was the likely culprit.

The problem was that the police had no hard evidence against Gacy, indeed no real evidence that a crime had occurred. After questioning Gacy about Piest but getting nowhere, the police sought and obtained a search warrant for Gacy's home. When officers searched the home, they soon found startling evidence that not only pointed to Gacy's likely involvement in Piest's disappearance but to the possibility that Gacy's crimes went well beyond what the police already knew. The search turned up, among other things, a class of 1975 high school ring with the initials J.A.S., driver's licenses issued to two young men, a hypodermic syringe, a variety of prescription pills, marijuana and rolling papers, a starter's pistol, a switchblade knife, police badges, an 18-inch dildo, a pair of handcuffs, a variety of men's clothing clearly too small to fit the 5-foot-7-inch, 250-pound Gacy, and many pornographic movies and publications with titles that included "Tight Teenagers," "Bike Boy," "Pederasty: Sex Between Men and Boys," "Heads & Tails," and "The Great Swallow."[8] But perhaps more alarming than any of these items was a kind of evidence that could not be seen: portions of Gacy's home and the crawlspace beneath them reeked with the odor of what some of the searching police officers described as sewage. When they looked for the source of the odor, they found that the ground in the crawlspace beneath the one-story home was covered with a light powder that appeared to be lime. Gacy's second wife had long noticed the same odor before she divorced him but accepted Gacy's repeated explanation that it was simply the inevitable result of dampness.

Soon the source of that awful odor would become apparent. But not before Gacy made every effort to stop that from occurring. Attempting to stop the police from tailing him everywhere he went and from conducting more extensive searches of his home and property, Gacy claimed that the investigation was harassing him and causing him mental anguish. He filed a civil rights lawsuit in U.S. District Court, seeking $750,000 in damages and an injunction that would block further surveillance and searches.

Cautious but undeterred by the lawsuit, police continued to press for answers. When they informed Gacy that they might have to tear up the floorboards in his home, he quickly volunteered that such destruction would not be necessary. He had, he told the officers, once killed a man in self-defense and buried his body under the garage. In the presence of his attorney, Gacy showed police the precise spot of this burial. Instead of digging in that spot, however, the police decided to begin their excavation in the ground beneath the crawl space at Gacy's residence.

After a single day of digging beneath Gacy's home, police uncovered the remains of two boys. As the excavating continued and more bodies were uncovered beneath his home, Gacy confessed to having killed at least 30 boys and young men since January 1972, most of whom he said he had buried beneath the 30-inch crawl space. As Gacy described it, his modus operandi was essentially the same in most of the killings: He would lure his victims to his home, handcuff them, stuff their mouths with their socks or underwear to muffle their cries, sexually assault them, and then strangle them with a rope or board while he raped them.

When the excavation of the ground beneath Gacy's crawl space was complete, a total of 27 bodies were uncovered. Two other bodies were uncovered at Gacy's home, one under the cement on his patio and the other beneath the floor in his recreation room. In addition to these 29 bodies, police eventually found the remains of three more of Gacy's victims floating in a local river. Gacy explained to police that he had begun disposing of his victims in the river when he ran out of burial space at his home. Gacy's final victim, Robert Piest, whose disappearance triggered the investigation that led to Gacy's arrest, had also been thrown in the river. His body, however, was not recovered until more than 3 months after Gacy's arrest.

By his own admission, Gacy had killed more people than any other known serial killer in American history, surpassing Ted Bundy's previous record of 28 murders committed between 1974 and 1978. Charged with 33 counts of murder by a prosecutor seeking the death penalty, Gacy had few legal options. Having confessed to all of the murders, the only potentially successful defense he could possibly muster was insanity. Under Illinois law, if a jury found that, at the time of the killings, "a mental disease or defect prevented him from appreciating the wrongfulness of his conduct or from conforming his actions to the requirements of law," Gacy could be acquitted by reason of insanity.[9]

Gacy entered pleas of insanity to all of the charges against him. As in virtually all American jurisdictions, in Illinois, when a criminal defendant pleads insanity, he waives his privilege against self-incrimination and must agree to be examined by the state's psychiatric and/or psychological experts or forfeit the insanity defense. Thus, in the approximately 13 months between his arrest and trial, Gacy was examined and/or tested by no fewer than a dozen psychologists and psychiatrists, some retained by his attorneys and others hired by the prosecution.

Gacy's trial, which began in January 1980, featured both lay and expert witnesses. Because Gacy did not testify, his 33 victims were dead, and many of their bodies were so badly decomposed that they could not be fully examined, the only knowledge the jury had of the true nature of Gacy's crimes came indirectly from witnesses who had been victimized but not killed by Gacy. The horrifying accounts of these victim-witnesses gave the jury a pretty good idea of what Gacy's murder victims had gone through.

Surprisingly, the first of Gacy's living victims to testify was called by the defense. Jeff Rignall testified that in 1978, when he was 26 years old, Gacy had picked him up on the street and offered him a ride to a gay bar. After offering

Rignall a couple of hits from a joint of marijuana he was smoking, Gacy shoved a chloroform-soaked rag into Rignall's face and held it there until the young man lost consciousness. Later, when Rignall regained consciousness, he found he had been stripped of his clothes and strapped to a pillory-like device that ensnared his head and both arms. Gacy then forced Rignall to perform oral sex and tortured him anally with a variety of instruments, tools, and dildos. Rignall eventually passed out and awoke to find himself lying in the snow near the park where Gacy had picked him up. He reported the incident to the police and spent a week hospitalized for facial burns and rectal injuries.

Gacy's attorney asked Rignall if he felt Gacy was able to appreciate the wrongfulness of his actions or to conform his actions to the requirements of law. Rignall said "No" and explained that he based that opinion on "the beastly and animalistic ways he attacked me."[10]

In rebuttal, the prosecution called Robert Donnelly to the stand. Donnelly testified that when he was in his late teens, Gacy had stopped him on the street, identified himself as a police officer, pulled a gun on him, handcuffed him, and forced him into a vehicle. Gacy drove Donnelly to his home, where he raped the boy anally and then held his head down in a bathtub full of water until he passed out. When Donnelly regained consciousness, Gacy urinated on him, forced him to watch "a gay porn flick," and then played a one-sided game of "Russian roulette" in which Gacy put a gun to Donnelly's head and repeatedly pulled the trigger.[11] Eventually the gun went off, but turned out to contain only a blank. After that, Gacy forced a gag into the youth's mouth and an unidentified instrument into his anus. Eventually Gacy released Donnelly but not before telling him, "You're going to die later, but don't tell, don't go to the police or anybody and don't tell them because they are not going to believe you."[12] Donnelly did report the incident to the police and, just as Gacy had warned, they did not believe him.

The expert testimony in Gacy's trial split predictably. Those experts who had examined him for the defense testified for the defense, whereas those hired by the prosecution testified against Gacy.

The first expert to testify was Dr. Thomas Elisio, a clinical psychologist who specialized in psychological testing and had examined Gacy on January 13, 1980, just a few weeks before the trial. Elisio, who acknowledged that he had not read any police reports and relied upon no source of information other than Gacy himself, told the jury that during all of the killings Gacy lacked the substantial capacity to appreciate the wrongfulness of his conduct or to conform his conduct to the requirements of law. "That does not mean he was overtly psychotic all the time," the doctor added, "but the condition was there, and probably he looked good, like most people do."[13]

Elisio further testified that Gacy was of superior intelligence and had suffered no brain damage. Asked for his diagnosis of the serial killer, Elisio replied, "Borderline schizophrenia or borderline personality, a person who on the surface looks normal but has all kinds of neurotic, antisocial, psychotic illnesses."[14] This diagnosis, Elisio testified, could have been made solely on the basis of the psychological testing results without knowing anything more about Gacy.

On cross-examination, Elisio acknowledged that he had seen "few" other cases in which a person had been psychotic for 17 to 20 years without being diagnosed.[15] Asked to name them, Elisio mentioned former president Richard Nixon and England's King George III. Asked "how he could determine whether [the] defendant was psychotic at certain points in time," Elisio replied, "It is a guess."[16]

Elisio's testimony was followed by that of three other mental health experts, all testifying for the defense. First came Dr. Lawrence Z. Freedman, a psychoanalyst who concluded that Gacy suffered "serious disturbances of thinking, his mood, and his behavior" and diagnosed Gacy with "pseudo-neurotic schizophrenia."[17] Freedman had interviewed Gacy for approximately 50 hours, reviewed all police reports, statements by the defendant, and reports from all other psychologists and psychiatrists in the case, and interviewed Gacy's mother and younger sister. He told the jury that Gacy's mental illness could be traced to the brutal ways in which he had been treated by his father while growing up. The "mixture of aggression and love" in Gacy's relationship with his father, Freedman testified, indicated "an enormous strain on the psychological structure of the individual."[18] In Freedman's view, Gacy's inability to attend his father's funeral because he was in prison in Iowa for sodomy "triggered the difference between serious neurosis [and] the development of a psychosis."[19]

Explaining the 33 homicides to the jury, the psychoanalyst opined awkwardly that Gacy "projected his own frightened awareness that [his sexual victimization of boys] was homosexual . . . and he thought of them as trash, to be put out of their misery . . . a projection of his own feelings—which might have been turned against himself—turned against them."[20]

When asked if Gacy met the legal criteria for insanity, however, Freedman balked, replying that "[t]he question goes to the legal and social thresholds of punishability. [I]t is not a psychiatric question but a legal question. And I feel these questions are outside my level of competence."[21]

Freeman was followed to the witness stand by Dr. Robert Traisman, a clinical psychologist. Relying largely upon the results of the Rorschach Inkblot Test—in which Gacy "saw flowers in many of the ink blots and birds or insects which were entering in to siphon the pollen, a response which was inappropriate to the card"[22]—Traisman concluded that Gacy was "a paranoid schizophrenic who had homosexual conflicts, marked feelings of masculine inadequacy, a man who had a lack of empathy, a lack of feeling for other people, an individual with an alarming lack of emotional control or ego control when under stress, who had strong potentials for emotional or ego disintegration and expressions of very hostile, dangerous impulses, either to others or to himself."[23]

On cross-examination, Traisman acknowledged that Gacy understood the nature of his crimes and might have been aware that they were wrong. Still, when pressed by the prosecutor, the psychologist maintained that even if Gacy knew that what he was doing was wrong, he might not have been able to control his homicidal impulses.

The last mental health expert to testify as part of the defense's case-in-chief was psychiatrist Dr. Richard Rappaport, who had examined Gacy for 65 hours over a period of 5 months and concluded that, as a result of mental illness, Gacy "did lack substantial capacity to control his behavior at the time of each of those crimes . . . and to conform his conduct to the requirements of law."[24] Rappaport diagnosed Gacy as suffering from "a borderline personality, or personality organization with a subtype of psychopathic personality also manifesting instances of psychotic or paranoid schizophrenic behavior."[25]

Like Freedman the psychoanalyst, Rappaport saw Gacy through the lens of Freudian theory, but his explanations were much wordier and more steeped in psychoanalytic theory. Gacy's perversions, he told the jury, were "representations of a block due to fear of castration" that arose out of unresolved Oedipal feelings.[26] As Rappaport further explained, "The little boy, in wanting to possess his mother, wants to do away with his father . . . However, in John Gacy, because of the abuse that he received . . . he developed heightened feelings of wanting to get rid of his father, tremendous homicidal feelings with rage."[27] Gacy's fetishism, which Rappaport defined as "use of an inanimate object to heighten sexual pleasure and take the place of an actual sex object," was a "symbol for the penis which helps the individual deny the expectation of castration.[28] He sees that as an object symbolizing a penis and then can, in his mind, deny the fact that this castration might take place."[29]

Explaining the homicides, Rappaport told the jurors that Gacy was a sexual sadist who had "identifie[d] with the aggressor . . . his father, the person who inflicted all of the pain on him . . . He was able to take out his hostility on helpless victims who were either tied up, who were in some way degraded, humiliated, and this gave him a great deal of relief in feeling this control."[30] As the psychiatrist further explained, "He [Gacy] is then the father in identifying with the aggressor, and these victims, these boys, are then himself. He can ... kill them ... and in a way rid himself forever of these qualities that are inside of himself: the hostile threats and frightening figures that pervade his unconscious. He is so convinced that these qualities exist in the other person, he is completely out of touch with reality ... and he has to get rid of them and save himself ... he has to kill them."[31]

Rappaport was the last witness before the defense rested its case. The first expert to testify for the prosecution in rebuttal was Dr. Leonard Heston, who had examined Gacy in Iowa over a decade earlier in regard to the sodomy charges there. Heston could give no opinion as to Gacy's mental state at the time of the crimes with which was now charged—33 counts of murder—but he testified that in 1968 he had diagnosed Gacy as "an antisocial personality ... a personality who comes into repeated conflict with society and social norms."[32] Antisocial personality, Heston added, was a "defect in personality," not a mental illness.[33]

Employing a common technique in cross-examining opposing experts, Gacy's attorney tried to use Heston to bolster the testimony of Freedman, his own witness. The defense attorney asked, "If I told you that Dr. Freedman's reports state that Mr. Gacy is a complex combination of manic compulsivity and obsessiveness with a paranoid personality, extraordinary dissociation between the most violent action and idea and the appropriate responsive emotion, what does that indicate to you?"[34]

Heston responded, "Sir, that, I'm afraid means nothing to me. There are six or eight diagnostic terms there that are all thrown in a pudding."[35]

The next expert to testify for the prosecution was Dr. Arthur Hartman, a psychologist, who had interviewed Gacy for about 25 hours in 12 interviews over 2 months. Hartman told the jury that Gacy was "a psychopathic or antisocial personality with sexual deviation" and "minor symptoms or characteristics of paranoid hysterical reactions."[36] In Hartman's view, Gacy did not meet the legal criteria for insanity and had never suffered from any psychotic condition.

Hartman was followed to the witness stand by Dr. Robert Reifman, a psychiatrist, who gave his own opinions and then attacked those of the defense experts. In Reifman's view, Gacy presented a narcissistic personality disorder, which the psychiatrist did not regard as a mental illness. This diagnosis, he testified, did not exclude a second diagnosis of antisocial personality disorder. "Antisocial personality is a subtype of narcissistic personality," Reifman explained, adding, however, that "I don't think it would be completely fair to call Mr. Gacy an antisocial personality."[37] Nor did Reifman believe that Gacy was a borderline personality because "in my experience ... they do not function very well." Gacy, the doctor noted, had "a very successful contracting business," was a "reasonably successful politician," "was a reasonably successful clown," and "was, generally speaking, a very efficient, successful person."[38] Apparently unable to resist the temptation to gild the lily, Reifman added that "[e]ven with respect to the crimes, [Gacy] was extremely efficient."[39]

Similarly, Reifman refuted the notion that Gacy suffered from pseudoneurotic schizophrenia. "Mr. Gacy functions extremely well," the psychiatrist testified.[40] "A pseudoneurotic schizophrenic is a frightened, constricted person who is teetering on the brink of psychosis and can't function."[41] By the same token, Reifman observed that there was "no evidence that Mr. Gacy was psychotic" and "no evidence to support a diagnosis of paranoid schizophrenia" because Gacy demonstrated "no delusions, hallucinations, [or] loss of contact with reality."[42]

The last two experts to testify in the prosecution's rebuttal case were Dr. Richard Rogers, a forensic psychologist, and Dr. James Cavanaugh, a psychiatrist. Rogers testified that Gacy was an obsessive-compulsive personality with hypomanic features and evidence of sexual sadism, who tried to exaggerate his mental illness on the psychological testing done by Dr. Elisio. Rogers further told the jury that Gacy appreciated the criminality of his behavior and had the capacity to conform his conduct to legal requirements.

Cavanaugh testified that Gacy suffered from a "mixed personality disorder" with obsessive-compulsive, narcissistic, hypomanic, and antisocial features.[43] He agreed with the other prosecution experts that Gacy had not been insane at the time of the killings.

Cavanaugh's testimony would have added little to the evidence against Gacy, but for his response to a couple of questions, one of which led Gacy's attorney to seek a mistrial.

In a blatantly improper attempt to bolster the psychiatrist's opinion, the prosecutor asked Cavanaugh if he kept statistics on the evaluations he and his colleagues at the Isaac Ray Center (a Chicago forensic mental health clinic) completed for the court system, adding, "You keep statistics as to any correlation with your decision as to what the ultimate factfinders find?"[44] Cavanaugh replied, "Yes . . . the coefficient correlation which really means the degree of agreement between our opinion and the factfinder, the judge or jury's opinion, was .8, which basically means eight out of ten times . . . "[45] Gacy's attorney objected, and the court sustained his objection.

The prosecutor also asked Cavanaugh, "Is it possible to guarantee a person found not guilty by reason of insanity, and then committed to a mental hospital, Department of Mental Health in Illinois, will remain there for the rest of his life?"[46] To which Cavanaugh replied, "Absolutely impossible. We find it very difficult to keep people in hospitals who in fact need to be there because of concern, which I can understand, that to hospitalize is a deprivation of civil rights."[47]

Gacy's attorney objected that the question and answer were not only speculative but likely to mislead the jury into believing that, if found insane, Gacy might soon be released from state custody. The judge denied defense counsel's motion for a mistrial, leaving the attorney only his cross-examination of the psychiatrist for damage control. The lawyer asked Cavanaugh if he thought Gacy needed to be in a psychiatric hospital. Cavanaugh said Gacy did not. Next, counsel asked Cavanaugh to explain to the jury what it would take for the state to keep an insanity acquittee hospitalized against his will. Cavanaugh replied that "[t]he individual must demonstrate imminent danger to himself or others, or be adjudged essentially unable to care for himself."[48]

In response to further cross-examination on the same issue, Cavanaugh was able to tell the jury, "I believe if he was found not guilty by reason of insanity, he would not meet the state's involuntary commitment standards" and "If the law were followed, I believe he would have to be released."[49] Finally, when Gacy's attorney asked Cavanaugh if Gacy was found guilty by reason of insanity and committed, and Cavanaugh examined him, whether Cavanaugh would recommend Gacy's release. The prosecutor objected, and the judge allowed Cavanaugh to leave the stand without giving an answer.

Ordinarily this would have been the end of the expert testimony in an insanity case, but Gacy was no ordinary case. After presenting their expert witnesses and hearing from those of the prosecution, the defense was allowed the chance to rebut the prosecution experts' testimony. Gacy's attorney called Dr. Tobias Brocher, a neurologist and a psychiatrist, to the stand. Brocher, who had examined Gacy only once, testified that the serial killer demonstrated a borderline personality with schizophrenic tendencies. Brocher's opinion was that "parts of [Gacy] 'split off' and he projected these bad parts onto his victims, and then destroyed the victims, believing that he was doing a service to society by ridding it of 'human trash.'"[50] Brocher testified, "My diagnosis proves the psychotic process because only persons who are psychotic can split off so far that they negate reality."[51] Brocher also told the jury, however, that Gacy's conscience "looks like a Swiss cheese with big holes in it."[52] He did not state an opinion as to whether Gacy met the legal standard for insanity.

Brocher was followed to the stand by Dr. Helen Morrison, another psychiatrist, who testified that Gacy suffered from a "mixed psychosis or atypical psychosis."[53] Morrison was adamant that Gacy had been insane at the time of the killings. On cross-examination, Morrison was asked if she thought Gacy would have killed Robert Piest, his final victim, "if there was a uniformed police officer in the home with him at the time."[54] Morrison responded, "Yes, I do."[55]

Trying to make sure that the defense experts did not have the last word on the question of Gacy's sanity, the prosecution called one last psychiatrist to the stand to rebut the views of Brocher and Morrison. Dr. Jan Fawcett testified that there was no basis for Morrison's diagnosis of mixed or atypical psychosis. Fawcett opined that Gacy suffered no mental illness and did not meet the legal test for insanity.

On cross-examination, Gacy's attorney reminded Fawcett that he had first been asked to examine Gacy for the defense but had refused. On redirect examination, Fawcett explained that he had declined to examine Gacy for the defense because he preferred to be a "friend of the court" witness whose report would go to both the prosecution and defense attorneys.[56] Fawcett further explained that Gacy's attorney "wanted me to be a private witness, which, as he said, would mean that he didn't have to use my report if he didn't want it."[57]

After Fawcett's testimony, one last witness, a Chicago police officer, testified for the prosecution before the attorneys made their closing arguments and the judge instructed the jury. After less than 2 hours of deliberations involving nearly three dozen separate murder charges, the jury rejected Gacy's insanity defense and found him guilty on all 33 counts. Next the jury would hear arguments as to why Gacy should or should not be sentenced to die for his crimes. Again the jury deliberated for only about 2 hours, this time unanimously sentencing Gacy to death.

On May 10, 1994, almost 14 years after his conviction and sentencing, John Wayne Gacy was executed via lethal injection.

5

Arthur Shawcross

In May 1972, 10-year-old Jack Blake disappeared in Watertown, a small city in the northernmost reaches of New York State. Perhaps because Jack came from a dysfunctional family, local authorities quickly wrote him off as a runaway despite his tender age. As the months passed with no sign of the boy, Jack's mother repeatedly told the police she was sure her son had been kidnapped and possibly killed; she also named the man she believed had taken the boy.

The man named by Mrs. Blake was Arthur Shawcross, then a 27-year-old Vietnam veteran with a history of suicide attempts, domestic violence, psychiatric treatment, two divorces, and incarceration for larceny and arson. During one incarceration, a prison psychiatrist had seen "latent projected homicidal intent in at least two of his arsons."[1] Mary Blake knew little if any of this background. But she did know that a few weeks earlier Shawcross had taken her sons, Jack and his younger brother, fishing without her consent.

Under relentless pressure from Mary Blake, the local police eventually interviewed Shawcross and quickly dismissed him as a suspect, emphasizing that Shawcross was an arsonist, not a child molester, and had given them no reason to believe that he had kidnapped young Jack.

As the weeks went by without any sign of her son, Mrs. Blake continued to point the finger at Shawcross. And the police continued to resist the idea that Shawcross might be involved, even though he had recently been arrested and placed on probation for an incident in which he had thrown one young child into a trash barrel and shoved grass down the shirt and pants of another, before spanking him. The police certainly had to have been aware of this incident but probably were not aware that around the same time—summer 1972—Shawcross's parole officer sent him to a nearby clinic for a mental health evaluation because of problems he was having with his third wife. Clinic staff reported that Shawcross had "borderline . . . intelligence" and "defective moral and social development."[2] They found him uninterested in pursuing mental health services at that time.

By early September, Jack Blake had been missing nearly 4 months. What had passed for an investigation into his disappearance took a new turn when, on Labor Day weekend, another young child, 8-year-old Karen Hill, went missing in Watertown. Karen had wandered out of the home she and her mother were visiting. Unlike Jack Blake's, Karen's disappearance triggered an enthusiastic response from law enforcement. The child had gone missing in the early afternoon and was found hours later, lying face down beneath a bridge, the victim of strangling, rape, and sodomy. Police immediately suspected Arthur Shawcross, not because of Mary Blake's repeated accusations but because he was known to have spent time fishing near the crime scene and had been spotted there shortly after Karen Hill's disappearance.

Questioned by the police, Shawcross was cooperative during two interrogations but denied any involvement in the child's death. Well into a third marathon round of questioning, Shawcross finally told the police, "I musta done it. But I don't actually recall doing it."[3] Within days, Shawcross would hint to police that he also killed Jack Blake and even give them an approximate idea of where they might find the boy's remains. Although Shawcross would not confess, he implicated himself in the murder of Karen Hill and gave police enough to go on that they soon turned up what was left of Jack Blake: a skeleton, with one tooth knocked out. Scattered some 35 feet from these remains were the clothes the boy was wearing the day he disappeared.

Though Shawcross was quickly indicted for murder, the prosecutor was not confident of convicting him. To begin with, the incriminating statements Shawcross made to the police were arguably inadmissible, given the findings of two mental health experts that the alleged killer was of below normal intelligence and mentally ill, most likely as a result of his service in Vietnam. Indeed, Shawcross's attorney quickly put the court on notice that he would argue that the charges should be dropped because his client had been unable to knowingly and intelligently waive his right to counsel and right to remain silent when the police questioned him. Additionally, not a single witness was found who could place Shawcross with either child at or near the times they disappeared. Moreover, there was not a shred of physical evidence linking Shawcross to either crime. Indeed, the district attorney felt that the case against Shawcross for killing Jack Blake was so weak that he did not even bother charging him.

Still, after hearing the evidence, a local judge determined that there was enough to take the case to trial. While awaiting trial, Shawcross was examined at a nearby state psychiatric hospital, where he was found competent to stand trial although he claimed that he was subject to command hallucinations (voices telling him to do things) and did not wish to be released until he had obtained the necessary psychiatric treatment.

As part of negotiations regarding a plea bargain in the case, conversations that all agreed could not be used against Shawcross at trial, the alleged killer admitted to killing Jack Blake but denied sexually abusing the boy. In a somewhat strange twist, in exchange for this admission the prosecutor agreed not to prosecute Shawcross for killing Jack Blake and to reduce the murder charge stemming from the killing of Karen Hill.

In court, the prosecutor invoked New York State's "extreme emotional disturbance" law to justify charging Shawcross with manslaughter instead of murder.[4] Under New York Penal Law, a crime that would otherwise be murder may be deemed the lesser offense of manslaughter if, at the time of the killing, "the defendant acted under the influence of extreme emotional disturbance for which there was a reasonable explanation or excuse."[5]

Neither Shawcross's statements nor any of the evidence indicated that he was under the influence of extreme emotional disturbance when he killed Karen Hill. Thus, the prosecutor's reliance upon this law was based upon convenience rather than fact. He wanted to put Shawcross away for as long as possible but feared that if he took the case to trial a jury might acquit the serial child killer.

As agreed, Shawcross pleaded guilty to manslaughter and was sentenced to serve up to 25 years in state prison. In theory, given the governing law at the time, under this sentence Shawcross could have been released from prison by the state parole board after serving as little as 10 months. But given the nature of the offense and Shawcross's record, the prosecutor had every reason to believe that Shawcross would spend the full 25 years behind bars.

Once Shawcross was transferred from the local jail to state prison, the likelihood that he would not be released before serving 25 years seemed to increase exponentially. Shawcross was diagnosed as a "dangerous pedophile" with an "intermittent explosive personality."[6] As the years went by, Shawcross became increasingly institutionalized, resisted psychotherapy and sex offender treatment, was routinely denied parole, and appeared destined to serve the maximum sentence. Nine years into his sentence, Shawcross began to participate in counseling, claiming posttraumatic stress arising from his service in Vietnam, where he now claimed to have engaged in numerous wartime atrocities. The parole board, however, remained unimpressed, classifying Shawcross as a "psychosexual maniac."[7]

Five years later, however, after Shawcross had served just 14 years in prison, the parole board heard from a prison psychiatrist that the child killer was "emotionally stable" and "not mentally ill."[8] Within months, on April 28, 1997, the board ordered Shawcross released to a men's shelter in Binghamton, New York, operated by the Volunteers of America. Shawcross's parole officer was so concerned by this turn of events that he warned his supervisors that he considered "this man to be possibly the most dangerous individual to have been released to this community in many years."[9]

Shawcross's presence in Binghamton, a city of about 50,000 people, was soon noted by the local police and one of the city's three television stations. But by the time local residents were informed by the media that they had a paroled child killer in their midst, parole authorities had already moved Shawcross to Delhi, a small, rural town located about 70 miles northeast of Binghamton. Within a week, however, reporters had tracked Shawcross to his new home and publicized his address. Again parole officials secretly moved Shawcross, this time to a hotel in a Binghamton suburb, before eventually placing him in Rochester, the state's third largest city.

Parole officials believed that Shawcross could fly beneath the radar in this city of some 250,000 people, and they were correct. Living with a woman he would soon marry while having an affair with another, Shawcross bounced from one minimum-wage job to the next before settling into work cutting up vegetables and making salads for a restaurant food supplier. The two women in his life knew of his criminal background but loved him anyway. His bosses knew that he was an ex-convict but had no idea what crime had put him behind bars. What they did know was that Shawcross was a good, clean, dependable worker who did his job and caused no trouble. Shawcross's neighbors in Rochester knew him as likeable handyman who readily offered to help them and took food to the homeless and needy.

What none of the people around Shawcross knew was that, using cars belonging to his fiancée and his lover, he prowled the streets of Rochester's "red light" district, looking for sex with prostitutes or that, over a period of about 2 years, from the time he arrived in Rochester, he raped and strangled at least 11 women. Nine of these women were prostitutes, 1 was an acquaintance of Shawcross, and another was a friend of his fiancée. Shawcross's modus operandi involved having or attempting to have sex with these women before and/or after their deaths. In most cases, he choked them to death with his bare hands and then dumped their bodies in out-of-the-way places.

While the police were looking for the serial killer who turned out to be Arthur Shawcross, he was leading an otherwise very ordinary and normal life. Parole officers who kept tabs on him reported that his relationship with his fiancée was strong and mutually supportive and that Shawcross had made a positive adjustment to life in Rochester. Meanwhile, a psychiatric social worker, assigned to provide psychotherapy for Shawcross, reported that the ex-convict was doing well:

> [S]ocial adjustment shows great improvement . . . He has re-established contact with his parents after eighteen years, has a pleasant apartment with his girlfriend and seems to have made friends . . . He reports that he is doing well at his employment and is now working full time . . . In brief, his coming is only in response to request of his PO . . . [T]here has been no recurrence according to his report of any impulses or inclination toward the sort of behavior which landed him in prison for a number of years . . . I have left it with him that he contact me on his own initiative should he feel the need for ongoing help . . . I've scheduled no further visits and do not feel he should be compelled to come.[10]

Perhaps because he appeared so normal and well adjusted, Shawcross eluded the police manhunt for the unknown serial killer for many months. In perhaps the most extensive investigation in the history of Rochester, a police dragnet that is estimated to have cost local taxpayers between $900,000 and $2 million,[11] Shawcross was finally apprehended when he returned to the scene of one of the crimes that was under surveillance. Even then, however, he would not likely have been charged with these murders had he not confessed to the crimes.

In a lengthy and coherent 79-page confession, Shawcross detailed how and why he killed the 11 women and where he disposed of their remains. In each instance, Shawcross explained what the woman had done to trigger his homicidal urge. His first victim, he said, had bitten his penis while giving him oral sex and then taunted him with epithets such as "faggot," "queer," and "little man."[12] His second victim, he told the police, infuriated him by announcing, "I'm going to have a baby."[13] His third victim, he claimed, threatened to tell his wife of their sexual affair. Two of his victims, he reported, had been trying to rob him. And so it went until Shawcross had provided an explanation for each killing.

Though Shawcross's explanations for the killings were self-serving, portrayed him as a victim of the women, and offered no legal justification for any of the homicides, none was delusional or patently irrational. The only bizarre aspect of his confession was his claim that he had not only sexually mutilated some of the women but had actually eaten parts of their genitals.

While the police had plenty of physical evidence, none of it tied any of the killings to Shawcross. Moreover, they had no eyewitness evidence linking Shawcross to the deaths. Thus, without Shawcross's confession, they would have had no case.

Even with a detailed confession, however, convicting Shawcross would not be easy because the nature of his crimes, combined with his past history, quickly led his attorneys to the suspect that, at the time of the killings, their client might have been insane or at least suffering from extreme emotional disturbance.

Their decision to pursue these defenses, although certainly justified from the perspective of criminal defense lawyers, led to what might well be described as a complex and expensive psychiatric and legal debacle.

All but one of Shawcross's homicides occurred in Monroe County, where Rochester is located. One of his victims was found in nearby Wayne County. Each county had its own public defender's office. The Monroe County office had a conflict in the case and was unable to represent Shawcross, so he was assigned two of Rochester's leading criminal defense attorneys. In the much smaller Wayne County, he would be represented by the public defender, also a very accomplished criminal defense lawyer. Though working for the same client and hoping for the same defenses, the Wayne County public defender hired a local psychiatrist, Dr. Richard Kraus, to examine Shawcross, whereas the Rochester attorneys retained the services of a Rochester psychiatrist, Dr. David Barry.

Kraus, who would spend months reviewing documents related to the case, examining medical test results and interviewing Shawcross, was initially puzzled by Shawcross. As the psychiatrist later said,

> He listed a bunch of silly excuses for killing: one woman bit him, one grabbed his wallet, one called him a "faggot," one talked too loud, one claimed she was a virgin . . .
> I thought, Jesus Christ, you're offering these as justifications for murder? He presented so differently from what I expected, made no secret about his crimes, talked a lot of nonsense. I thought, well, he's got antisocial tendencies, but what else? He wasn't like any sociopath I've ever seen.[14]

In interview after interview, Shawcross told Kraus increasingly implausible if not impossible tales of horror. In one interview, Shawcross told the psychiatrist that after one of his Rochester victims had been dead 4 days, he had returned to the body, cut out her vagina, and eaten it: "Ate it raw, cold, frozen, driving down the road."[15] In another, Shawcross claimed to have eaten young Jack Blake's genitals as well as the Watertown boy's heart.

In still other interviews, Shawcross claimed to have witnessed and committed numerous atrocities while in combat in Vietnam. Among Shawcross's stories were those of a prostitute whose head he claimed to have blown off by inserting a fire hose into her vagina and a another Vietnamese woman spy he said was tied between two trees and "split down the middle with a machete."[16] Kraus found it telling that despite his many horror stories of combat in Vietnam, Shawcross could not name a single person with whom he had served in the Southeast Asian conflict. As it would turn out, there was a reasonable explanation for Shawcross's inability to name anyone with whom he had served in combat: Army records indicate that while he served in Vietnam, Shawcross was never even close to combat.

Eventually, the persistent and thorough Kraus would discover that Shawcross suffered from XYY syndrome—a genetic anomaly in which a male is born with an extra Y chromosome—a disorder that has been linked in some studies to violent behavior. Overall, however, Kraus told the defense attorneys, "I can't give you *any* kind of psychiatric defense. This is a very disturbed guy, aberrant, definitely abnormal. But he hasn't told me anything that would absolve him of these crimes. As you know, our New York [insanity] rule is cognitive, a rule of knowledge: Did he know what he was doing? Did he know the consequences of his act? Did he know it was wrong? The answer is yes, yes, and absolutely."[17]

Similarly, Dr. Barry concluded that he could not support any psychiatric defenses for Shawcross.

When an expert retained by the prosecution in an insanity case concludes that a defendant was insane at the time of the offense, the prosecution has a legal duty to make that opinion known to defense counsel, who is then free to use it to his or her client's advantage. Thus, usually when a prosecution expert reaches the conclusion that a defendant meets the legal criteria for insanity, the case is resolved by stipulation—defense and prosecution agree that the defendant was insane, and the court enters such a verdict without a trial.

However, when an expert retained by the defense, such as Dr. Kraus or Dr. Barry, concludes that the defendant does not meet the criteria for a defense of insanity, defense counsel is under no obligation to reveal that opinion to the prosecution. Indeed, the defense attorney is under an ethical obligation not to reveal that opinion to the prosecution. Moreover, in such an instance, if funds permit, the defense lawyer may simply seek other expert opinions.

Had the opinions of Kraus and/or Barry been favorable to Shawcross's insanity plea, it is almost certain that defense counsel in Rochester (Monroe County) would have called one or both as an expert witness. But given the two psychiatrist's conclusions, Shawcross's attorneys had little choice but to find another opinion if they were to proceed with the planned insanity defense. Giving up on local doctors, Shawcross's appointed defenders in Monroe County turned to Dr. Dorothy Lewis, a professor of psychiatry at New York University with a national reputation for the study of criminal violence.

Although Kraus and Barry concluded that Shawcross did not meet the legal criteria for insanity in New York, Lewis disagreed.

As part of her forensic examinations of Shawcross, Lewis utilized hypnosis and purportedly uncovered a great deal of previously unknown information about the serial killer's childhood. According to Lewis, hypnotic interviews revealed that, as a child, Shawcross had been sexually "tortured" by his mother and her friend.[18] From Shawcross's statements and behavior while presumably hypnotized, Lewis concluded that as a young boy Shawcross had been forced to have oral sex with a friend of his mother whom he regarded as an "aunt."[19] Lewis also found evidence that convinced her that Shawcross's own mother repeatedly and brutally assaulted the young boy anally—for example, forcing him to take and hold 1-gallon enemas and shoving various objects, such as a broomstick, a toilet brush, and a large thermometer deep into his rectum to punish him for showing sexual interest in his sister. Through hypnosis, Lewis also purportedly learned that both of Shawcross's parents had beaten him as a child and that, on numerous occasions, his mother had threatened to cut the child's penis off with a knife if he did not stop masturbating.

In her interviews, both with and without hypnosis, Lewis explored Shawcross's experience serving in the U.S. Army in Vietnam more than 2 decades earlier. Shawcross maintained that he was a witness to and participant in many atrocities during his year of service in the Southeast Asian conflict. For instance, he claimed that he had seen many Vietnamese women and children killed, that he had raped two Vietnamese girls, and that he had participated in the torture of four others. One of these victims, he said, was a prostitute who had "black syph" and gave the disease to a number of soldiers.[20] According to Shawcross, he and his comrades shoved a fire hose into the woman's vagina and inflated her with water until her head essentially exploded. A second woman, Shawcross claimed, had placed a razor device into her vagina to injure American troops with whom she had sex. Shawcross reported that he and his fellow troops tied her between two trees and then cut her up the middle until she was torn in two. Two other women, he reported, had been decapitated.

Lewis also learned that Shawcross had purportedly wandered alone into a Vietnamese jungle after surviving an incident in which 1200 people were massacred, that Shawcross had personally killed 26 people by sneaking onto an enemy encampment and shooting them with a high-powered firearm silenced by the use of baby bottle nipples, and that one of Shawcross's fellow soldiers had been killed by the enemy and died in his arms.

Based upon the "torture" she believed Shawcross had experienced at the hands of his mother and others as a child and the atrocities he had witnessed or been a part of in Vietnam, as well as his reaction to these events, Lewis concluded that Shawcross suffered from posttraumatic stress disorder (PTSD) so severe that he had been in a dissociative state during each of the 10 killings with which he was charged in Monroe County. As she explained to the jury,

> Dissociative state is a pathological psychiatric state usually brought on by extraordinary trauma . . . either psychological or physical. The more ongoing the trauma, the earlier the trauma, the more severe the dissociative symptoms are. In a dissociative state, the individual is not really in touch with reality[;] there is a kind of splitting off, where the person is operating sometimes as though he or she were a totally different individual. But the person, in essence, is not in touch with reality.[21]

Months after reaching and reporting this diagnosis, and after filing at least three reports in the case, Lewis added another diagnostic conclusion. Having reviewed additional information and having consulted with a neurological colleague, Lewis later opined that Shawcross was not only in a dissociative state at the time of the killings but was also undergoing a "complex partial seizure" secondary to a "small, fluid filled cyst"[22] on his brain revealed by an electromagnetic scan.

As Lewis explained years later,

> I had no question that Mr. Shawcross had been severely abused and suffered from dissociative episodes . . . I also knew that a psychiatric defense, especially one based on the diagnosis of a dissociative disorder, would never fly. If for years I had doubted the very existence of the diagnosis, there was no reason to think a judge or jury would buy it. A neurologic defense, however, based not only on clinical findings but also on visible MRI evidence of brain damage, was likely to be far more convincing. Letters and phone calls flew back and forth, as I begged the Shawcross attorneys to obtain the computerized EEG and the specialized neurologic evaluation . . .
>
> Here is where I made my first big mistake. I buckled and agreed to write my report in the absence of all the data I requested. Therefore, all I could do is describe the dissociative phenomena I saw and hint at the existence of a possible seizure disorder, while I awaited proof of it . . . The lawyers assured me that by the time I came to Rochester to testify, the examinations I requested would be completed.
>
> I arrived in Rochester two days before I was to testify, only to discover that neither the neurologic examination by the eminent neurosurgeon nor the computerized EEG he had recommended had been obtained . . .

> I should have turned around and gone home. I should have refused to testify. I didn't. I didn't have the courage. That was my second big mistake . . . [23]

If, as Lewis says, her failure to make sure that the needed tests were completed prior to preparing her report was her "first big mistake" and testifying was her "second big mistake," these errors certainly were not the only ones she made as an expert witness in *People v. Shawcross*.

Linking Shawcross's purported posttraumatic stress disorder, dissociative reactions, and seizure disorder, Lewis testified that Shawcross was insane (i.e., unable to appreciate the nature and consequences or the wrongfulness of his homicidal acts), was in a state of extreme emotional disturbance at the time of each of the killings, and had been unable to form an intent to kill any of the 10 women for whose murders he was being tried.

Though most of her testimony was about the trauma that she claimed triggered Shawcross's posttraumatic stress disorder, when it came to explaining why the serial killer should be acquitted by reason of insanity or found guilty of a lesser charge on the theories that he was acting in a state of extreme emotional disturbance and unable to formulate an intent to kill his victims, Lewis stressed not PTSD, nor dissociation, but seizures. As she told the jury,

> I believe that at the time of these deaths that something in the interaction between Mr. Shawcross and the person with whom he was engaged at the time triggered a response in him and indeed an emotional response at first and since emotional kinds of response in patients with this kind of temporal lobe dysfunction frequently trigger seizures, that something, be it his penis feeling bitten, be it some other thing, be it the word [sic] I'll tell triggered an emotional response which then, in turn, triggered a physiologic response. And at such times, he was experiencing the auras which are caused by the beginning of abnormal brain activity, then a period of time in which deep in the brain there is much more significant abnormal brain activity at which times a person really does not remember clearly what had happened, followed by a post epileptic stage at which he either slept or felt dizzy or out of it. I cannot tell you at which point the strangulations occurred . . . However, it is my clinical opinion that these strangulations occurred in the context of one of these seizure episodes and that at that time there is no way that he could have controlled his behavior or could even have been clearly aware of what he was doing.[24]

When cross-examined about the report of a local neurologist who had reviewed the MRI and CT scans of Shawcross's brain and pronounced them within normal limits, Lewis testified that "it did not matter what [he] said," adding that in her view "there are only about five or six people in the country who are competent to work on this kind of case," and that she was led to believe that one of this select handful of doctors had been retained by Shawcross's lawyers.[25] Pressed by the judge to limit her answers to the questions asked, a direction he gave her repeatedly throughout her testimony, Lewis immediately failed to comply, turned to the judge and said, "Your honor, these questions have to do with the very areas in which I was lied to by defense counsel."[26]

As a result of Lewis's attack on Shawcross's lawyers, who had retained her and presented her as a witness, the attorneys asked the court to declare a mistrial on the theory that Lewis's claims would bias the jury against the defendant, whose defenses rested almost exclusively on the jury's reaction to Lewis's testimony.

The judge refused to grant a mistrial, perhaps reasoning that by the time Lewis made these allegations against defense counsel, she had already completely undermined her own testimony in the eyes of the jury.

For instance, much of what Lewis reported about the sexual "torture" Shawcross purportedly underwent as a child came from a session in which she hypnotized Shawcross and asked him pointed questions about such abuse. In a withering cross-examination, prosecutor Charles Siragusa first got Lewis to acknowledge that she was not an expert in hypnosis and that hypnosis is controversial and not a reliable tool for getting at the truth, particularly in forensic settings such as this one. Siragusa then got the psychiatrist to acknowledge that there are standard procedures that should be followed when utilizing hypnosis in such a setting—for example, exhausting the recollection of the subject before hypnotizing him, making a complete record of what the subject knew about the case prior to hypnosis, videotaping all hypnotic sessions, avoiding leading and suggestive questions, and remaining unemotional during the hypnotic sessions—and that she did not follow these procedures in her hypnosis of Shawcross. Finally, in a remarkable exchange, Siragusa asked Lewis, "Are you telling me that you knew the right way to do it but you didn't do it the right way?"[27] To which Lewis replied, "Absolutely. I am telling you that, yes, absolutely, yes."[28]

Following up on Lewis's conclusion that Shawcross had been subjected to brutal sexual abuse by his mother and her assertion that this was one of the two major causes of his PTSD and dissociative episodes (his experiences in Vietnam being the other), Siragusa asked, "So if it never happened, never happened, it wouldn't change your opinion, is that correct?"[29] Lewis replied, "Correct."[30]

Similarly, Siragusa attacked Lewis's reliance upon claims Shawcross had made about his many traumatic experiences in Vietnam. After Lewis had testified that Shawcross's traumatic experiences in Vietnam played a significant role in his PTSD, dissociative episodes, and mental state at the time of the killings— "I believe that the most significant trauma contributing to his psychiatric illness occurred throughout his childhood, however, had he not been traumatized again in Vietnam, he might not have expressed the disorder in so violent a fashion"[31]—Siragusa confronted her with the purported traumatic events, one by one, getting the psychiatrist to acknowledge that many of these events were unlikely to have occurred and that not a single one was ever verified.

Indeed, Lewis acknowledged that she had spent 45 minutes interviewing Shawcross in an effort to get him to provide the names of any individuals who could corroborate his accounts of his exploits in Vietnam. Pressed by Siragusa, Lewis admitted that Shawcross could name only one person, Sgt. Edwards, and that "[t]o the best of my recollection, Sergeant Edwards said that these things did not happen and that he could not confirm them."[32]

Finally, and perhaps most damning in the eyes of the jury, which had to render a separate verdict on each of the 10 indictments, was Dr. Lewis's admitted failure to go into the details of each of the 10 killings with Shawcross. When the prosecutor asked her repeatedly about the specifics of a particular killing, Lewis was able to give few if any details. Finally, after failing to answer repeated questions, the psychiatrist explained,

> Again, they were confused and similar to the other—to the other women that he had killed and they were not distinct in my mind from the others that he had done and there were discrepancies between what he had said in his statements to the police and his statements to others, so that I did not take note of exactly what he said about each one of the murders. I was satisfied that he—that in each one he was confused, he had an impaired memory for it.[33]

In rebuttal to Dr. Lewis's testimony, the prosecution called Dr. Park Dietz to the witness stand. Dietz who, like Lewis, was a board-certified psychiatrist but not board certified in forensic psychiatry, has testified in many of America's most high profile insanity cases, including those of Jeffrey Dahmer, John W. Hinckley, Jr., and Andrea Yates, and is a well-regarded and frequent witness for the prosecution.

Dietz, who was paid more than twice what Lewis earned on the case ($97,000 versus $47,000), proved to be worth the cost to the prosecutor's office. Dietz conducted a thorough, methodical, and detailed—some might say tedious—evaluation of Shawcross. His testimony, unlike Lewis's, was organized, succinct, and calculated to be intelligible to lay jurors. Indeed, even Dr. Lewis complimented Dietz's methodology of leaving no stone unturned and acknowledged that she learned a great deal about Shawcross from the videotapes and transcripts of Dietz's examinations of the serial killer.

Dietz not only concluded that Shawcross had been sane at the time of the killings, had not been suffering from an extreme emotional disturbance, and had been able to form the intent to kill, but disputed Lewis's diagnoses of Shawcross and the purported facts she used to substantiate those diagnoses.

First, with regard to Lewis's conclusion that Shawcross had been brutally sexually abused as a child, Dietz disagreed, indicating that in over a thousand pages of correctional and mental health records, witness statements, and other accounts of Shawcross's life preceding the killings, he found not a single mention anywhere of childhood physical or sexual abuse. Dietz also testified that the kind of physical damage one would expect to see caused by the anal abuse to which Shawcross was reportedly subjected by his mother would likely have been fatal and, if not, would have required surgery. He told the jury he found no evidence of any treatment, much less any surgery, for such injuries.

Next, with regard to Shawcross's claims of traumatic incidents in Vietnam, incidents that Lewis believed formed a large part of the basis for his mental illness and lack of criminal responsibility in the 10 killings, Dietz testified flatly that "they're not true. Obviously not true because they're impossible."[34]

To begin with, Dietz testified,

> [T]he military records concerning Mr. Shawcross do not indicate that he saw combat while he was in Vietnam. Rather, they indicate that he was assigned to a supply and transportation unit. And there's no indication that he was out of that unit during the time he served overseas ... The records also don't indicate that he received any combat injuries, though he's repeatedly talked about receiving such an injury ... Sergeant Edwards, who had the occasion to discipline the defendant once, indicated in his statement that none of the stories that Mr. Shawcross told could possibly have happened in the supply and transport unit, that none of that was true.[35]

Dietz further testified that some of Shawcross's Vietnam stories were anatomically impossible. For example, he cited the story "in which a firepump is inserted into a prostitute's vagina causing her neck to jump from her body," adding that, "The anatomy does not work that way."[36] Dietz also made reference to Shawcross's description of having decapitated two Vietnamese women: "His description is that the neck hanged down, the tissue was hanging from the head. Whereas, in fact, the neck retracts. It's just skin stretched between where the head is and where the chest and thorax begins and it does not hang down in that way."[37]

Finally, with regard to Shawcross's claims about his experience in Vietnam, Dietz testified that he had personally conducted an experiment on a police firing range to test the serial killer's assertion that he had used baby-bottle nipples to silence an M-16 rifle he used to ambush and kill 26 enemies. As Dietz told the jury, "It's not often in psychiatry that we're told a lie and can, within hours, prove that it was a lie. And this was obviously such an occasion ... [The baby-bottle nipples] didn't silence anything. The report was equally loud with and without the baby-bottle nipple."[38]

Given that Dietz did not believe Shawcross's claims of trauma as a child or as a soldier in Vietnam, it came as no surprise that he disagreed with Dr. Lewis's diagnosis of posttraumatic stress disorder. As Dietz testified, "So the fact that he doesn't have the signs and symptoms of the disorder is one good indication that he doesn't have it. Second is that the stressors [Dr. Lewis] claimed had caused it, namely sexual torture on the one hand and Vietnam combat atrocity experiences on the other, in my opinion did not occur. So he has neither the causes of such a disorder nor the symptoms of it."[39]

Dietz also disagreed with Lewis's diagnosis that Shawcross suffered from complex partial seizures at the times of the killings. Asked why, Dietz explained,

> Well, on the basis that Mr. Shawcross has never had a seizure. In order to have a diagnosis of complex partial seizures, someone has to have seizures. Mr. Shawcross has never had a witnessed seizure. All of the materials that I've reviewed—and I mentioned before they include family members and friends and acquaintances and co-workers, that they also include all of the time he served in correctional facilities, his time in the military, the time he's been in jail awaiting trial here, there are documents concerning Mr. Shawcross in a way that isn't true for most people because more than half his life has been spent in places where they keep records—he has never been witnessed to have a seizure ...
>
> Second indication is that he has had the usual tests designed to see if seizure activity in the brain can be measured. Namely electroencephalograms, also known as brain wave tests. On at least four

occasions the electrical activity in Mr. Shawcross's brain was measured by having such a test done. And on all four of those occasions the electrical activity in his brain was normal . . .

It's also significant, at least in this instance where [it] seems to be Dr. Lewis's opinion that seizures have had something to do with these crimes, that his behavior during the crime is organized behavior of locating a victim, taking a victim to a secluded location, killing that victim in ways he remembers and can describe in detail, often taking the victim's remains to another location, and in all instances finding the means of hiding the victim's remains, often disposing of their possessions, and escaping the scene. In fact, he evaded detection for quite some time. That organized criminal behavior is inconsistent with the behavior occurring during complex partial seizures . . . [40]

Citing Shawcross's history—which included all of the diagnostic criteria for conduct disorder as a juvenile (e.g., running away, initiating fights, using a weapon, cruelty to animals and humans, stealing, and repeatedly lying before the age of 15) as well as inability to sustain consistent work, repeatedly performing antisocial acts that are grounds for arrest, failing to honor financial obligations, lying and showing no regard for the truth, recklessly disregarding his own personal safety and that of others, failing to sustain a monogamous relationship, and lacking remorse, all as an adult—Dietz used the criteria laid out in the American Psychiatric Association's *Diagnostic and Statistical Manual* (then the "Third Edition-Revised" and referred to as *DSM-III-R*) to diagnose Shawcross with antisocial personality disorder, the modern-day version of what was formerly called a psychopath or sociopath.

Finally, unlike Lewis, Dietz went through the specific details of each homicide and explained why the facts did *not* indicate that Shawcross lacked the substantial capacity to know or appreciate either the nature and consequences or the wrongfulness of his actions, had acted in extreme emotional disturbance, or had been unable to form the requisite intent to kill his victims. In most of the killings, for example, Dietz noted that Shawcross had taken the victims to secluded places for purposes of engaging in acts of prostitution, had gone to great lengths to conceal the crimes, and had repeatedly lied about them to the authorities. In a number of instances, Dietz observed, Shawcross claimed he had killed the women when they threatened to reveal his actions to the authorities or to his wife; indeed, he claimed that one of his victims had threatened to identify him to police as the serial killer who had been terrorizing local prostitutes.

After deliberating just 6 hours, the jury rejected all of Shawcross's defenses—insanity, extreme emotional disturbance, and lack of capacity to form an intent to kill—and found him guilty of 10 counts of murder. Questioned about the verdict, a number of jurors were extremely critical of Dr. Lewis and her testimony. For instance, jury foreman Robert Edwards said, "If she could have kept her feet on the floor instead of in her mouth, she would have been O.K. The more she talked, the worse it got . . . It's just too bad she didn't leave after she read her qualifications."[41]

Such criticism was not unexpected, apparently even by Dr. Lewis. As she said later,

> Not only did the jury not believe me, they hated me. Then again, so did the rest of Rochester. My testimony extended over a three-week period as the prosecutor relished raking me over the coals . . . Night after night during the course of my testimony I would return to my hotel, almost punch-drunk from the new information hurled at me in court, information the defense should have shared with me . . . I would then switch on the news and watch the man (or woman) in the street belittle me and my testimony. Jingles were written about me and played on talk radio. It was a nightmare.
>
> The prosecution had hired one of the most highly regarded forensic psychiatrists in the nation . . . He was a handsome, confident man who never appeared hassled. Compared to him I looked clumsy and disorganized. I looked as though the courtroom vapors had gotten to me. In truth I was angry. I had been tricked. I have learned since then that one should never take the stand angry. It wreaks havoc with one's memory and, of course, one's demeanor.[42]

After Shawcross's conviction, but prior to sentencing, his attorneys asked the trial judge to overturn the jury's verdict, alleging that Shawcross had been denied a fair trial by Lewis, who was the only witness for the defense. Defense counsel argued that "Dr. Lewis, through her conduct, created the impression that the attorneys were liars and were trying to pull wool over the jury's eyes."[43] Her behavior on the witness stand, they claimed, "tainted the right of the accused to a fair consideration of his mental state at the time of the conduct alleged in the indictment."[44] "In short," they concluded, "Dr. Lewis, by her own testimony, undermined the opinions which she had earlier given before the jury."[45]

The judge rejected this argument, upheld the verdict, and sentenced Shawcross to a minimum term of 250 years in prison. An appellate court later addressed the complaint that Lewis had "sabotaged" Shawcross's defense.[46] In affirming the serial killer's conviction, the appeals court said,

> [W]e cannot conclude that defendant was deprived of competent psychiatric assistance. At State expense, defendant was provided with "a competent psychiatrist who did conduct an appropriate examination and assisted in evaluation, preparation, and presentation of the defense." The psychiatrist selected by defendant is an internationally recognized expert in the field of violent criminal behavior and possesses outstanding qualifications. She conducted appropriate and thorough examinations of defendant and assisted in the evaluation, preparation, and presentation of the defense. Moreover, numerous tests and evaluations were performed at her request concerning defendant's mental condition and she consulted with several neurologists. The report of one neurologist, with whom she had frequently consulted in the past, was received in evidence. No fault can be found with the witness's presentation on direct examination. Under all of the circumstances, her loss of composure under vigorous cross-examination did not rise to the level of incompetent psychiatric assistance.[47]

6
Scott Panetti

As early as his teenage years, Scott Panetti showed signs of mental illness. As his mother would later concede, "There was something dreadfully wrong with Scott."[1] But as Mrs. Panetti also noted, Scott's illness went undiagnosed and untreated: "Looking back, I remember the danger signs but I then associated his behavior with typical teenager weirdness. After all, this was the early 1970s. Mental illness was not publicized or admitted to. I told myself that Scott was just a unique person. There were no support groups to contact that I know of, where one could go to for advice. Psychiatry was eyed with suspicion."[2]

Like many troubled youngsters of his generation, Panetti dropped out of high school to join the military, perhaps looking for the kind of control he could not exercise over his own behavior. Before long, however, he was medically discharged from the Navy. Although he claimed that he was discharged due to arthritis in his hands, his parents suspected that their son was actually discharged due to his psychological problems.

After his discharge from the Navy, Panetti moved with his parents to Texas, where he married Janie Luckenbach. Though the couple had three children, their marriage was doomed by Panetti's worsening mental illness. By 1986, when Janie filed for divorce, Panetti had already twice been hospitalized for mental illness—both times for threats to kill his wife and her family—and diagnosed as suffering from chronic undifferentiated schizophrenia.

In 1986 alone, Panetti spent time in eight different psychiatric hospitals and was treated with various antipsychotic medications. Psychiatrists and psychologists repeatedly confirmed the diagnosis of schizophrenia, based in part on his delusion that he was being followed by federal agents and his hallucinations of a voice telling him to kill his family and himself.

Though Panetti was certified as disabled, found unable to work, and granted Social Security disability benefits, he moved from his parents' home and adopted a cowboy persona, "swagger[ing] around town like Clint

Eastwood in his cowboy hat and leather boots and silver belt buckle."[3] Soon he met and began dating Sonja Alvarado. Sonja became pregnant and gave birth to a daughter, Amanda. A year after Amanda's birth, Sonja married Scott, whom she described as a good father, even though he was obviously mentally ill, drank heavily, smoked marijuana, and could not work steadily because of his illness and the side effects of the medications he was taking for it.

Although Scott frequently became drunk, screamed and threw things, caused his neighbors to call the police, and led the family to move at least twice, Sonja had trouble accepting the consensus of family, friends, neighbors, and the police that Scott was mentally ill. As she would later say, "I loved Scott so much that I didn't see that he was mentally ill."[4]

But even an adoring wife could not ignore the increasing threats and abuse that led to two psychiatric hospitalizations for Panetti. In 1990, Panetti was hospitalized involuntarily after threatening to kill his wife, daughter, father-in-law, and himself. In 1992, Panetti was again hospitalized for threatening his family. During this inpatient stay, Panetti complained of hearing several different voices, which he appeared to identify as separate aspects of his own personality. He was diagnosed with schizoaffective disorder—an illness essentially combining symptoms of schizophrenia and bipolar disorder.

In August 1992, following this last hospitalization, Panetti argued with Alvarado and struck her in the face with a rifle butt. Alvarado responded by leaving Panetti and moving in with her parents. Panetti moved into a cabin about 5 minutes away. In the following weeks, Panetti called Alvarado and threatened to burn down the house and kill her and her parents if not allowed to see his daughter. Several times, Panetti went to the Alvarado home. On one occasion, Panetti threatened to kill the family with a sword. Another time, when Sonja Alvarado's father ordered Panetti to leave, Panetti threatened to shoot his father-in-law. Sonja called the police several times and pleaded with them to take away her husband's guns—a deer rifle and a sawed-off shotgun—but the responding officers refused and allowed Scott to keep the firearms.

On September 2, 1992, Sonja obtained a court order of protection against Panetti, but it was too late to do much good. Five days later, Panetti met with a friend and discussed the restraining order. The friend suggested that Panetti abide by the order and encouraged him to leave town. Instead, Panetti purchased and drank a bottle of whiskey and fell asleep in his cabin. The next morning, September 8, 1992, Panetti awoke, shaved his head, dressed in camouflage fatigues, grabbed his rifle, shotgun, and a number of knives, and drove to the Alvarados' home. There he used the shotgun to smash a window and confront his wife. Sonja ran from the house but Panetti soon caught her, hit her in the face with the butt of his rifle, and then ordered her back into the home. Inside the house, Sonja locked Panetti out and tried to call the police. Before she succeeded, however, Panetti shot the knob off the door, and asked Sonja whom he should kill first, Sonja or her parents.

With his 3-year-old daughter watching, Panetti then shot both Mr. and Mrs. Alvarado in the chest. The couple was killed, and blood from Mrs. Alvarado sprayed on both Sonja and the child. Panetti then forced his wife and daughter into his Jeep and drove them to the cabin in which he had been staying since the separation. Inside the cabin, holding Sonja and his daughter at gunpoint, Panetti refused Sonja's request to be allowed to check on her parents. Panetti told her, "I just shot your parents. No more mommy, no more daddy; get that through your head."[5] He then proceeded to blame her for the killings, telling her that she had betrayed him by going to the police and repeatedly forcing her to read the order of protection. Finally, Panetti allowed his wife and daughter to leave before turning himself in and confessing to the police.

Representing a mentally ill client charged with capital murder and facing a possible death sentence if convicted, Panetti's attorney requested a hearing regarding Panetti's competence to stand trial. Did the confessed killer have "a factual understanding of the proceedings against him" and "sufficient present ability to consult with his lawyer with a reasonable degree of rational understanding"?[6]

A competency hearing held in April 1994 resulted in a mistrial after the jury deadlocked. Three jurors believed Panetti was competent, four concluded that he was not, and the remaining five were undecided.

When the competency issue was retried before another jury in September 1994, one of Panetti's attorneys testified that in the 2 years he had been representing Panetti he had not been able to engage in any meaningful discussion regarding the case. The attorney further testified that Panetti's thought process appeared bizarre and he seemed to have multiple personalities. On cross-examination, the prosecutor emphasized the attorney's admission that for "various reasons" he had waited 2 years to seek a hearing on Panetti's competence to stand trial.[7]

Defense counsel also presented the testimony of Dr. Richard Coons, a psychiatrist, who told the jury that Panetti had been diagnosed with schizophrenia, demonstrated tangential thinking, needed to be treated with psychotropic medications, was not competent to stand trial, and would further decompensate under the stress of a capital murder trial. Under cross-examination, however, Coons acknowledged that it was "not beyond the realm of possibility" that Panetti was feigning some of his symptoms.[8]

In response, the prosecution offered the testimony of three law enforcement officers and a court-appointed psychiatrist. The officers testified that

Panetti appeared to be rational and seemed calm when he got what he wanted. Surprisingly, one of the police officers was allowed to testify that, in his opinion, Panetti was not mentally ill. That opinion, however, was promptly contradicted by the testimony of the prosecution's only expert witness. Psychiatrist Dr. Lee Simes told the jury that Panetti suffered from schizophrenia but was nonetheless competent to stand trial.

The ink was barely dry on the jury verdict finding Panetti competent to stand trial before the mentally ill defendant decided to fire his attorneys and represent himself in the forthcoming capital murder trial. Although the judge repeatedly warned Panetti of the difficulties he would likely encounter as a layman defending himself against murder charges in a trial that could result in a sentence of death, and cautioned that he would not in any way bend the rules of evidence to accommodate the defendant's ignorance, Panetti stated on the record that he understood the pitfalls of self-representation and expected no special treatment.

Although Panetti's request to represent himself was opposed by his counsel, the prosecutor, and the judge, the judge had no choice but to grant the defendant's request.

In 1975, the U.S. Supreme Court held that a criminal defendant's right to represent himself in court is guaranteed by the Sixth Amendment. In *Faretta v. California*, the high court concluded that

> [t]he Sixth Amendment does not provide merely that a defense shall be made for the accused; it grants to the accused personally the right to make his defense. It is the accused, not counsel, who must be "informed of the nature and cause of the accusation," who must be "confronted with the witnesses against him," and who must be accorded "compulsory process for obtaining witnesses in his favor." Although not stated in the Amendment in so many words, the right to self-representation—to make one's own defense personally—is thus necessarily implied by the structure of the Amendment. The right to defend is given directly to the accused; for it is he who suffers the consequences if the defense fails.[9]

In *Faretta*, the Court recognized that even though choosing to represent oneself in court may be foolish and detrimental to a defendant's interests, such a choice must be respected. As the Court explained,

> It is undeniable that in most criminal prosecutions defendants could better defend with counsel's guidance than by their own unskilled efforts. But where the defendant will not voluntarily accept

representation by counsel, the potential advantage of a lawyer's training and experience can be realized, if at all, only imperfectly. To force a lawyer on a defendant can only lead him to believe that the law contrives against him. Moreover, it is not inconceivable that in some rare instances, the defendant might in fact present his case more effectively by conducting his own defense. Personal liberties are not rooted in the law of averages. The right to defend is personal. The defendant, and not his lawyer or the State, will bear the personal consequences of a conviction. It is the defendant, therefore, who must be free personally to decide whether in his particular case counsel is to his advantage. And although he may conduct his own defense ultimately to his own detriment, his choice must be honored out of "that respect for the individual which is the lifeblood of the law."[10]

Eighteen years after deciding *Faretta*, the U.S. Supreme Court considered how courts must respond when a mentally ill defendant wishes to waive counsel and represent himself.

In 1993, in *Godinez v. Moran*, capital defendant Allan Moran waived his right to be represented by an attorney, pleaded guilty, and ultimately was sentenced to death. The trial court held that Moran's waiver of counsel was legal because he was competent to stand trial. A federal district court reversed Moran's conviction, holding that competence to waive counsel requires a higher degree of understanding and reason than does mere competence to stand trial. After a federal appeals court rejected the district court's decision and sided with the trial court, the U.S. Supreme Court agreed with the trial court that if a defendant is competent to stand trial he is competent to waive counsel and to represent himself if he so chooses. As the Supreme Court concluded,

> [T]here is no reason to believe that the decision to waive counsel requires an appreciably higher level of mental functioning than the decision to waive other constitutional rights. Respondent suggests that a higher competency standard is necessary because a defendant who represents himself "must have greater powers of comprehension, judgment, and reason than would be necessary to stand trial with the aid of an attorney." But this argument has a flawed premise; the competence that is required of a defendant seeking to waive his right to counsel is the competence to *waive the right*, not the competence to represent himself. In *Faretta* v. *California* (1975), we held that a defendant choosing self-representation must do so "competently and

intelligently," but we made it clear that the defendant's "technical legal knowledge" is "not relevant" to the determination whether he is competent to waive his right to counsel, and we emphasized that although the defendant "may conduct his own defense ultimately to his own detriment, his choice must be honored." Thus, while "[i]t is undeniable that in most criminal prosecutions defendants could better defend with counsel's guidance than by their own unskilled efforts," a criminal defendant's ability to represent himself has no bearing upon his competence to *choose* self-representation.[11]

In keeping with *Faretta* and *Godinez*, Panetti represented himself at trial. A standby attorney was appointed by the court to be present throughout the proceedings in case Panetti changed his mind about representing himself. Wearing a plaid shirt, bandana, cowboy boots with spurs, and a broad-brimmed Stetson hat slung over his shoulder on a strap, and accompanied everywhere he went in the courtroom by two Texas Rangers (one on of each side of him), Panetti struggled through a trial that later was variously labeled a "circus," a "farce," a "mockery" and a "big joke."[12]

In his statement to potential jurors, Panetti said,

> Maybe now, to wind this up, acquit, innocence, yeah . . . as far as insanity talk, I can tell you what, I restore to Sandy, would flat be wacko . . . The death penalty doesn't scare me, sure, but not much. Be killed, power line, when I was a kid. I've got my injun beliefs as a shaman. I sent the buffalo horn to my sister. Adjustment, Jesus wrote . . . but I don't love injuns and Mexicano and Mexicano know, but . . . I was named "he Who Doesn't Cry" because I didn't cry when I should have, and I must admit, though, in Gillespie County Jail when I was in my little suicide box there was old boy committed suicide, I went through a week of pretty much scuba diver's tears, although, I don't scuba.[13]

During voir dire, when asked if he wanted to exercise his right to strike a potential juror from serving on the panel, Panetti flipped a coin and told the judge, "Strike him, Your Honor."[14]

On the day that opening arguments were to be given, Panetti requested a brief continuance, telling the judge, "I definitely need a couple of days to get the medicine, to see my doctor and to prepare my case . . . [to] get medicine, to see my psychiatrist, to be prepared to cross-examine, to think clearly, to cross-examine witnesses clearly."[15] Not only did the trial judge refuse to grant Panetti the requested brief delay but an appeals court later affirmed that decision, noting that because Panetti did not make the motion in writing and under oath, the judge's decision could not be reviewed on appeal.

Prior to the commencement of the trial, Panetti had sought to subpoena over 200 witnesses, including Jesus Christ and John F. Kennedy. Many of these subpoenas were quashed because the person sought was dead or would not have offered any relevant testimony. Panetti did, however, manage to subpoena, among others, Dr. Simes, the psychiatrist who testified at his competency trial that Panetti suffered from schizophrenia. Clearly confused about who would testify when, Panetti failed to object when the trial judge released Simes from the subpoena and thus forfeited the opportunity to present the psychiatrist's testimony at trial.

Although Panetti was not allowed to present Dr. Simes's testimony, he did offer the testimony of several other doctors who had treated him. Dr. John Ramsay, Panetti's former family physician, who was not a psychiatrist, testified that as early as 1984, Panetti had been rambling, grandiose, manic, and depressive. Dr. Eugene Waters, a psychiatrist who had examined the defendant while he was jailed awaiting trial, testified that Panetti was delusional and preoccupied with "almost mythological characters."[16] Dr. F. E. Seale, a psychiatrist who treated Panetti in the 1980s, testified that Panetti showed symptoms of thought disorder and suffered from schizophrenia. Seale admitted on cross-examination that he had not treated Panetti since 1986. Another psychiatrist, Dr. Wolfgang Selck, who also had not seen Panetti since 1986, testified that the defendant had been psychotic and at times could not differentiate right and wrong.

Panetti also presented the testimony of his mother and his sister-in-law, who confirmed that Panetti had long shown obvious symptoms of mental illness and had spoken of an alternate personality named Sarge years before the killing. The testimony of these lay witnesses was critical because Panetti testified that it was Sarge, not he, who committed the killings. In that regard, Panetti told the jurors,

> Sarge woke up. Cut off Scott's hair. Sarge suited up. Shells, canteen, pouch, 30.06, tropical hat, tropical top, bunkhouse, fast, haircut fast, suited up fast, boom, ready fast, fast, haircut, webgear, top, brush hat, boots, out the door, in the jeep, driving, wife, the bridge. Why is it taking so long? In front of Joe and Amanda's house . . . Sarge, everything fast. Everything fast. Everything slow. Tapped on the window, shattered window. Sonja screams, runs, follow her. She runs out, out the front, knife, Birdie, Birdie [Panetti's daughter]. Where's Birdie? Pick her up, she's in bed . . .

> Scott, what? Scott, what did you see Sarge do? Fall. Sonja, Joe, Amanda, kitchen. Joe bayonet, not attacking. Sarge not afraid, not threatened. Sarge not angry, not mad. Sarge, boom, boom. Sarge, boom, boom, boom. Sarge, boom, boom. Sarge is gone. No more Sarge. Sonja and Birdie. Birdie and Sonja. Joe, Amanda lying kitchen, here, there, blood. No, leave. Scott, remember exactly what Scott did. Shot the lock walked in the kitchen. Sonja, where's Birdie? Sonja here. Joe, bayonet, door, Amanda. Boom, boom, boom, blood.
> Demons. Ha, ha, ha, ha, oh, Lord, oh, you.[17]

When the judge cut Panetti off at that point, telling the defendant, "Mr. Panetti, let's stop," Panetti replied, "You puppet."[18]

Panetti ended the guilt-innocence phase of his trial with a rambling, almost incoherent summation, which concluded with the following remarks to the jury:

> How long did this deliberate and that deliberate? I don't think—I think that you are all way beyond, and this ain't no show, and there ain't no body in this point, any evidence, and I proved without a preponderance of a doubt that I didn't know right from wrong and that I was insane, not lay experts or doctors, and in your hearts everybody knows. Do you honestly think any of you are going to go home after making the decision and second guess it? I think without a hesitation you won't, and God bless Texas. Thy will be done. Oh, the law sometimes sleeps, but it never dies.[19]

Because Panetti had never presented any evidence regarding his mental state at the time of his crime, an essential element in any insanity defense, it came as no surprise to anyone—other than perhaps the defendant himself—that the jury convicted him of capital murder after less than 2 hours of deliberations.

The same jury that convicted Panetti would then hear evidence regarding whether or not he should be put to death for his crimes. To impose a sentence of death, the jury would have to conclude that if not executed, Panetti would pose a continuing threat to society. They would also have to conclude that—considering all of the evidence including the offense, the defendant's character and background, and the defendant's moral culpability—there were insufficient mitigating circumstances to warrant that a sentence of life imprisonment rather than a death sentence be imposed.

The prosecution presented lay testimony about assault and death threats Panetti allegedly made to law enforcement officers during his pretrial incarceration. The state was also allowed to present the expert testimony of a notoriously controversial Texas psychiatrist, Dr. James P. Grigson, known in Texas and elsewhere as "Dr. Death" for his well-established track record of testifying for the prosecution in the sentencing phase of capital murder trials.[20] In response to a hypothetical question crafted by the prosecutor to match the facts of Panetti's case, Grigson—who was expelled that same year from the American Psychiatric Association for making predictions of dangerousness about capital defendants (such as Panetti) he had never examined[21]—told the jury that Panetti would be a future danger to society if not executed. Grigson also testified that the danger posed by Panetti could not be reduced by any psychotropic medications.

After 4 hours of deliberation, the jury sentenced Panetti to death by lethal injection.

Observers of the trial were appalled, and jurors said they would not have sentenced Panetti to death had he been represented by counsel. A psychiatrist who attended the trial said, "My main impression was why was the Judge allowing this crazy man to defend himself. I thought to myself 'My God. How in the world can our legal system allow an insane man to defend himself? How can this be just?' I not only thought that Scott was incompetent, but that it was not moral to have him stand trial. It was terribly wrong. I did not know that our legal system would allow an insane man to represent himself in his own trial."[22]

Another psychiatrist who observed the trial commented that

> Scott literally enjoyed the spectacle of the Courtroom where he was the center of attention. Scott enjoyed the trial since he was getting attention and was being allowed to act like an attorney . . . Scott was acting out a role of an attorney as a facet of the mental illness, not a rational decision to represent himself at trial . . . Scott was acting as his own attorney from his paranoid fear that the attorneys were out to get him . . . Scott gave a rambling presentation that showed he could not think clearly nor understand what information was important in his trial . . . The trial gave Scott the opportunity to get the attention that a paranoid person so desperately needs.[23]

Panetti's standby attorney, who sat through the entire trial unable to offer any assistance, said, "This was not a case for the death penalty. Scott's life history and long term mental problems made an excellent case for mitigating evidence. Scott did not present any mitigating evidence because he could not understand the proceeding . . . In simple terms, by representing himself, he hung himself. Scott's incompetence prevented him from asking for or using my assistance as his standby. I was not able to assist Scott in any meaningful way because he was so mentally incompetent. As a result, his trial was truly a judicial farce, and a mockery of self-representation. It should never have been allowed to happen or, at least, stopped."[24]

This same attorney later reported that he had interviewed two of the jurors after the trial: "[They] told me that Scott probably would not have received the death penalty if the case had been handled differently ... In short, the jury was grossly 'over-exposed' to Scott. Since Scott presented no real evidence of insanity other than his own behavior, the jury had no trouble with a guilty verdict. Unfortunately, they were also scared to death of Scott and they were fearful that somehow, someway, Scott might get out of prison. They gave him the death penalty to avoid this possibility."[25] Another attorney discussed the case with a couple of other jurors. As he reported, "They said that if Scott had been represented by attorneys that he would not have received the death penalty ... They knew he had a long term mental history, but, because he scared them they voted for death."[26]

Following his conviction and sentencing, Panetti was represented by counsel on appeal, but the courts routinely rebuffed arguments that Panetti should never have been found competent to stand trial, should not have been permitted to represent himself, should have been found insane, and should not have been sentenced to die. With regard to Panetti's decision to represent himself—which the courts have all upheld—one appeals court held that "whether he [was] competent to represent himself is immaterial; the appropriate question is whether he [was] competent to choose the endeavor."[27] Once Panetti's self-representation was affirmed, the appeals courts had no difficulty justifying his conviction and death sentence. He had the burden of proving his insanity, they said, but presented no evidence whatsoever regarding his mental state at the time of the killings. Moreover, the fact that he represented himself in court while taking no psychotropic medications, the courts said, undercut his argument that he was psychotic at the time of the killings because he had not taken his prescribed medications during the preceding week. As for the death sentence, the courts held that Panetti's criminal acts, his threats and assaults on others, and Dr. Grigson's testimony all established his dangerousness and overcame any argument for mitigating circumstances that would warrant a sentence of life in prison rather than death.

After exhausting Panetti's appeals to the Texas state courts, his appellate attorneys turned to the federal courts in an effort to prevent the convicted murderer's execution. In the face of Panetti's scheduled February 5, 2004, execution, the attorneys asked a federal district court on January 26, 2004, to stay the execution on the grounds that their client was incompetent to be executed.

Two days later, the stay was denied. In denying the stay, the court concluded that because Panetti's attorneys were relying on psychiatric evaluations from 1997 they had thus presented no evidence regarding his *current* mental state. As a result, the court held, "the defendant has failed to raise a substantial doubt of the defendant's competency to be executed."[28] After denying a second request for a stay, the court also denied Panetti's request for funds to employ an expert to examine him and opine as to his current mental state.

Literally fighting for their client's life just days before he was to be executed, Panetti's attorneys had him examined by a renowned forensic psychologist, Dr. Mark Cunningham. Dr. Cunningham, who has been honored by the both the American Psychological Association and the Texas Psychological Association for his work on death penalty cases, evaluated Panetti on death row just days before he was to be executed. On February 3, 2004, Cunningham reported,

> 1. Mr. Panetti's thought processes are markedly disorganized, so that it is impossible for him to maintain a linear and logical train of thought. More specifically, he exhibits flight of ideas (spontaneously shifting in conversation from one topic to another with no obvious connection), tangentiality (using any inquiry as a starting point to expand into other subjects), and circumstantiality (providing excessive and irrelevant detail). His responses to inquiry were repeatedly irrelevant, and he had to be continually interrupted and redirected. Often he answered in ways that seemed satisfactory to him, but in fact had not addressed the inquiry at all or only in the most oblique fashion.
>
> 2. Mr. Panetti exhibited delusional beliefs incorporating both grandiosity and paranoia. He expressed a conviction that he is the target of evil forces that would seek to prevent him from preaching the gospel. He described that the Satanic forces arrayed against him included not only the Wicken [sic] national headquarters in Wisconsin, but also reached even into "the administration." Mr. Panetti attributed the primary reason for his execution to the efforts of these evil forces to prevent him from continuing to preach the gospel.
>
> 3. Mr. Panetti expressed the belief that God may render him invulnerable to lethal injection so that he may go on preaching the gospel.
>
> 4. Mr. Panetti reported that he promptly tears up and flushes any legal correspondence or documents regarding his case, as these

are "classified documents" and he fears they may fall into "enemy hands."

5. He has no insight into his psychotic thought processes or continuing mental illness, describing that he is a "born again April fool" who God has healed from Schizophrenia and any associated need for medication or treatment.

My diagnostic impression is that Mr. Panetti is actively psychotic, and suffers from a disorder on the Schizophrenic and/or Schizo-affective spectrum.[29]

One day before Panetti was to be executed, the federal court issued a stay of execution based on Dr. Cunningham's report. The legal underpinnings of that stay of execution lay in the U.S. Supreme Court's 1986 decision in *Ford v. Wainwright*. Like Panetti, Alvin Ford had been convicted of capital murder and was sentenced to die. Though neither his competence nor his mental state at the time of the crime was an issue in his trial or appeals, Ford became seriously mentally ill while on death row. Seeking to block his execution, his counsel invoked a Florida law governing the determination of an inmate's competency for execution.

The Florida law barred execution of a convicted capital defendant unless he had "the mental capacity to understand the nature of the death penalty and the reasons why it was imposed upon him."[30] Florida law also provided that such a determination was to be made by mental health experts appointed by the state, with the final determination resting with the governor. Ford was examined by three state-appointed psychiatrists in a 30-minute, jointly conducted group interview. Although these state-appointed psychiatrists concluded that Ford understood the death penalty, four other psychiatrists found him psychotic, unable to understand the death penalty, and unable to understand why it was being applied to him. Accepting the findings of the state-appointed panel, the governor issued a nonreviewable decision that Ford was competent to be executed.

Ultimately, Ford's case made its way to the U.S. Supreme Court, which took the occasion to hold that "[t]he Eighth Amendment prohibits the State from inflicting the penalty of death upon a prisoner who is insane"[31] and that the level of process provided by the Florida law was constitutionally inadequate. Although the plurality of four justices did not define "insanity" in this context, Justice Powell, in a concurring opinion, wrote that "I would hold that the Eighth Amendment forbids the execution only of those who are unaware of the punishment they are about to suffer and why they are to suffer it."[32] As for the type of process required to determine whether a death row inmate was "insane" and thus unfit for execution, Justice Powell, also concurring with the plurality, wrote,

> I would not require the kind of full-scale "sanity trial" that Justice Marshall appears to find necessary ... We need not determine the precise limits that due process imposes in this area. In general, however, my view is that a constitutionally acceptable procedure may be far less formal than a trial. The State should provide an impartial officer or board that can receive evidence and argument from the prisoner's counsel, including expert psychiatric evidence that may differ from the State's own psychiatric examination. Beyond these basic requirements, the States should have substantial leeway to determine what process best balances the various interests at stake ... [33]

In Panetti's case, after granting a stay of execution, the federal court determined that the process Texas followed in determining Panetti's "sanity" or competence to be executed was flawed and did not comport with the mandates of *Ford v. Wainwright* or even those imposed by the state's own law. Specifically, the court held that the state's "failure to 'receive evidence and argument from the prisoner's counsel, including expert psychiatric evidence that may differ from the State's own psychiatric examination,' was a violation of due process under *Ford* ... "[34]

Having concluded that the Texas authorities failed to provide due process in adjudicating Panetti's claimed "insanity" or lack of competence to be executed, the federal court took the unusual step of conducting its own evidentiary hearing into the question. Panetti's attorneys presented the testimony of three psychologists, Cunningham, Dr. Mary Alice Conroy, and Dr. Susana Rosin, and a psychiatrist, Dr. Seth Silverman. The prosecution countered with the testimony of a psychologist, Dr. George Parker, and a psychiatrist, Dr. Mary Anderson.

On the defense side, Dr. Conroy testified that Panetti suffered from a form of schizophrenia and did not understand that he was to be put to death for killing his in-laws but rather believed his punishment was "part of a spiritual warfare that's been going on since the middle 1980s"[35] and was aimed at keeping him from preaching the word of God. Dr. Rosin also testified that Panetti suffered from schizophrenia and lacked a rational understanding of why he was to be executed: "He told me that he has been on death row, basically been put there to preach the gospel, that he's there to help and save other inmates; that there has been a conspiracy to kill him for years; and that the forces of evil, demons, devils, are basically set against him."[36]

Dr. Silverman testified that he found Panetti to be paranoid, irritable, grandiose, tangential, and pressured. Silverman told the court that "[h]e can't keep all his thoughts together, and at times, they just don't make a lot of sense . . ."[37] The psychiatrist added that "[h]e doesn't believe or doesn't understand that the reason he's going to be executed is because he killed his in-laws. He doesn't believe that that's the reason . . ."[38] Asked what Panetti told him regarding his understanding of why he was to be executed, Silverman replied, "Because he preaches the word of the gospel."[39]

Dr. Cunningham testified in rebuttal to the prosecution's two witnesses that although Panetti understood that the State of Texas was going to execute him, his delusions kept him from recognizing the state as "a lawfully constituted authority."[40] Instead, Cunningham told the court, Panetti saw the state "as being in league with the forces of evil to prevent him from preaching the Gospel."[41] As Cunningham explained,

> I asked him why he is on death row, why he is going to be executed . . . He said, for preaching the gospel of Jesus Christ, and he went on to say that they don't want him to go back to Wisconsin preaching the gospel, and that the anti-Christians were there. And I said, who are they? And he said, well it's the national headquarters for the Wickens [sic]. And then he went on to describe that this conspiracy goes up into the highest levels of the administration.[42]

The two experts called by the prosecution, Drs. Parker and Anderson, had jointly interviewed Panetti for "a little over an hour" and written a joint report on Panetti's competence for execution.[43] On direct examination, Parker testified that, upon interview, Panetti had insisted on discussing religion and had been uncooperative. Thus, the psychologist testified, he had been unable to reach any conclusions based upon the interview alone. Instead, he testified further, he relied on a review of records and correspondence, some written by Panetti. Having reviewed some of Panetti's letters, Parker said, "Well, I mean, it's—he can be reasonably clear and lucid at times, so I don't know why in the world he couldn't understand what the state is up to here and what this is all about."[44]

Parker went on to testify as to the five opinions included in the report he prepared jointly with Dr. Anderson:

> The first one is that Mr. Panetti is able to understand direct questions about his past as well as his present. And he could answer questions about relevant legal issues regarding his execution if he were willing to do so. Number two, Mr. Panetti consciously chose

not to answer our interview questions about his past and present, as well as questions about legal aspects of his execution. Number three, Mr. Panetti deliberately and persistently chose to control and manipulate our interview . . . by deflecting the interview into religious topics.

Number four, Mr. Panetti knows that he is to be executed and that his execution will result in his death. And number five, although Mr. Panetti chooses not to discuss the reason that he is to be executed, he has the ability to understand the reason that he is to be executed.[45]

On cross-examination, Panetti's attorney was able to establish that, despite what Parker had testified to on direct examination, Panetti had not been uncooperative with the prosecution experts' interview:

Q. He didn't attempt to leave the room, did he?
A. I don't think so, no.
Q. He remained in the room?
A. Yes.
Q. He didn't stand mute?
A. He didn't?
Q. Stand mute? Say nothing?
A. Oh, no.
Q. He responded in some fashion to your questions?
A. Well, let's say he responded. I'm not sure it was always to my questions. But he was—he talked most of that hour, yes.
Q. During your interview, you asked him, why are you in prison and he said, in order to preach the gospel of the living king, didn't he?
A. Yes.
Q. So he answered your question, didn't he?
A. Yes.
Q. So he answered your question, didn't he?
A. That question, I think he did.
Q. Okay. You asked him, you are on death row right now. Why? And he said, they don't want me to preach the word of God, right?
A. Right.
Q. So he answered your question then, too, didn't he?
A. Right.[46]

Dr. Anderson's testimony was challenged on the grounds that it would violate the attorney-client privilege. From the evidence it appeared that a decade earlier Panetti had been evaluated by another psychiatrist, Dr. Coons. According to Coons, he had been accompanied by Anderson during one of his interviews of Panetti. If Anderson had participated in or even observed that evaluation, any information she derived from that contact would have been protected by the attorney-client privilege because Coons, who was apparently her mentor, had been retained by Panetti's appellate counsel. Anderson denied any recollection of having met Panetti prior to her joint evaluation of him with Parker. Surprisingly, the judge held that even if Anderson had been part of the evaluation of Panetti by Coons, her current testimony was admissible because the objection to it should have been made "way long before the last minutes of any hearing" and because "anything that occurred with, if it did occur with Dr. Anderson—she says she doesn't remember it—would have been derivative of Dr. Coons just taking her to see his client—I assume it was because I don't know one way or the other."[47]

After this lengthy argument over privilege, Anderson testified that she had been unable to evaluate Panetti's competence for execution, largely because Panetti had not been cooperative in the single-hour interview she conducted jointly with Parker. Contrary to Parker's admission on cross-examination, Anderson testified that Panetti would not directly answer the question of why he was on death row awaiting execution. Minutes later, however, Anderson engaged in the following dialogue with the prosecuting attorney:

> Q. Did you ever ask Mr. Panetti if he understood why he was going to be executed?
> A. I did.
> Q. What was his response?
> A. I asked him a number of times, but ultimately, he talked about his belief that people were wanting him to be executed for preaching. And I can quote that, if you like.
> Q. So, essentially, he was telling you that he was being executed to prevent him from preaching the gospel?
> A. Yes.
> Q. In your opinion, does that render him unable to understand why he's being executed?
> A. No.
> Q. Why not?
> A. Well, I think one can have a belief that there is—everything has a purpose, and I think he may believe that he is now there for

a purpose, which is to preach the bible [sic], and that if he's executed, then he is being stopped from doing so. But his capacity to understand the bible [sic], to understand history, movies, other things that he referenced, tells me that he has the capacity to understand the facts of why he's being executed.[48]

Based upon all of this expert testimony as well as the testimony of several other lay witnesses, the court concluded that Panetti was competent to be executed because he met three criteria: (1) he knew that he committed two murders; (2) he knew that he was to be executed; and (3) he knew that the reason given by the state for his execution was his commission of the murders.

Panetti's attorneys appealed the federal district court's ruling, maintaining that the court had applied an improper legal standard in determining Panetti's competence to be executed. They argued that under *Ford v. Wainwright*, the proper standard is not simply whether the convicted capital defendant knows the reason the state has given for his pending execution, but whether he has a rational understanding of the state's reason for the execution. Panetti, the defense attorneys argued, lacked such a rational understanding because he believed that, despite what the state said about its motives for executing him, the state's actual motivation was to prevent him from preaching the gospel.

In 2006, the U.S. Court of Appeals for the Fifth Circuit affirmed the trial court's determination, holding that the proper standard was that enunciated by Justice Powell in his concurring opinion of *Ford v. Wainwright*, namely that "the Eighth Amendment forbids the execution only of those who are unaware of the punishment they are about to suffer and why they are to suffer it."[49]

In 2007, the U.S. Supreme Court reversed the decision of the U.S. Court of Appeals for the Fifth Circuit and remanded the case to the U.S. District Court "for further proceedings consistent with this opinion."[50] In a 5–4 decision, the Supreme Court held that the lower court's test for competency to be executed was "too restrictive" because it "treats a prisoner's delusional belief system as irrelevant if the prisoner knows that the State has identified his crimes as the reason for his execution."[51]

Acknowledging that "[t]he opinions in Ford . . . did not set forth a precise standard," the Court observed that "the Ford opinions nowhere indicate that delusions are irrelevant to 'comprehension' or 'awareness' if they so impair the prisoner's concept of reality that he cannot reach a rational understanding of the reason for the execution. If anything, the Ford majority suggests the opposite."[52]

Although the Court declined to "attempt to set down a rule governing all competency determinations," a majority of the justices agreed that "[g]ross delusions stemming from a severe mental disorder may put an awareness of a link between a crime and its punishment in a context so far removed from reality that the punishment can serve no proper purpose."[53] Thus, they held, Panetti's "submission . . . that he suffers from a severe, documented mental illness that is the source of gross delusions preventing him from comprehending the meaning and purpose of the punishment to which he has been sentenced . . . should have been considered."[54]

7

Eric Smith

On the morning of August 2, 1993, Derrick Robie's mother packed him a lunch and sent the 4-year-old off to a summer recreation program, just several hundred yards from the family's home. Derrick had never walked the short distance alone, but this day his mother, Doreen, was caught up caring for Derrick's infant brother, who was teething, so she let the preschooler set out on his own.

And who could blame her? The program was right at the end of the Robie's short, quiet street. The path was straight, and there were no roads to cross. Derrick was independent for his age and knew the way—indeed knew his way all around the tiny, close-knit upstate New York village of Savona. Of course, Doreen Robie had warned her son to stay away from strangers, but the odds Derrick would encounter a stranger on his short walk down an isolated dead-end street in this rustic rural town with a population of about 970 were somewhere between slim and none because virtually everyone in town knew each other.

But that morning Derek Robie did run across a person he had seen before but did not know. The person Derrick encountered offered to show him a shortcut to the recreation program. Was this person a "stranger," the sort of individual his mother had warned him to stay away from? Derrick thought so and said so, responding that his mother had told him "not to go with strangers."[1] Derrick stood his ground but was finally persuaded by the promise that if he took the shortcut he would "beat everyone else" to the program.[2]

Minutes later, indeed less than 5 minutes after he had left home, Derrick was lured into a thinly wooded vacant lot, grabbed from behind, placed in a choke hold, and strangled. His lunch was dumped to the ground and the Kool-Aid he was carrying was poured over him. Derrick was then repeatedly bludgeoned with rocks before suffering the final indignity of having his pants pulled down and part of a tree branch shoved four inches into his anus. Derrick's assailant rushed off but returned moments later to make sure that the youngster was dead.

Two hours later, when it was discovered that Derrick had never arrived at the recreation program, police officers and dozens of volunteers set out to find the missing child. Within about 4 hours they found his 40-pound, 45-inch body right where the killer had left it—less than 100 yards from his home. An autopsy showed that Derrick died from multiple blunt force injuries and manual strangulation. Despite the desecration of the body, no semen or other evidence of sexual trauma was found.

State and local police immediately closed off the area surrounding the village, stopping all cars entering or exiting Savona. A state police profiler was called to the scene and quickly pronounced the killer an older pedophile, possibly a sex crime parolee. While police combed parole records looking for a suspect, searched for a pickup truck seen near the crime scene, fielded hundreds of calls offering tips, and interviewed over 500 people, the townspeople, especially those with children, were paralyzed with fear and anguish.

One of those parents worried about the perpetrator, dubbed an "animal"[3] by many local residents, was Tammy Smith, a Savona mother of three older children. Like other parents in the community, Smith was horrified by the crime but she was also especially concerned because her 13-year-old son, Eric, had been in the vicinity of the recreation program around the time Derrick Robie was killed. Smith questioned Eric and came away with the thought that he might have seen something or been threatened by someone that morning.

Three days after the slaying, Smith took Eric to the police command post, where he was questioned by detectives. In two morning interviews totaling 45 to 50 minutes, Eric told the police very little, but they were struck by what they later identified as "discrepancies" in his story.[4] Later that day, three officers questioned Eric and he admitted for the first time that he had seen Derrick the morning of the killing. Twice during this interview, Eric became tearful; once he asked, "Do you think I did it?"[5] The police reassured Eric that they did not believe he had killed the 4-year-old, but later that day they asked Eric to come to the crime scene area and review his actions from the morning of the killing. While doing so, Eric asked the officers, "What would happen to the person who did it?"[6]

The next day, at the request of the police, Eric again reenacted the events of the morning Derrick was slain, this time while being filmed with a video camera. Later that day, detectives again questioned Eric, pressing him on what they saw as inconsistencies among his stories and reemphasizing the need for complete accuracy. Getting no further with the boy, police sent Eric home, where, for the next 2 days, he discussed the case with his parents, grandfather, and great-grandfather, a former police officer.

Eric's family felt that the boy was hiding something. As his stepfather later said, "Something inside me just kept saying, 'There's something wrong here. Something's not right.'"[7] Two days after his last encounter with the police, Eric was gently pressed by his parents to tell them the truth. In his mother's words, "[W]e stressed how important it was that he tell the truth, that this is serious. And that if someone threatened him, to tell us. If he knows anything to tell us."[8]

The Smiths suspected that Eric had seen Derrick's killer and was perhaps too frightened to tell them what he had observed. After about half an hour of prodding from his mother and great-grandfather, Eric turned to his mother and confessed to the crime. "Mom, I did it,"[9] he said. "I snapped and I done it."[10] "I'm sorry, Mom. I'm sorry. I killed that little boy," he added.[11] Tammy Smith responded by shaking her son, demanding more details, and asking why Eric had committed such a heinous crime. As she would later recall, "He just kept saying, 'I don't know. I don't know. I don't know why. I'm sorry. I'm sorry.' And I'm yelling and screaming and bawling and everything at once."[12]

Eric's great-grandfather, a retired sheriff's deputy, responded by calling a current deputy and telling him that Eric was the killer and that "[t]he boy needs help."[13] The deputy then set up a meeting with the local prosecutor, who arranged to have police question Eric in the district attorney's office. Eric was given his *Miranda* warnings (the familiar statement of a suspect's right to silence and counsel). Eric said he understood these rights but then had to ask what an attorney was. After being told that an attorney was a lawyer, Eric was questioned for about 3 hours and gave a detailed confession to the grisly killing of Derrick Robie. Among other things, Eric told the police the following:

> I looked to the left and saw a little kid with blonde hair, a whitish tee shirt, carrying a bluish/brown with designs bag. He was walking toward Rec. I turned around and went up behind him and when I was within ten feet I said "Hey kid." The kid turned around as I caught up with him. At that point I knew I wanted to take him someplace and hurt him . . . I asked the kid if he wanted to go to Rec by way of a short cut, through the woods and beat everybody there. The kid said "No I'm not supposed to." I said "It's OK, I'm right here." . . . The kid then followed me through the empty lot . . . I let the kid go in front of me. When we got inside the trees . . . I put my arm around his neck. I was standing behind him. The kid then dropped his lunch. I continued squeezing harder as the kid made fists and swung his arms trying to get away . . . I was going to hold him against the tree and choke him with my hands. As I started to

release him, he made a noise like he was trying to gasp some air, a weird noise. So I said "forget it" and squeezed harder. I let go after 30 seconds or so. He didn't make any noise so I let him down on the ground . . . His eyes were closed and I don't know if he was breathing. There was a little rock lying beside him and I hit him in the head three times. I picked up a bigger rock . . . I threw the rock with both hands down onto his head. At this point blood began running from his nose and the rock fell to the side. Two more times I picked up the rock and threw it onto his head . . . I then picked up another big rock . . . I threw that rock into the middle of his chest.

Now I remember that while he was lying on the ground, before I hit him with any rock, he was gasping for air. I dumped his lunch out onto the ground which consisted of a sandwich, cookie, koolaid [sic], plastic reusable container and something else which I can't recall. Also I saw a paper napkin and put it in his mouth . . . As I tried to stuff the baggie in his mouth he bit me . . . It hurt but left no marks. I pulled my finger and the baggie out and threw the baggie down. I then began hitting him in the head with the rocks.

. . . I picked up the koolaid [sic] and poured it on his face on the right side of his temple area where I had hit him with the small rock and on his chest. At this point I don't know whether I had pulled down his pants or not . . . I must have taken them down. I then looked around for a stick and picked one off a tree . . . I then flipped him over and put the stick up his butt . . . I then left the area . . . After about 5 minutes at Rec I went back to the body . . . I was worried if he wasn't there he might say something . . . I figured if he's dead, and I believed he was I won't have to worry about anything . . . When I arrived back at Rec it started thundering and stuff and Bill Horn the director told everyone to go home . . . [14]

Following his confession, Eric's family felt betrayed because instead of pressing charges against the 13-year-old in Family Court, where he could be remanded to a juvenile treatment facility for the "help" they felt he needed, the prosecutor almost immediately announced that he planned to charge Eric with murder and require him to stand trial in adult criminal court. Under New York's "juvenile offender" law, minors as young as 13 may be tried as adults when charged with murder; to be tried as an adult for any other serious violent crime, a youngster must be at least 14 years old.[15] Although the statute allows the criminal court judge to transfer such a case to Family Court, the judge may not do so without the consent of the prosecutor.

Almost as soon as he was appointed, Eric's attorney realized that his client had to be a seriously disturbed youngster. He pleaded with the prosecutor to have the boy examined by a psychologist or psychiatrist before condemning him to an adult criminal trial and possible life sentence. The prosecutor, however, refused to consider any psychological or psychiatric evidence in making his decision not to permit the case to be heard in Family Court. In explaining his judgment, the prosecutor seemed to be most concerned about the privacy that Family Court would permit the 13-year-old defendant. As he stated, "If this case were whisked into the 'black hole' of Family Court, the public would never learn the outcome of the matter."[16]

Questioned later about why he did not want a psychological and/or psychiatric evaluation of Eric before requiring him to stand trial as an adult at the age of 13, the prosecutor said, "Oh, I suppose I could have recommended it, yes . . . It wasn't something I considered, OK? Under our system, that's not my job. It's not my burden, OK?"[17] As he also explained, "This isn't an accident of youth, this is a calculated act . . . "[18] Moreover, the prosecutor said, "I truly believe that Eric Smith was a budding serial killer."[19]

Referring to Eric and his crime, the prosecutor made it clear that he believed Eric to be evil, not mentally ill: "There are clearly people who make choices which reflect pure evil. In—in my view, this heads the list."[20]

When it was suggested by a journalist that "[a]ny 13-year-old who commits murder must be in some way nuts," the prosecutor replied, "I agree with you. That's not what's at issue here. Did he know what he was doing? Did he know when he was strangling Derrick, that he was strangling a child, a person? And if he knew that what he was doing was wrong, that he shouldn't have been doing it, then he can have every psychological, psychiatric problem in the world, and he's still responsible for what he did."[21]

Unable to shake the resolve of the prosecutor to try the case in adult criminal court, and faced with overwhelming evidence of his client's guilt, Eric's attorney began looking for evidence that would support a defense of insanity and/or extreme emotional disturbance. Under New York insanity law, Eric could be found "not responsible" (i.e., "insane") if his attorney could prove that when he killed Derrick Robie, as a result of mental disease or defect, he lacked substantial capacity to know or appreciate either the nature and consequences of his conduct or that his conduct was wrong.[22]

Even if the defense attorney failed to prove his client "insane," Eric could avoid a murder conviction if he could prove that at the time of the killing, Eric was suffering from an "extreme emotional disturbance for which there was a reasonable explanation or excuse."[23] In that event, Eric would be guilty only of the less serious offense of manslaughter—an offense that did not carry the potential of a life sentence. Indeed, a conviction for manslaughter would take Eric's case out of the adult system because, under New York State's juvenile offender statute, murder is the only crime for which a 13-year-old may be held responsible as an adult.

It did not take long to unearth evidence that would support both of these defenses. Eric's developmental and psychosocial history was replete with psychiatric red flags. Tammy Smith suffered from epilepsy and while pregnant with all of her children, including Eric, took anticonvulsant medications known to be capable of causing birth defects. Eric was born with a somewhat odd facial appearance, particularly his small, folded, low-set ears and epicanthal skin folds on his upper eyelids. Physicians initially reassured his mother that if she taped his ears back, they would eventually appear normal; she tried that remedy, but it did not work. Years later, physicians would attribute these defects to the medications she took while pregnant.

More significantly, some of Eric's early developmental milestones were delayed: He did not walk or talk until he was 2 years old. These developmental delays were also attributed to his mother's use of anticonvulsant medications while pregnant.

Eric also demonstrated serious behavioral problems early in life. By the age of 28 months, he was described by a pediatrician as "a child who is stubborn and who has temper tantrums at least daily."[24] From the age of 2 until about 3½, Eric also engaged in frequent head banging and breath holding.

Eric's impulsive acting-out would continue right up to and including the time of the killing. For example, he manifested the "triad"—three symptoms that some mental health professionals believe foretell later violence.[25] He wet the bed until age 11, was fascinated with fire, and killed small animals.

Moreover, just a few months before he killed Derrick Robie, Eric physically attacked his sister, screaming, "I'm going to hurt you."[26] After that incident, Eric told his stepfather, Ted Smith, "Dad, I need help."[27] Ted suggested that Eric take out his anger on a punching bag in the garage. Instead, Eric punched a tree until his were hands were torn and bloodied.

Academically, Eric was also behind. He had speech problems that required therapy and, until he was 8 or 9 years old, drooled when he spoke. Learning problems forced him to repeat the second and fourth grades. As a result, at the age of 13, he was in only the fifth grade, the same grade as his younger sister. His learning disability, diagnosed as "difficulties with recalling information he hears and with remaining on task in the classroom," was deemed "not severe enough to warrant special education placement."[28]

Because Eric was not placed in special education, he made little progress and by age 13 was achieving academically at only the third- or fourth-grade level. Worse, Eric's odd appearance, learning problems, and impulsivity made him not only the class clown but also the target of relentless teasing and bullying by his schoolmates. On an almost daily basis, they mocked his ears and his bright red hair and went out of their way to trip him on the school bus. The result was a depressed youngster with a low self-image, who smoked about a pack of cigarettes a day from age 9 on, cried nearly every day, constantly referred to himself as "stupid," and told his family, "I'm never going to be anybody."[29] One school year, after receiving his class picture, Eric scratched his face out of the photograph, telling his sister that he was not "good enough" to be included.[30]

Eric's history also revealed hints that all was not well in the Smith family. Eric and his older sister, Stacy, were fathered by Tammy Smith's ex-husband. It was not until Eric was 9 years old that he learned from a classmate that Ted Smith was not his biological father. The shock of that revelation was compounded by Eric's learning that although his natural father had remained close to Stacy after divorcing their mother, he wanted nothing to do with Eric. Although Eric always denied that he had been abused by either of his parents, Ted Smith responded to a question about abusing the children, saying, "Well, for quite a few years, I had a little hot temper myself, so it's hard to say. There's a lot of things I said: 'Kick their butts up over their shoulders,' 'sick and tired of their crap,' 'sick and tired of you,' 'swat them upside the head.'"[31] Worse, Eric's older sister Stacy, then 16, revealed that Ted Smith had sexually molested her when she was 11 and 14 years old.[32] Ted and Tammy Smith admitted that Ted had fondled Stacy's breasts on one occasion and that Ted had been forced out of the home for a week and had to receive psychotherapy as a result of his misconduct.[33]

Finally, Eric's history revealed that just minutes before he killed Derrick Robie, he had been threatened with great bodily harm, not by a parent but by a stranger. Tom Van Osdel, a local insurance agent, reported that just before the time Derrick Robie was killed, he had been meeting with several other agents around a picnic table not far from the crime scene. According to Van Osdel, Eric, whom he described as "kind of comical looking," had been bumping the picnic table with his bicycle when one of the agents threatened Eric.[34] As Van Osdel told it,

> Here's a 270-pound guy saying, "I bet I could beat you up." Or "I bet I could beat your head in." The final comment was, he said, "I bet you I have a gun in my glove compartment and I can shoot you." And I said, "Enough of this."
> On Eric's part, he left very quietly and very nicely. I mean, there wasn't like—you know, he didn't go off and start throwing rocks or

anything like this. He wasn't upset. That is why it just leaves you wondering.[35]

It was while Eric was leaving this encounter that he first saw Derrick Robie. Within minutes Derrick was dead.

Although Eric's history, coupled with the almost inexplicable nature of the crime, raised doubts about his sanity, his defense attorney realized that in order to convince a jury that Eric was insane or at least acting in a state of extreme emotional disturbance at the time of the killing, he would need input from a psychologist and psychiatrist. With the court's approval, which was required largely for financial reasons (the doctors' fees would be paid from public funds), Eric's attorney asked Dr. Peter Cormack, a Rochester clinical child psychologist, and Dr. Stephen Herman, a Connecticut pediatrician and child psychiatrist, to examine Eric. Neither man was a full-time forensic practitioner, but both had plenty of experience in the courts and had testified in other high-profile cases.

Dr. Cormack conducted intellectual and projective testing with Eric and reported that

> [Eric] harbors a great deal of anger and rage . . . that relates to feelings of rejection and/or abandonment . . . On occasions when this rage builds up to a sufficient intensity that it is directly expressed, he can become rather detached from his own actions, taking little personal responsibility for what is occurring and not giving consideration to anything other than what is happening in the moment . . . Depressed mood as well as anger, including angry or hostile outbursts, result when his efforts at control do not serve to block painful feelings . . .
>
> [A]lthough Eric does not demonstrate any signs of significant cognitive or intellectual impairment, the mental disease from which he suffers is such that he was unable to appreciate either the legal or moral implications of his actions at the time of the crime. [It is] doubtful that he appreciates these factors even at the present time.[36]

Dr. Herman ordered numerous studies of Eric—including physical, endocrinological, and neurological examinations as well as an electroencephalogram (EEG)—all of which showed normal results. He concluded that Eric suffered from intermittent explosive disorder, the diagnostic criteria for which are the following:

> A. Several discrete episodes of failure to resist aggressive impulses that result in serious assaultive acts or destruction of property.

B. The degree of aggressiveness expressed during the episodes is grossly out of proportion to any precipitating psychosocial stressors.

C. The aggressive episodes are not better accounted for by another mental disorder (e.g., Antisocial Personality Disorder, Borderline Personality Disorder, a Psychotic Disorder, a Manic Episode, Conduct Disorder, or Attention-Deficit/Hyperactivity Disorder) and are not due to the direct physiological effects of a substance (e.g., a drug of abuse, a medication) or a general medical condition (e.g., head trauma, Alzheimer's disease).[37]

Herman summarized his forensic psychiatric evaluation of Eric as follows:

> Eric was born with certain constitutional or organic vulnerabilities ... born with fetal trimethadione syndrome ... [D]evelopmental delay, school and speech problems [were] all part of this syndrome ... [Eric] suffered from pathological rage attacks, as evidenced by his abnormal temper tantrums, breath-holding spells, and headbanging. As he grew, [he was] unable to modulate his anger appropriately ... [He] grew up with serious self-esteem problems ... unable to ignore the teasing of other children ... academic problems and difficulties with peers ... low self image ... [His] family did not provide much in the way of intellectual challenges or psychological support. [He] grew up a lonely child, easily hurt ... cried frequently ... also developed a sadistic side ... expressed in ... cruelty to animals and ... in his attack on [Derrick Robie]. At the time of that attack, however, I do not believe that Eric meant to kill the child. I believe that his rage overtook him ... and he was completely driven by pathological anger, which was then out of his control. Thus, I can say with a reasonable degree of medical certainty, that the attack ... was not a premeditated murder but rather a tragic result of Eric's pathological rage.[38]

If a jury were to accept Herman's assessment of Eric and his state of mind at the time of the homicide, they would certainly have little difficulty finding that he had acted in a state of extreme emotional disturbance and that this disturbance had a reasonable explanation. Indeed, although Eric's attorney pleaded his client not guilty by reason of insanity, he explained to Herman that he was hoping for a manslaughter verdict based on extreme emotional disturbance.

The defense attorney's strategy in that regard may well have been influenced by the relative consequences of the possible verdicts. A finding of guilt on the murder charge would expose Eric to a sentence of 9 years to life in prison. An insanity verdict would see the teenage defendant committed to a state forensic unit—a secure psychiatric hospital where he would be surrounded by severely mentally ill patients who had also been found insane—until such time as a court found him no longer dangerous or mentally ill. In view of the nature of Eric's crime and the community fear it engendered, that would likely mean a lifetime commitment. But a finding that Eric was guilty of manslaughter would have precluded both a prison sentence and a commitment to a secure forensic hospital and required a time-limited placement in a state youth facility.

Having raised psychiatric defenses, Eric was required by law to submit to an examination by an expert selected by the prosecution. As a practical matter, the opinion of the prosecution's expert would be pivotal and possibly dispositive. If the prosecution expert agreed with Cormack and Herman, the prosecutor would have little choice but to stipulate to a finding of insanity or allow Eric to plead to manslaughter. If the prosecution expert disagreed with the defense doctors, the case would go to trial and a jury would decide Eric's fate.

The prosecutor selected Dr. Kathleen Quinn, a general, child, and forensic psychiatrist to examine Eric. As is usually the case in matters such as this one, Quinn had the benefit of knowing what Cormack and Herman had already determined. Based upon her review of the evidence, Quinn determined that Eric suffered not intermittent explosive disorder, but rather attention deficit hyperactivity disorder, which she said was neither a major mental illness nor an explanation for the killing.

One day short of a year after Derrick Robie was killed, Eric Smith's trial began, following several days of jury selection in which a panel of six men and six women were seated. With one notable exception, the prosecution case, consisting of 19 witnesses, was routine. Eleven police officers detailed the results of their investigation, including the circumstances and substance of Eric's confession. The coroner gave perfunctory testimony about ordering an autopsy, and the medical examiner testified to the cause of death: blunt trauma to the head with asphyxiation as a contributing cause. Several lay witnesses testified, largely to establish a timeline for the homicide.

The one prosecution witness whose testimony was not routine was Doreen Robie, Derrick's mother. Her testimony could have been fairly routine, had it been kept to the facts as the rules of evidence generally require. But, over defense counsel's strenuous objection, the judge allowed the prosecutor to question the grieving mother about Derrick, his activities, interests, personality, and interactions with other people. After Doreen Robie gave lengthy and touching responses to these questions, the judge felt constrained to remind the jury that her testimony was "elicited and will be used in some probative manner . . . and not elicited solely for the purpose of sympathy."[39] The court, however, never instructed the jury regarding the issue or issues, if any, upon which this testimony was purportedly probative.

The case for the defense consisted of eight witnesses: four of Eric's teachers, one of his neighbors, both his parents, and Dr. Herman. For unknown reasons, Dr. Cormack, whose report clearly supported the defenses of insanity and extreme emotional disturbance, was not called to testify.

Eric's teachers described him as basically a normal child who was not a discipline problem but had problems completing his school work. One teacher reported that Eric had once told him that he wanted to punch someone who had picked on him. Eric's neighbor, who had known him for a decade, testified that he was a "nice, bright child," whose behavior changed when he turned 13 and he began being less respectful to adults.[40] Tammy and Ted Smith provided the jury with much of Eric's developmental, familial, and social history.

Clearly the key witness for the defense was Dr. Herman. Because Eric did not testify, Herman's testimony would be the only chance—other than the confession—the jury had to hear Eric's description of the killing. Unfortunately, Eric had been unable or unwilling to provide the psychiatrist with many details, frequently saying that he did not remember or simply responding, "I don't know."[41]

Eric did, however, tell Herman how he was feeling and what he was thinking at the time of the homicide. As Herman related to the jury, during their first interview, exactly 1 month after the killing, Eric "said that he just became angry when he saw [Derrick Robie] and said to himself that he wanted to hurt him . . . that he was feeling very angry and that he had to let the anger out . . . began to choke [Derrick] and . . . said to himself, 'I can't let go.'"[42]

Herman then testified that a day later, in his second interview, he had asked Eric "why he choked [Derrick], why he used the rocks, why he used the stick."[43] Eric again replied that he was "just angry."[44] Herman asked, "Did you want to kill him?" and Eric replied, "I didn't think of killing him . . ."[45]

Herman further testified that when he examined Eric about 6 months later, Eric said, "[I]t was the mad switch. I got mad. I got angry. I wanted to get it out. I thought about people picking on you, spitting, sister hitting you, screaming at you, taking cigarettes and not caring."[46] Herman added, "He said he thought about a girl that he had asked out who supposedly said to him, 'You're too ugly. I don't want to go out with you' . . . and he said [of Derrick] 'He's smaller and practically helpless. I had to get my anger out on him. I wanted to hurt him.'"[47]

Faced with at best a vague explanation for the homicidal act from the perpetrator himself, Herman explained to the jury his opinion that Eric had been in a "deadly rage" symptomatic of intermittent explosive disorder.[48] Herman told the jury what it was like to be a child experiencing this disorder:

> They can become angry very quickly and . . . it can get out of control very quickly. They may feel a pressure build-up, a tension that is almost unbearable that they can only relieve by doing something which is usually violent. People who have this disorder describe feeling as if they are about to explode, feeling as if they have pressure building up like they're a pipe and both ends of the pipe are closed off and there is no place for the pressure to go . . . [T]here's a sense of building up of incredible tension, almost palpable physical tension, that is only released at the time of the rage and the violence and after that there is almost a kind of calming that occurs and so that after the episodic rage the child may . . . appear to be normal.[49]

Herman went on to explain to the jury that, in his clinical experience, a child such as Eric, suffering from intermittent explosive disorder could go "from normal to having a rage attack to being normal again sometimes within ten or fifteen minutes."[50] He also detailed the nature of the stimulus and response involved in such attacks:

> [E]xternally the stimulus for it may be very slight, it may be nothing. It may be somebody coming into their vision that reminds them of something else or it may be a word or phrase that somebody used that just rubbed them the wrong way . . . [O]ther reasons in their life [become] almost like the bellows that causes their sort of kindling embers to flare up at that time way out of proportion in a very pathological and sick way . . . [T]hey can do damage and it's often to other people . . . [T]he person's self awareness is either severely diminished or disappears entirely and they become dissociated or separated from themselves and at times in an automatic fashion do things in their rage and they either are somewhat aware or not aware of what they are doing until afterwards and then they may remember some of it, all of it, none of it and they can't explain, they can only explain up to a point.[51]

Finally, going from the abstract to the specifics of Eric's case, Herman linked his diagnosis of Eric to the legal questions before the jury. As the psychiatrist explained,

The mental illness . . . which Eric had on that day definitely impacted on his anger and rage which was way out of proportion to any kind of provocation . . . [A]t the time of the killing his anger put him basically out of control so that . . . [H]e was [so] consumed with rage and anger he was not able to monitor himself or modulate his anger . . . not able to have insight into what he was doing at that moment in terms of what the end result would be . . . Eric was in an altered state of mind such that he could not understand or take the time to appreciate what the ultimate result would be to his rage and anger. [S]o I don't feel that he was fully aware enough nor could he stop himself at the time.[52]

In rebuttal, the prosecution called five witnesses, including Dr. Quinn. The lay rebuttal witnesses were called to make very specific points that the prosecutor would later argue undermined Dr. Herman's opinion. For example, Herman had relied in part on Eric's claim that he sometimes could not control his anger after losing school wrestling matches; Eric's wrestling coach testified that Eric "never threw a tantrum or became physically difficult after wrestling match."[53] Similarly, Herman relied in part on Eric's statement that he killed a neighbor's cat and other small animals; a neighbor testified that Eric had not killed the cat but had placed an automotive clamp around its neck, which her father had to cut off.

Quinn told the jury that Eric "struggled with . . . life long emotional issues" but suffered only from attention deficit hyperactivity disorder, "not a major mental illness" such as intermittent explosive disorder.[54] She said she rejected Herman's diagnosis because the disorder is rare, mostly seen in adults, and unlikely to be seen in someone Eric's age. Moreover, she testified, "when I looked I could not find a history to substantiate severe and chronic aggression."[55]

On cross-examination, however, Quinn acknowledged that, although several discrete episodes of aggression grossly out of proportion to any precipitating stimulus were required to make the diagnosis, she was aware of cases in which this disorder arose suddenly and that an individual with this disorder may have the disorder at the time of the first episode of violence.

Although denying that Eric suffered from a major mental illness, Quinn also conceded on cross-examination that on the day Eric killed Derrick, Eric would have been "civilly committable" to a psychiatric hospital.[56] In New York, as in most states, an individual may not be civilly committed unless he or she is both mentally ill and poses a danger to self or others.

Quinn also stated, "[W]e are left with . . . purposeful behavior [by] a boy who . . . is comfortable and excited by aggression."[57] Eric's behavior was "purposeful," she testified, because he made rational choices such as moving the body to better conceal it and because he indicated that he felt normal at the time of the killing, told her he knew that killing Derrick was wrong, and said he had slept like "a baby" that night.[58]

Asked on cross-examination if she agreed with Dr. Cormack's assessment that Eric's rage builds up until it is directly expressed and that when that occurs he does not consider anything other than what is happening in the moment, Quinn replied, "I would not be able to have an opinion until I understood whether this is purely derived from the projective tests."[59] The psychiatrist's answer was odd in that she had earlier reviewed all of Cormack's reports, notes, and test data.

Pressed to explain why an apparently normal 13-year-old boy would suddenly commit such a heinous offense, Quinn speculated that Derrick Robie "may have been a very unusual or peculiar trigger [who] symbolized someone well cared for and as a child successful and competent, all the things Eric himself felt he was not."[60]

Finally, and most importantly from a legal perspective, Quinn testified that Eric was not under the influence of extreme emotional disturbance at the time of the killing and did not lack the capacity to appreciate the nature or wrongfulness of his act.

After 11 hours of deliberations, the jury rejected Eric's claims of both insanity and extreme emotional disturbance and convicted the teenager of intentional murder. One juror who agreed to be interviewed said the jury rejected insanity because "[w]e didn't feel [Eric] had an emotional defect or a disease."[61] As for the mitigating defense of emotional disturbance, she said, "We felt there were some emotional problems there, something of that nature, but we had to go with what the law read, which was extreme emotional disturbance."[62]

Eric was sentenced to serve a term of 9 years to life in prison, then the maximum sentence possible for a youth convicted of murder under New York's "juvenile offender" law. Both the conviction and sentence were appealed but were affirmed by the appeals court. In holding that "the jury's rejection of the defense of mental disease or defect is not against the weight of the evidence,"[63] the appellate court focused largely on the testimony of the competing expert witnesses:

> The opinion of Dr. Quinn that defendant does not have the "Intermittent Explosive Disorder" diagnosed by the defense psychiatrist is well supported by defendant's background, medical and educational records, and recent psychiatric examinations. There is no

history of extreme aggression or loss of control supporting Dr. Herman's conclusion that defendant, in response to stress, would enter a dissociative state in which he could neither control his anger nor understand the nature and consequences of his conduct. Although such lack of history presents the possibility that defendant's conduct in killing Derrick represented the acute onset of a mental disease, that theory was specifically eschewed by the defense psychiatrist. Moreover, the defense was undermined by independent proof contradicting several assumptions about defendant's background relied upon by Dr. Herman in forming his diagnosis and opinion. Dr. Herman's opinion was undercut further by the concession on cross-examination that defendant saw an opportunity to harm Derrick because there was no one else around, but that defendant could have "chosen" to control his anger if others had been around. Dr. Herman additionally conceded that defendant was sadistic, which Dr. Herman defined to mean intentionally cruel, and that a sadistic person, in order to derive pleasure from being cruel, must be consciously aware of his cruelty.[64]

After serving 9 years behind bars, in high-security juvenile detention facilities and state prison, Eric became eligible for parole in 2002. His application for release was summarily rejected. Two years later, in a written opinion rejecting Eric's second bid for release, the parole board wrote, "Despite your lengthy incarceration to this point, this panel is of the opinion that should you be released at this time, you would continue to pose a clear and present danger to the safety and welfare of society . . . Your release would pose an unreasonable and unacceptable risk to the safety and welfare of others."[65]

In 2006, 26-year-old Eric, having then spent half of his life behind bars, again applied for parole. Eric told the parole board, "I would like the opportunity to re-enter society, not because I feel I've done enough time . . . but I want an opportunity to help someone not commit a crime the way I have or help young kids coming into their teenage years . . . I am not trying to go out into society and commit another crime, because I know what would happen if I went out and violated in any way, minor or major. . . . I know I would never have an opportunity to re-enter society again."[66] Although noting that Eric had a record of good behavior in prison and had been making the most of educational and job training opportunities, the parole board again denied release.

8

Andrew Goldstein

Their lives intersected randomly one rainy Sunday in January 1999. Their momentary encounter on a New York City subway platform could easily have gone unnoticed and amounted to nothing more than an exchange of a few words between strangers. Instead, the chance meeting between Kendra Webdale and Andrew Goldstein not only resulted in a senseless homicide that destroyed two lives, but led to a legal precedent that may fundamentally alter the way expert testimony is presented in insanity trials.

Kendra and Andrew were living in the same city but had little else in common. Kendra, 33 years old, had grown up in rural Upstate New York, graduated from the University at Buffalo, and moved to the big city 3 years earlier in the hope of advancing her budding career in screenwriting. While her star had been rising for over a decade, Andrew had not been so fortunate. In the preceding 10 years, 29-year-old Andrew had gone from a promising graduate of the prestigious Bronx High School of Science to a "revolving door" psychiatric patient who had been hospitalized more than a dozen times since suffering a psychotic break when he was a freshman in college. In the 2 years leading up to January 1999, Goldstein had been hospitalized on 25 occasions, totaling 193 days.

In 1989, while a student at the University at Stony Brook, Goldstein accused his mother of poisoning him, pushed her, and was admitted to Creedmoor Psychiatric Center, a state inpatient facility for the mentally ill. At Creedmoor, Goldstein was described as suffering from delusions and hallucinations; he heard voices and believed that an organ was growing inside of him. He was diagnosed with chronic paranoid schizophrenia with an acute exacerbation. A year later, he was again hospitalized with a diagnosis of "bipolar disorder with psychotic features."[1] The next year he was rehospitalized at Creedmoor, described as "delusional, psychotic and dangerous" and suffering from "chronic undifferentiated schizophrenia."[2]

For the next 4 years, Goldstein was either hospitalized or living in a supervised residence for the mentally ill. During that period, from 1992 to 1996, he was variously described by mental health professionals as "actively psychotic," "highly delusional," "in need of inpatient psychiatric admission" and suffering from "schizoaffective disorder."[3] Goldstein assaulted staff members at Creedmoor, after accusing them of poisoning him, and attacked a fellow supermarket shopper who resembled his mother.

In 1997 and 1998, Goldstein's assaultive behavior continued, and he was in and out of various psychiatric hospitals. Annoyed by a child in a bookstore, Goldstein apparently tilted a table that bumped the child; fleeing the store, he knocked a woman into a bookshelf, injuring her face and eye. In a fast-food restaurant, Goldstein swung at two women without provocation. While waiting at an outpatient mental health clinic, he threw a female psychiatrist against the wall, knocked her to the floor, and banged her head. During an inpatient group therapy session, he struck a resident physician, claiming he had been unable to control his arms. Later, while aboard a subway train, he shoved a woman for no apparent reason.

As these events were unfolding in 1997 and 1998, doctors at the various hospitals were describing Goldstein with diagnostic terms such as "bipolar and manic with psychotic features" and "paranoid schizophrenic."[4] According to hospital records during this period, Goldstein was "malodorous," demonstrated "poor personal hygiene," and was experiencing hallucinations and "bizarre delusions"—for example, the hospital charts indicated that Goldstein reported "hearing voices telling him to hurt somebody" and believed he was being controlled by "Larry" who "likes to eat people's excrement with a knife and fork."[5]

Despite his assaultive behavior and his increasingly severe mental illness, Goldstein was repeatedly released from the hospitals to which he was committed. During his last hospitalization before his January 3, 1999, encounter with Kendra Webdale—an inpatient stay that began on November 15, 1998—Goldstein was described as experiencing "command hallucinations" and having "delusions of being controlled" by someone who was inhabiting his body and removing his brain.[6] On December 2, 1998, he was described in hospital notes as evidencing "bizarre delusions" and "thought disorder."[7] On December 6, the notes reported that he "remains delusional" and "still feels people are after him."[8] On December 9, he was described by hospital staff as "malodorous," "unwashed," and "very delusional."[9] Four days later, he was portrayed in the chart as having improved from psychosis, and on December 14, 1998, he was discharged from the hospital with a week's supply of antipsychotic medication and a referral to an outpatient clinic for counseling.

Soon after discharge, Goldstein stopped taking his prescribed medication. When he failed to follow through on the referral for counseling by December

26, the clinic mailed him a form letter indicating that unless he contacted them by January 6, 1999, his case would be closed.

On January 3, 1999, at about 5:00 P.M., just 3 weeks after he had been discharged from the hospital and three days before his outpatient case would have been summarily closed, Andrew Goldstein was pacing the subway platform of the 23rd Street station, creating anxiety among the others who were there waiting for a train. Kendra Webdale was also there, leaning against a wall, facing an oncoming train. Goldstein asked Webdale for the time. She glanced at her watch and replied, "[I]t's a little after five."[10] Suddenly, Goldstein grabbed Webdale, picked her up, and threw her onto the tracks in front of the train just as it entered the station. Webdale was crushed and died instantly.

After the incident, Goldstein made no effort to flee. Instead, he sat down and said, "I'm psychotic. Take me to a hospital."[11] A motorman operating the train confronted Goldstein, telling him, "You threw the woman in front of the train."[12] Goldstein replied, "Yes, can I get a doctor please?"[13] Soon, a police officer arrived, frisked Goldstein, found psychiatric appointment cards on his pockets, and handcuffed him. Goldstein made no effort to resist and told the arresting officer, "I don't know the woman. I just pushed her."[14]

Within hours, Goldstein gave police a videotaped statement, attributing the homicide to an overwhelming urge:

> I walked to the far end of the platform which would be the back of the train. As I'm walking I felt a sensation like something was entering me like a ghost or a spirit or something like that. While I was walking it fell out of me. When I have the sensation that something is entering me I get the urge to push, shove or sidekick. As the train was coming—it—the feeling disappeared and came back several times . . .
>
> As I was standing on the platform there was a woman standing waiting for the train. She was facing the incoming train and I was standing behind her. I got the urge to push, kick or punch. I pushed the woman who had blonde hair. I don't recall what she looked like. But I know she was a white female. When I pushed her she fell onto the track and was struck by the train . . .
>
> I feel like an aura, or a sensation like you're losing control of your motor systems. And then, you lose control of your senses and everything. And then you feel like something's entering you. Like you're being inhabited. I don't know. But—and then, and then it's like an overwhelming urge to strike out or push or punch . . .

This is like 10 times this has happened to me. Now this time, terrific, I mean bang zoom, you know it's right—right in front of a train . . .

I shoved her, not knowing which direction I was going, coming or going, and then she fell onto the track and then I went into shock, horror. I saw the body go under and then I walked away, and then I said, "I don't know." I threw my hands up and said, "I don't know."[15]

At the end of Goldstein's lengthy videotaped statement, he was questioned by a prosecutor, who obviously anticipated an insanity defense in the case and did his best to put words into Goldstein's mouth that would undermine any such defense:

Prosecutor: You certainly agree that you knew what you were doing and you knew it was wrong.
Goldstein: Uh Hugh. I got a cold. I don't know what the heck . . .
Prosecutor: That is you pushed her onto the tracks, it was the cause of her death?
Goldstein: I see.
Prosecutor: No, tell me.
Goldstein: No, I'm sorry?
Prosecutor: Were you listening to what I was saying?
Goldstein: Oh no, I'm sorry.
Prosecutor: Do you agree or disagree that you knew at the time you pushed her that it could cause her death?
Goldstein: Well, I wasn't thinking about anything about pushing her. When I—when it happens, I don't think. It just goes, push, you know? It's like a—like an attack of some kind. I pushed her. But I didn't push her thinking that she would wind up on the tracks. I didn't—didn't intend to push her in any direction. It just happened. It's like you break loose. I don't know.
Prosecutor: Well, did you expect that she would go off the platform?
Goldstein: No. No. No. No. I would never push anybody off the tracks.
Prosecutor: Because you know it's wrong.
Goldstein: Yeah.[16]

Goldstein was charged with murder and, as expected, pleaded not guilty by reason of insanity. Prosecutors countered with the theory that the killing of Kendra Webdale was the result not of mental illness, but of Goldstein's longstanding hatred of women. They accused Goldstein of using his mental illness to avoid being punished for his violent conduct.

Under New York law, Goldstein bore the burden of proving by a preponderance of the evidence that, by reason of mental disease or defect, he lacked the substantial capacity to appreciate the nature and consequence or the wrongfulness of his homicidal act. After hearing the testimony of several eyewitnesses and viewing the videotape of Goldstein's confession, the eight-man, four-woman jury heard from psychiatric experts for both sides.

Dr. Spencer Eth, director of psychiatry at one of the many hospitals to which Goldstein had been admitted over the years, explained in detail Goldstein's lengthy history of revolving-door inpatient treatment and testified that Goldstein suffered from "schizophrenia of the most severe and malignant sort."[17] Eth, who had reviewed all 3500 pages of the defendant's psychiatric history and examined him for 2 hours, opined that, as a result of this illness, Goldstein had not been able to appreciate the nature and consequences of his actions. As the psychiatrist explained, "His illness has him doing things that don't come from him.... It's internal, crazy thoughts and feelings that are driving the behavior."[18]

Eth further told the jury that the fault for the killing could be traced to the hospitals that generally discharged Goldstein within a matter of a few weeks. The hospitals, he testified, were "under enormous pressure ... to turn beds over quickly" and functioned like "MASH unit[s] ... patch[ing] up patients and send[ing] them out."[19] Tellingly, Eth recounted how as recently as the spring of 1998, less than year before Kendra Webdale was killed, doctors concluded that Goldstein needed long-term inpatient care and persuaded Creedmoor Psychiatric Center, a state hospital, to admit him. Creedmoor, however, had a lengthy waiting list, so Goldstein was instead discharged to the streets and left to his own devices.

Another defense witness, Dr. Wilfred Van Gorp, a forensic psychologist, concurred with Eth's conclusion that Goldstein was suffering from severe schizophrenia and was insane at the time of Kendra Webdale's killing. Van Gorp testified that Goldstein demonstrated classic symptoms of schizophrenia, including "a slowed ability to think ... an inability to understand what details are important, an emotionless demeanor and an inability to concentrate."[20] Van Gorp had also administered psychological tests to Goldstein and found that the defendant's full-scale IQ had dropped from 122 (superior range) when he was a child to 94 (below normal) when tested prior to trial. The former score placed Goldstein's intellect in the top 8 percent of the population, whereas the latter score fell within the bottom 34 percent of the population. Van Gorp attributed this sharp drop in intellectual functioning to the ravages of Goldstein's mental illness.

Testifying for the prosecution was Dr. Angela Hegarty, a psychiatrist who concluded that Goldstein did not meet the criteria for insanity. Hegarty told the jury that Goldstein was a woman-hating, sexually frustrated predator with an antisocial personality, who was "malingering," "lying," and "exaggerating" his illness and its effects.[21] According to Hegarty, Goldstein killed Kendra Webdale because she aroused him sexually. "To use the colloquial," she testified, "I think he was turned on."[22] When Goldstein saw the attractive blonde standing on the subway platform, Hegarty told the jury, "It was a reminder of how he couldn't, to use the colloquial, 'make it.'"[23]

Under intense cross-examination, Hegarty admitted that Goldstein was "probably schizophrenic."[24] Pressed on the issue of malingering, Hegarty backed off, telling Goldstein's defense attorney, "I don't believe the defendant is making up his mental illness," but adding quickly, "I do not believe that is the reason he killed Kendra Webdale."[25]

Explaining her opinion further, Hegarty said of Goldstein, "He knows he's charged with murder and he could go to jail for a long time if he's convicted of murder. He'd rather go to a hospital . . . The analogy I use is the dog ate my homework. It is very clear the defendant has a dog. He has a mental illness . . . What is not clear is whether this illness interfered with his ability to know what he was doing."[26]

Despite Hegarty's concession on cross-examination that Goldstein probably suffered from schizophrenia, a psychologist called by the prosecution testified that his testing of Goldstein suggested that the defendant may have suffered from attention deficit disorder and not schizophrenia. The psychologist, Dr. William Barr, also cast doubt upon the notion that Goldstein had briefly been psychotic at the time of the killing. Barr told jurors that "[p]eople don't usually have brief psychotic episodes. They have episodes through several days—most typically a week."[27]

On cross-examination, however, Barr declined to present any diagnosis for Goldstein, admitting that he had not read any of Goldstein's 3500-page, decade-long psychiatric history, in which the defendant had been repeatedly diagnosed as suffering from schizophrenia. Without such a review, Barr agreed, he could not determine Goldstein's diagnosis. "I don't have any conclusion on what his mental illness is," the psychologist finally stated.[28]

On cross-examination, Barr also backed down with regard to the importance of some of the psychological test results. For example, he acknowledged that Goldstein had simply responded "true" to all of the items on one psychological test. In the end, the psychologist conceded, "I was unable to come up with a conclusion to what they represented. I couldn't make any sense of it."[29]

Despite overwhelming evidence that Andrew Goldstein was suffering from a severe mental illness, most likely paranoid schizophrenia, at the time he killed Kendra Webdale, and despite what appear to have been devastating cross-examinations of the prosecution's two expert witnesses, the jurors (at least most of them) were not inclined to regard Goldstein as insane. After 5 days of deliberations, the jury was deadlocked and unable to reach a verdict.

Accounts of the jury deliberations vary, but by all accounts 10 or 11 jurors wanted to convict Goldstein of murder, whereas 1 or 2 adamantly believed that he was not guilty by reason of insanity. What is not disputed, however, is that the main (and perhaps only) holdout on the jury was Octavio Ramos who, just 2 weeks before the trial, had been convicted of resisting arrest and harassment following a dispute with his landlord. At the time of the Goldstein trial, Ramos was awaiting sentencing and facing the possibility of spending up to a year in jail.

Ramos had been allowed to serve on the jury because during jury selection neither the judge nor the prosecutor followed the routine procedure of asking potential jurors if they had ever been arrested or convicted of a crime. Ironically, Ramos was the last juror selected and ended up on the jury in part because the prosecutor had complained about defense counsel's repeated challenges of potential jurors with Latino surnames. The critical significance of the jurors' backgrounds and beliefs in insanity trials was also highlighted by what the judge and the attorneys all knew prior to seating Ramos on the jury without objection or challenge: He worked in a hospital as an advocate for patients' rights, he was a tenants' rights activist, and two of his daughters were psychiatrists.

The jury's inability to reach a verdict led to a mistrial, which, in turn, forced a second trial. Having seen how the evidence, particularly the expert testimony, had played out in the earlier trial, attorneys for both sides were able to alter their approaches in the second trial. For example, newly appointed defense counsel offered another defense in addition to insanity. They offered to prove, through expert psychological testimony, that at the time of the killing, Goldstein had been suffering an extreme emotional disturbance for which there was a reasonable cause or explanation. Under New York law, if defense counsel proved this defense to a jury, Goldstein could not be convicted of murder, only first degree manslaughter, a much less serious offense.

Goldstein's attorneys also requested a court order to allow their client to undergo positron emission tomography, a so-called PET-scan, which would visually depict the functioning of various regions of Goldstein's brain. Because the PET scans of patients with schizophrenia are said to demonstrate physical manifestations of the disease, defense attorneys argued that allowing such a test in this case might effectively answer the prosecution expert's opinions that Goldstein was malingering.

The trial judge, the same jurist who presided over the first trial, rejected both defense motions, refusing to allow any evidence regarding extreme emotional disturbance and denying the defendant the opportunity for a PET scan. According to the judge, defense counsel had waited too long to give notice regarding extreme emotional disturbance. The defendant was not entitled to a PET scan, the judge ruled, because the test would cost too much "public money," its results (even if positive) might not be admissible, and it would require taking the defendant to a hospital, which she said would "threaten security."[30]

In the second trial, prosecutors also tried a somewhat different approach to the expert testimony. This time, Hegarty would testify that Goldstein suffered from a disorder "in the schizophrenic spectrum" but one that was "relatively mild" and "substantially in remission" at the time of the killing.[31]

In the second trial, prosecutors would also go out of their way to paint Hegarty's evaluation of Goldstein as more thorough and comprehensive than that conducted by Eth. In cross-examining Eth, one prosecutor asked him, among a barrage of seemingly irrelevant questions, whether he had visited the crime scene and walked the entire length of the platform, visited the bookstore in which Goldstein had once allegedly assaulted a woman, explored the geography of a place in Delaware Goldstein had once visited, or inquired into Goldstein's rent payments and bank withdrawals. Eth's answer to all of these questions was "no."[32] As the psychiatrist explained, to him "the critical issue was that day [January 3, 1999]" and "most particularly on the platform."[33] Eth responded essentially and reasonably that although he did not dismiss the events leading up to the killing, he was a psychiatrist and not a detective.

Whatever relevance, if any, these investigations may have had upon the legal question of Goldstein's sanity is unknown. But clearly the prosecutor wanted to leave the jury with the impression that Eth had not done a thorough evaluation. Also unknown, however, and certainly never revealed to the jury, was whether the defense had the financial resources to pay Eth to conduct such an investigation even if he had been inclined to do so. Goldstein was indigent, and his defense was funded by the taxpayers solely upon advance approval from the court. The cost of the prosecution of this case, although also funded by taxpayers, was almost entirely within the discretion of the prosecutor. To put it another way, the prosecution had almost unlimited resources to fund its experts. Though the trial judge had the discretion to require greater funding for the defense evaluation of Goldstein, it is worth recalling that she denied Goldstein's request for a PET scan because it would require too much "public money."[34]

The import of this line of cross-examination, obviously intended to undermine the reliability of Eth's expert opinions, became most clear when Hegarty took the stand in rebuttal. Unlike Eth, Hegarty apparently had the resources to pull out all the stops and no qualms about doing her own detective work. She not only reviewed Goldstein's records and interviewed him repeatedly but also interviewed victims and witnesses to Goldstein's many past assaults, his past and present roommates and their girlfriends, and Goldstein's landlady. Hegarty also testified that she visited the scene of the crime both alone and with a police detective, visited the scenes of the prior assaults, and visited Goldstein's prior residences. Moreover, Hegarty informed the jury that she had reviewed, among many other items, a transcript of Goldstein's parents' divorce proceedings and his banking, social security, and telephone records.

Whatever relevance, if any, some of these more obscure investigations had upon the legal question of Goldstein's sanity is unknown. But clearly Hegarty and the prosecutors wanted to leave the jury with the impression that unlike Eth, she had left virtually no stone unturned.

Hegarty described her sweeping approach to the evaluation of Goldstein as having employed a "new" theory of forensic psychiatry that had recently emerged as forensic mental health experts abandoned their traditional roles as advocates for patients and began to see their mission as a "search for the truth," but conceded that "many good forensic psychiatrists might disagree" with this approach.[35] In fact, this approach was hardly new in 1999 and had been the professional standard in insanity evaluations for 15 years or more. In a chapter published in 1985, but written earlier, forensic psychologist Dr. David Shapiro wrote that in insanity evaluations,

> [i]nterviews with the defendant, of course, provide one source of information. But the conscientious expert should also consult all available secondary sources . . . It should be a rule of thumb, for example, never to prepare a report without first reviewing a complete police report of the offense. Wherever possible the expert should also interview witnesses to the offense as well as family members, friends, employers, teachers, and so forth—anyone who can describe what transpired and/or what the defendant's functioning was like at or around the time of the offense.[36]

Although the prosecution obviously and understandably sought a strategic advantage in comparing Eth's standard clinical approach with Hegarty's apparently scorched earth method of evaluation, in the end the prosecutor and the expert witness went too far. Repeatedly, Hegarty drove nails into the coffin of Goldstein's insanity defense by quoting directly from interviews she conducted with six people who had known Goldstein in the past. All of the quoted statements were damaging to Goldstein's claim of insanity and tended to support Hegarty's hypothesis that Goldstein was not seriously mentally ill, killed Kendra Webdale because he had issues with women, and had a history of using his alleged mental illness to shield himself from punishment. Hegarty's testimony regarding what she learned from four of these interviews was summarized by the New York Court of Appeals as follows:

> John P. was a security guard at Waldbaum's in late 1996, about two years before the fatal attack on Kendra Webdale, when defendant assaulted a woman who was shopping there. John P. restrained defendant immediately after the assault, and he described to Hegarty, who repeated to the jury, defendant's reaction when he was seized. According to Hegarty's account of John P.'s statement, defendant said, "I'm sick, I'm sick, I'm schizophrenic," kept repeating those assertions, and said that he had just got out of the hospital. Defendant made a similar statement—"I'm psychotic, take me to the hospital," or words to that effect—immediately after throwing Kendra Webdale to her death. John P.'s statement thus supported Hegarty's and the prosecution's theory that defendant had repeatedly used his schizophrenia to minimize his misconduct and avoid punishment.
>
> Kimberly D. was the girlfriend of a man who shared an apartment with defendant in November 1998—about two months before Kendra Webdale's death—when Stephanie H., the girlfriend of another resident, visited the apartment. Hegarty testified that Kimberly D. had told Hegarty that Stephanie H., who worked in a strip club, "would tease" defendant. Hegarty also testified, apparently still recounting what Kimberly D. said to her, that Stephanie H. "bears a rather remarkable similarity [in] appearance to Kendra Webdale." Thus, Hegarty suggested to the jury that defendant identified the woman he killed with another woman who had frustrated him sexually.
>
> Serita G. had been defendant's landlady twice, first in 1996 and then in 1998–1999 up to the date of Kendra Webdale's death. According to Hegarty, Serita G. told her "that on one occasion . . . her maid went downstairs and the defendant was lying on his bed exposed and he didn't cover himself." This was part of the basis for

Hegarty's testimony that defendant had "been sexually inappropriate with women."

Isaac V. was one of defendant's roommates in the month preceding Kendra Webdale's death. Hegarty testified to Isaac V.'s description of defendant's personality: She said that Isaac V. said that defendant was "a little weird . . . didn't act his age . . . wanted to go to college and . . . wanted to be somebody . . . was never disrespectful and never violent and very calm. . . . " This description corroborated Hegarty's overall picture of defendant as someone suffering from a relatively mild mental illness, not a hopelessly out-of-control schizophrenic.[37]

Goldstein's defense attorney repeatedly objected to this testimony, asserting that allowing it to be heard by the jury violated Goldstein's Sixth Amendment right to confront his accusers. Allowing Hegarty to present this hearsay (or in the case of the landlady's statement, hearsay upon hearsay) to the jury provided no opportunity to cross-examine the individuals (John P., Kimberly D., Serita G, and Isaac V.) who made the statements and thus test the reliability of their statements. In response, accepted by the trial judge who overruled the defense objections, the prosecution argued that New York case law allowed (as did the law in most states) an expert witness to explain to the jury the information comprising the basis of his or her opinions as long as such information was of the sort ordinarily relied upon by experts in the particular field. Because Hegarty had testified that in the "new" methodology of forensic psychiatry, experts relied upon, among other things, interviews with individuals other than the defendant (so-called "collaterals"), the trial judge had no trouble overruling defense counsel's repeated objections and allowing Hegarty to testify to what she had been told.

This time, jurors did not need 5 days to deliberate Goldstein's fate. Indeed, after just 45 minutes of deliberation, the jury rejected Goldstein's insanity defense and convicted him of second degree murder. Shortly thereafter, Goldstein was sentenced to serve from 25 years to life in prison. And there the matter would likely have rested had it not been for the intervention of the U.S. Supreme Court in a seemingly unrelated case from the State of Washington.

During an argument in which Michael Crawford claimed that Kenneth Lee had raped Crawford's wife, Crawford stabbed Lee. Crawford claimed that he had acted in self-defense, but his wife, who witnessed the altercation, gave police a tape-recorded statement conflicting with her husband's claim of self-defense. Tried for assault while armed with a deadly weapon, Crawford invoked the state's marital privilege, thereby preventing the prosecution from calling his wife as a witness against him. In response, over defense counsel's objection, prosecutors offered and were allowed to play for the jury Mrs. Crawford's tape-recorded police statement.

Crawford was convicted. A series of appeals of that verdict ultimately led to the U.S. Supreme Court, which decided the case on March 8, 2004, by which time Andrew Goldstein had already been imprisoned (including pre-trial detention) for over 5 years. The Supreme Court held that the tape of Mrs. Crawford's police statement was inadmissible and that her husband's conviction must be overturned because testimonial statements of witnesses who do not testify at trial may be admitted against a criminal defendant only when the witness is unavailable and the defendant has had prior opportunity to cross-examine the witness.

As the appeal in *Crawford v. Washington*[38] was making its way to the U.S. Supreme Court, Goldstein's appeal was slowly moving through the appeals courts in New York. The first appellate court to hear it, New York's Appellate Division, readily dismissed every one of Goldstein's arguments for a new trial, including, among others, denial of the PET scan, refusal to allow testimony on extreme emotional disturbance, and the alleged hearsay testimony given by Hegarty. On the last point, the Appellate Division noted the Supreme Court's recent decision in *Crawford* but distinguished the hearsay in Goldstein from that in *Crawford,* holding that the statements made by witnesses to Hegarty were not "testimonial" in nature:

> [C]ontrary to defendant's contentions . . . New York cases and *Crawford* do not preclude admission of the prosecution's forensic psychiatrist's testimony regarding the background information upon which she relied in arriving at her expert opinion as to defendant's sanity. Rather, the former specifically encourage the use of such background information for that purpose, and the latter impliedly distinguishes its admission into evidence from that of "testimonial" hearsay directed towards proof of defendant's guilt or innocence.[39]

The statements of the witnesses interviewed by Hegarty were *not* "testimonial hearsay directed towards proof of [Goldstein's] guilt or innocence"? The Court of Appeals had a hard time believing that. As the state's highest court observed and held in granting Goldstein a third trial,

> We think the statements made to Hegarty by her interviewees were testimonial. Hegarty was an expert retained to testify for the

People. The record does not specifically show that the interviewees knew this, but it would be strange if Hegarty did not tell them; we infer that they knew they were responding to questions from an agent of the State engaged in trial preparation. None of them was making "a casual remark to an acquaintance"; all of them should reasonably have expected their statements "to be used prosecutorially" or to "be available for use at a later trial."

While it is true that the Supreme Court referred, in describing testimonial hearsay, to "formal" statements made to "government officers," we do not think that these words exclude the statements at issue here. Responses to questions asked in interviews that were part of the prosecution's trial preparation are "formal" in much the same sense as "depositions" and other materials that the Supreme Court identified as testimonial. *Crawford* itself shows that the statements need not be under oath and need not be formal in their language; the statement held excludable by the *Crawford* Court was unsworn and used colloquial phrasing. Nor do we think the difference between an expert retained by the State and a "government officer" is of constitutional significance here. The Confrontation Clause would offer too little protection if it could be avoided by assigning the job of interviewing witnesses to an independent contractor rather than an employee.

In short, defendant's rights under the Confrontation Clause were violated when Hegarty was allowed to tell the jury what witnesses defendant had no chance to cross-examine had said to her.[40]

Following the New York Court of Appeals decision, Goldstein's prosecutors sought review by the U.S. Supreme Court, which refused to hear the case. Although the Supreme Court's refusal to hear the case does not make the New York court's decision in Goldstein the law of the land, certainly it may be read as a signal that testimony such as that given by Hegarty against Goldstein will not be tolerated under *Crawford*. Thus, it appears that the efforts of the prosecutors in this case not only backfired but may have fundamentally altered the way psychologists and psychiatrists give expert testimony for the prosecution in insanity and other mental defense cases.

Although the court's decision in Goldstein is the law only in New York, the New York Court of Appeals is one of the most influential appellate courts in the United States. Thus, it is not unlikely that other courts in other states will follow that court's lead in *Goldstein* when confronted with the same issue.

Rather than pursue yet another trial on its murder charge against Goldstein, the prosecution offered to allow him to plead guilty to manslaughter. Goldstein agreed, pleaded guilty to, and was sentenced to prison for, the lesser charge. Although under his original sentence for murder, Goldstein could have been incarcerated for the rest of his life, and would not even have been eligible for parole for 25 years, his sentence for manslaughter requires that he be released from prison after serving no more than 23 years. Indeed, with good behavior, he may be conditionally released from prison after serving 20 years behind bars.

9

Eric Michael Clark

There was never any real dispute that Eric Michael Clark was severely mentally ill. But the Arizona teen had not always been so troubled. Early on in high school, Clark had been a solid student and a standout football player—a running back for the varsity team with ambitions to one day play professional football. He was also popular with his peers and had been elected freshman homecoming king.

Then suddenly, at age 16, Clark changed. He became obsessed with the dire predictions for Y2K (the turn of the new millennium), quit school, and charged $1,700 worth of survival gear on his father's debit card. When January 1, 2000, came and passed without incident, he quietly went back to school. Even then, however, his behavior remained odd and puzzling. For example, for 2 years after a house fire he refused to drink tap water, talked of worrying about lead poisoning, and drank only bottled water.

Not long after, Clark lost interest in sports, became heavily involved with drugs, especially LSD, and started talking about aliens in the community, even accusing his parents of being aliens. Clark also began having inexplicable mood swings, episodes in which he would scream and whisper gibberish. Fearful that he was being poisoned, he refused to sleep in his bedroom and moved instead to a small computer room in his family's home. There he rigged the room with fishing line, wind chimes, and beads designed to alert him to any intrusion. Similarly, he carried a bird in a cage to serve as a first alarm for any attempt to gas him. He let his appearance go and began to demonstrate bizarre hygiene and grooming habits. At the same time, Clark began turning up the volume on the television and radio in what appeared to others to be an attempt to drown out auditory hallucinations.

People at home, at school, and in the community began to observe Clark's bizarre behavior and soon he was an outcast, a friendless loner telling anyone who would listen that his hometown of Flagstaff was overrun with aliens who were trying to capture and kill him. To avoid what he regarded as certain death, Clark refused to eat food that wasn't either in sealed packages or from a restaurant.

Eventually Clark's parents were so worried about their son that they had him arrested, taken to a juvenile facility, and ultimately admitted to a psychiatric hospital. Released from the hospital against medical advice, Clark was arrested on charges of drug possession and driving while intoxicated. Soon, acquaintances heard Clark talking about luring a police officer to a secluded place and then shooting him and any others who came to his aid.

Not knowing where to turn for help, Clark's parents sought in vain to have their 17-year-old son committed to a psychiatric institution, consulting but getting no help from at least five hospitals and two lawyers.

Before long, Clark was committed to a state hospital but only after a tragedy that would essentially destroy two lives. On June 21, during the early hours of the first day of summer in 2000, Clark stole the keys to his brother's truck, armed himself with a pistol, and drove the truck around a nearby neighborhood where, for about 40 minutes, he circled the block more than 20 times, blaring rap music from the vehicle's stereo. Among the lyrics heard from the truck early that morning were "fuck the cops."[1] Not surprisingly, at least one neighbor who observed the spectacle called 911 for police assistance.

Minutes later, at 4:42 A.M., Flagstaff police officer Jeffrey Moritz responded to the call, spotted the truck, activated the patrol car's emergency flashers and siren, and tried to pull Clark over. When Clark did not comply, Officer Moritz radioed his intention to go after him. "I have one running on me," he told the dispatcher.[2] But less than a minute later, the officer added the truck's license plate number and said, "I'll be out with him."[3] Moritz directed Clark to remain in the vehicle. Half a minute later, Moritz told the dispatcher, "999, I've been hit. 999, I've been hit."[4] The numeric phrase 999 is police code for "officer needs assistance immediately."[5] Neighbors reported hearing an exchange of gunfire, several small caliber shots followed immediately by two larger caliber blasts. Within seconds, Officer Moritz was stumbling toward a house, calling, "Help me. Somebody help me."[6] Moritz had been shot in the shoulder, and soon died from a bullet wound that severed major blood vessels.

After shooting Officer Moritz, Clark fled and was not captured until about 16 hours later, when a police officer found him crouched behind some rocks near his family's home and chased him down when he tried to run away. Clark asked, "What's this all about?" and the police responded by asking him where the gun was.[7] Clark said, "What gun? I don't know anything about any gun."[8] The evidence, however, suggested that he did. Police soon found a .22-caliber revolver stuffed in a knitted cap and hidden close to a nearby shed. Clark was found to have gunpowder residue on his hands, and the cap contained biological material that matched Clark's DNA. Finally, a ballistics examination established that the handgun found in the cap had fired the bullet that killed Officer Moritz.

Immediately after Clark was arrested and charged with murder, a judge determined that he was "suffering from psychosis and paranoid schizophrenia and therefore gravely disabled and a danger to himself and others."[9] As a result, Clark was committed to the Arizona State Hospital for psychiatric treatment. In a separate proceeding, a judge found that Clark was incompetent to stand trial and ordered an additional commitment to the state hospital for treatment aimed at restoring Clark's competency. As it turned out, Clark was so seriously mentally ill that it took 3 years of intensive treatment to restore his capacity to understand the nature of the charges against him and to assist counsel in his own defense. Indeed, during Clark's 3-year pretrial hospitalization, mental health professionals who examined him unanimously agreed that he suffered from paranoid schizophrenia and that he was actively psychotic at the time of the shooting.

Once deemed competent to stand trial, Clark waived trial by jury and agreed to have his case determined by a judge alone. At trial, Clark did not deny shooting and killing Officer Moritz. Instead he offered two psychological defenses. Clark's first defense was that he was "guilty except insane." Under Arizona's version of the insanity defense, "A person may be found guilty except insane if, at the time of the commission of the criminal act, the person was afflicted with a mental disease or defect of such severity that the person did not know the criminal act was wrong."[10] Clark's second defense was that because of his mental illness, he did not intentionally or knowingly kill a police officer, thus lacked the requisite mental state (*mens rea*) for the offense of first degree murder, and accordingly could be convicted only of a less serious form of homicide not requiring proof of such intent or knowledge.

Although the trial court agreed to hear expert and lay evidence bearing on Clark's insanity, it refused to consider such evidence for purposes of rebutting Clark's alleged *mens rea*.

The primary evidence regarding Clark's mental state at the time of the offense came from three witnesses, one a former classmate of Clark's who testified against him, the second a psychiatrist who testified for the defense, and the third a psychologist called to the witness stand by the prosecution.

Clark's former classmate Jason Tackett testified that in April or May of 2000 he heard Clark "mumble to himself at a fast-food restaurant that someone had been arrested unjustly and that he wanted to prove his point to the police."[11] Tackett also testified that "a couple of weeks" before the fatal shooting, Clark approached Tackett, who was at a barbeque with acquaintances in a local park.[12] According to Tackett, when he greeted Clark, Clark "kind of went off about [how] he wanted to shoot Officer Moritz to get the emergency response out there, and [said] he was going to hide up in the hills with a rifle and start picking them [police officers] off like a sniper would."[13] Clark, he added, said, "If I came up here with my .22 caliber hand pistol . . . and started firing off, when the police come, I will get their cars and start—I have rifles and I'll start shooting them in the head."[14]

Dr. Barry Morenz testified for the defense that he had examined Clark, found him suffering from paranoid schizophrenia, and concluded that he did not understand right from wrong when he shot and killed Officer Moritz. Explaining some of the bases for this diagnosis and conclusion, the psychiatrist told the court,

> Um, I think that the—probably one of the better examples is his continual reference to his mom periodically that they are after him; his references and actions based on these beliefs that the water in his house was being poisoned; that the food was being poisoned, those are also evidence of delusional beliefs, evidence of psychosis; his statements that he made about, um, that a rap star was going to talk to him and somehow he was going to become president, you know, evidence of a grandiose delusion; and then his discussions at times asking his mom if she was really his mom or were they aliens, again, evidence of delusional beliefs; and then his behaviors around the time that he's experiencing these delusional beliefs, washing of the clothes, the—the turning on of water in the house, the shutting the blinds, the turning of volume up on all of the TVs and radios, which, by the way, I think probably was evidence that he was experiencing auditory hallucinations and that this turning up of all the volume, which schizophrenics often describe, is an attempt to drown out the voices that they are experiencing. I don't know that for sure. He's never admitted to these hallucinations, but I'm still suspicious that that was going on . . .
>
> And then he stops grooming himself, he is attempting to cut his own hair, he's wearing a shower cap, he, I guess, wears these stocking caps on his head, is really getting to look just fairly bizarre. And it seems that this may have been in the service of preventing himself from being poisoned by the aliens. And I'm imposing a little bit of logic here that may not exist, you know. I'm inferring that this may have been part of the motivation, but I don't know for sure, because he's never been able to really fully communicate why he did all these

things. Other evidence was his putting the strings with beads in his room and in his car, carrying a bird around in his car . . . all apparently to prevent others from intruding into his personal spaces, for what fear is not completely clear, but the behavior was becoming increasingly bizarre and reflected his delusional beliefs and confusion.[15]

Asked about the prosecution's theory that Clark had deliberately and with premeditation lured Officer Moritz to the crime scene in order to create a confrontation in which he could kill one or more police officers, Morenz replied, "I can't imagine that."[16] Asked to explain, he testified,

> Eric's behaviors were just—there wasn't much purpose or, you know, didn't seem there was much rhyme or reason to his behaviors. You know, he was continually a surprise to his parents. They didn't know what he was going to do next, which is what they were so concerned about and why they wanted him in the hospital, you know, he wasn't functioning in school, you know, he really wasn't functioning at all. To hypothesize that he was sort of planning, you know, kind of a scheme to lure police I think is a bit of a stretch. I have trouble imagining that.[17]

Asked about the significance of Eric's ability to remain at large more than half a day after the killing, Morenz said,

> I think that it reflected that Eric was afraid and had been afraid for months, had been very frightened, you know. He was frightened that the end of the world was going to come, frightened that aliens were taking over people, were manipulating people, that his own parents might be aliens. He really had a tremendous amount of difficulty perceiving reality as you and I see it. And there is, you know, reference that he became kind of preoccupied by this movie, *The Matrix*, which I saw once and was a pretty bizarre movie, but basically had to do with, you know, government forces, police forces, you know, basically alien police forces somehow inhabiting people's bodies and so forth, and he kept saying to his mom that these were real. So Eric may have had some kind of particularly enhanced fears of the police or people in authority were somehow in, you know, particularly controlling positions with this sort of alien presence in the community of Flagstaff.[18]

On cross-examination, however, Dr. Morenz conceded that he could not conclusively state that Clark did not know that killing Officer Moritz was wrong. He also acknowledged that simply because Clark was psychotic before and after the killing was "alone not enough for an insanity finding."[19] Finally, he acknowledged that the disturbance Clark created early in the morning in a quiet residential neighborhood was consistent with an intention to lure a police officer to the scene.

Testifying for the prosecution, Dr. John Moran agreed that Clark suffered from paranoid schizophrenia but concluded that "Mr. Clark knew that he was committing a criminal act when he shot Officer Moritz."[20] Asked to explain why he had reached that opinion, the psychologist testified,

> I reached that opinion because, with the variety of data that I relied upon, would include, I guess, beginning with the statements that he made regarding his intent to shoot police officers . . . comments about anti-police attitude, that if he was intoxicated at the time of the shooting, that that would mean that he would not qualify as being insane and he may have been intoxicated, though we don't know. The evidence that we have, the best data that we have to base a conclusion then is the information about his functioning around the time of the crime. And for me that included the fact that he had been dating a girl, I think as recently as the end of April. And though he was somewhat bizarre on some of those dates, he was capable of having a dating type of relationship at that time, at least in her opinion. That he continued to work out regularly at the club and to be paying attention to his hygiene and his physical status that way. That he continued to socialize to some extent; he went to the party, at the party he engaged in that act of fisticuffs, he broke the kid's nose. We know that he was intoxicated at that time. We know that then the following Friday, that was on a Wednesday, and the following Friday he went to The Museum Club where he was observed socializing. He was by himself but still placing himself in the presence of his peers. That around this time, school was completing, and I think he completed the school year and earned some passing grades, as well as completing the correspondence courses that he had begun in the fall of 1999. Then we have the reports of the fellow at the Sizzler who says he seemed to be doing better than he typically had been when he was at the Sizzler restaurant, and he was engaging in that conversation of having been in a fight. So, again, his aggressive behavior is emerging as a theme, as a conscious theme, as a theme of selected behavior rather than reactive behavior against aliens. That the parents then report that he was

doing relatively well on that night. His mother spent from roughly 2:30 in the afternoon with him until 9:30 at night, and she reported him to be normal, which I'm sure means normal for Eric as opposed to doing worse, given his typical range of functioning, but doing better in his typical range of functioning. That then we don't have any evidence of a stressor between 9:30 at night and 4:30 in the morning that would accommodate or explain the precipitous drop in his level of functioning that must have occurred if one adopts an insanity theory. So that, ultimately, I suppose there's two primary theories at work; one would be an insanity theory that his mental status took a nose dive and he saw the policeman as an alien and attacking him. And I don't think that it's my job to engage in theorizing. I think it's my job to opine about the mental state at the time of the offense; however, I did note that there was no where in the data that Mr. Clark had mentioned the police as trying to get him or attack him. And I also noted that all of his concerns about being killed were about being poisoned. And so, suddenly, we would have to have that at the moment of the crime for the first time his delusional system incorporates the police as aliens engaging in active acts of aggression other than trying to poison him.

On the other side—and it's also important to me that that theory is based on inference and speculation—that on the other side of the theory that would hold that he was volitional, that he was acting with a purpose, that the purpose was either to shoot the cop or possibly to evade apprehension because he thought he was being busted for burglary, that the—there's more data on that side, which is let's call it first degree data or primary data, physical evidence, whether that is the attempt to evade the policeman, the hiding successfully for 16-and-a-half hours, the hiding the gun, the attempting to avoid the policemen at the time of his capture. And then, additionally, I do think it's significant that between the time that he left the theater and when he shot Officer Moritz, that he had to have the wherewithal in order to get into the house without being detected and steal his brother's truck, which apparently was an unusual behavior for him. So all of those things together led me to the conclusion that he probably knew what he was doing, that he knew that what he was doing was wrong.[21]

On cross-examination, Clark's attorney got Moran to agree that at the time of the shooting, Clark was suffering from persistent delusions, that

Clark's "entire behavior" at that time was continuously "one of complete paranoia," that his moods could change suddenly and with little or no provocation, and that he was experiencing schizophrenic symptoms 24 hours a day.[22] Clark's attorney also got Moran to concede that he believed that it was part of his role as a psychologist in this case to strategize with the lawyers who retained him (i.e., the prosecutors).[23] Under questioning, Moran also admitted that he had never testified for the defense in an insanity case. Finally, and most significantly, defense counsel asked Moran if he would agree "that insanity is merely a gross impairment of reality."[24] When Moran said he disagreed with that definition, the attorney produced a transcript of a pretrial interview he had conducted with the psychologist. That transcript showed that when asked by the attorney about how mental health professionals determine the legal standard of insanity, Moran had replied, "Well, gross impairment of reality testing is a common standard that's used in the community, and I think that there are symptoms that are associated with that."[25] After a lengthy colloquy between the attorney and the psychologist, Moran was asked whether he had given any answers in the previous interview that he now felt were necessary to change. Moran's reply: "I guess I would change that one."[26]

The judge, acting as trier of fact in the bench trial, found that the state had proven Clark's guilt beyond a reasonable doubt. As for Clark's defense of insanity, the judge found that "[b]oth experts, all lay witnesses, and the attorneys agree that the defendant suffers from a qualifying mental disease: paranoid schizophrenia" and noted that the prosecution's own expert testified that "there seems to be little doubt that on June 21, 2000, the Defendant was suffering from paranoid delusions."[27] The judge also found, however, that Clark had failed to prove that his "mental illness . . . distorted his perception of reality so severely that he did not know his actions were wrong."[28]

Clark was sentenced to life in prison without hope of parole for 25 years. He appealed, and the Arizona Court of Appeals affirmed his conviction. The appellate court noted that the two experts disagreed regarding Clark's sanity and went on to hold that "[t]o the extent that the trial court may have accepted Dr. Moran's evaluation over Dr. Morenz's, it was entirely within the trial court's province to do so. As the trier of fact in the case, it was free to believe or disbelieve the testimony of either expert and resolve any conflicts in the psychological testimony."[29] The appeals court also approved the way the judge handled the other evidence in the case:

> In reaching its decision that Clark had not proven insanity, it also appears that the trial court gave significant consideration to Clark's own actions both before and after the shooting. For example, its

judgment specifically noted Clark's own actions in driving through residential neighborhoods with loud music "to attract law enforcement," as well as his behavior in evading capture before his arrest at gunpoint and in disposing of the murder weapon afterwards . . .[30]

The Court of Appeals also rejected Clark's arguments that his constitutional rights to due process were violated by Arizona's overly restrictive insanity statute and by Arizona case law that precluded the trial court from considering evidence of his mental illness in determining whether he had the requisite *mens rea* for first degree murder.

On the insanity issue, Clark argued that Arizona's insanity statute (which limited an insanity verdict to cases in which the defendant's mental disease or defect prevented him from knowing that the criminal act was wrong) was unconstitutional because "it did not allow him to present a 'complete defense' under the *M'Naghten* test for insanity to show that he did not appreciate the nature and quality of his acts . . . "[31] In response, the appellate court noted that "there is no constitutional requirement that a state recognize an insanity defense," that "the United State's [sic] Supreme Court has recognized that individual states are free to recognize and define the insanity defense as they see fit," and that "Clark therefore fails to prove how eliminating the first prong of the *M'Naghten* test establishes a violation of due process under either the Arizona or United States Constitutions."[32] Additionally the Court of Appeals reasoned that *M'Naghten's* "nature and quality" standard was not necessary: "It is difficult to imagine that a defendant who did not appreciate the 'nature and quality' of the act he committed would reasonably be able to perceive that the act was 'wrong.' Therefore we do not find that the language would add significantly to the test available under the statute."[33]

Finally the state appeals court held that the trial judge's refusal to consider evidence of Clark's mental illness as evidence that he lacked the necessary *mens rea* for the crime charged was mandated by the state's Supreme Court's holding in an earlier case that "Arizona does not allow evidence of a defendant's mental disorder short of insanity either as an affirmative defense or to negate the *mens rea* of a crime."[34] Stating the obvious, the appellate court added, "This court is bound by decisions of the Arizona Supreme Court and has no authority to overturn or refuse to follow its decisions."[35]

Not surprisingly the Arizona Supreme Court refused to even hear Clark's appeal. However, the United States Supreme Court did agree to hear the case. The high court gave short shrift to Clark's claim that the Arizona insanity law violated his constitutional right to due process.

The Court initially noted that "[w]hen the Arizona legislature first codified an insanity rule, it adopted the full *M'Naghten* statement [but] in 1993 . . . dropped the cognitive incapacity part, leaving only moral incapacity as the nub of the stated definition."[36] In rejecting Clark's claim that this amendment "offends [a] principle of justice so rooted in the traditions of and conscience of our people as to be ranked as fundamental,"[37] the Court said, "History shows no deference to M'Naghten that could elevate its formula to the level of fundamental principle, so as to limit the traditional recognition of a State's capacity to define crimes and defenses."[38]

After observing that the U.S. Supreme Court has never ruled as to whether the insanity defense is constitutionally mandated, and pointing out that they were not called upon to do so in this case, the Court held that the definition of insanity is and should be a matter left to the states, such as Arizona:

> [I]t is clear that no particular formulation has evolved into a baseline for due process, and that the insanity rule, like the conceptualization of criminal offenses, is substantially open to state choice. Indeed, the legitimacy of such choice is the more obvious when one considers the interplay of legal concepts of mental illness or deficiency required for an insanity defense, with the medical concepts of mental abnormality that influence the expert opinion testimony by psychologists and psychiatrists commonly introduced to support or contest insanity claims. For medical definitions devised to justify treatment, like legal ones devised to excuse from conventional criminal responsibility, are subject to flux and disagreement. There being such fodder for reasonable debate about what the cognate legal and medical tests should be, due process imposes no single canonical formulation of legal insanity.[39]

The Court also found that, as a practical matter, deleting the cognitive capacity prong of the *M'Naghten* standard had little if any effect and certainly did not signal "that some constitutional minimum has been shortchanged."[40] As the Court explained,

> The *M'Naghten* test is a sequential test, first asking the factfinder to conduct the easier enquiry whether a defendant knew the nature and quality of his actions. If not, the defendant is to be considered insane and there is no need to pass to the harder and broader enquiry whether the defendant knew his actions were wrong. And, because, owing to this sequence, the factfinder is to ask whether a

defendant lacks moral capacity only when he possesses cognitive capacity, the only defendants who will be found to lack moral capacity are those possessing cognitive capacity. Though, before 1993, Arizona had in place the full *M'Naghten* test with this sequential enquiry, it would appear that the legislature eliminated the cognitive capacity part not to change the meaning of the insanity standard but to implement its judgment that a streamlined standard with only the moral capacity part would be easier for the jury to apply.[41]

Pointing specifically to Clark's case, the Court found that Clark's defense counsel had, in effect, utilized this same approach at trial:

> Clark, indeed, adopted this very analysis himself in the trial court: "[I]f [Clark] did not know he was shooting at a police officer, or believed he had to shoot or be shot, even though his belief was not based in reality, this would establish that he did not know what he was doing was wrong." The trial court apparently agreed, for the judge admitted Clark's evidence of cognitive incapacity for consideration under the State's moral incapacity formulation. And Clark can point to no evidence bearing on insanity that was excluded. His psychiatric expert and a number of lay witnesses testified to his delusions, and this evidence tended to support a description of Clark as lacking the capacity to understand that the police officer was a human being. There is no doubt that the trial judge considered the evidence as going to an issue of cognitive capacity, for in finding insanity not proven he said that Clark's mental illness "did not . . . distort his perception of reality so severely that he did not know his actions were wrong."[42]

Turning to Clark's claim that the Arizona rule disallowing evidence of mental illness to be used to negate the requisite *mens rea* violated due process, the Supreme Court first rejected "the State's argument that *mens rea* and insanity, as currently understood, are entirely distinguishable, so that mental-disease and capacity evidence relevant to insanity is simply irrelevant to *mens rea*."[43] Instead the Court reasoned that "[n]ot only does evidence accepted as showing insanity trump *mens rea*, but evidence of behavior close to the time of the act charged may indicate both the actual state of mind at that time and also an enduring incapacity to form the criminal state of mind necessary to the offense charged."[44]

Furthermore, the Court explained that "evidence tending to show that a defendant suffers from mental disease and lacks capacity to form *mens rea* is relevant to rebut evidence that he did in fact form the required *mens rea* at the time in question; this is the reason that Clark claims a right to require the factfinder in this case to consider testimony about his mental illness and his incapacity directly, when weighing the persuasiveness of other evidence tending to show *mens rea*, which the prosecution has the burden to prove."[45]

But the analysis did not end there. The Court went on to observe that

> [a]s Clark recognizes, however, the right to introduce relevant evidence can be curtailed if there is a good reason for doing that. "While the Constitution . . . prohibits the exclusion of defense evidence under rules that serve no legitimate purpose or that are disproportionate to the ends that they are asserted to promote, well-established rules of evidence permit trial judges to exclude evidence if its probative value is outweighed by certain other factors such as unfair prejudice, confusion of the issues, or potential to mislead the jury." And if evidence may be kept out entirely, its consideration may be subject to limitation, which Arizona claims the power to impose here. State law says that evidence of mental disease and incapacity may be introduced and considered, and if sufficiently forceful to satisfy the defendant's burden of proof under the insanity rule it will displace the presumption of sanity and excuse from criminal responsibility. But mental-disease and capacity evidence may be considered only for its bearing on the insanity defense, and it will avail a defendant only if it is persuasive enough to satisfy the defendant's burden as defined by the terms of that defense. The mental-disease and capacity evidence is thus being channeled or restricted to one issue and given effect only if the defendant carries the burden to convince the factfinder of insanity; the evidence is not being excluded entirely, and the question is whether reasons for requiring it to be channeled and restricted are good enough to satisfy the standard of fundamental fairness that due process requires. We think they are.[46]

The Court then listed several "characteristics of mental-disease and capacity evidence giving rise to risks that may reasonably be hedged by channeling the consideration of such evidence to the insanity issue on which, in States like Arizona, a defendant has the burden of persuasion"[47] and explained why they cut against allowing such evidence to be used to rebut evidence of *mens rea*.

First, the Court noted that "diagnosis may mask vigorous debate within the profession about the very contours of the mental disease itself . . . Though we certainly do not 'condemn mental-disease evidence wholesale,' the consequence of this professional ferment is a general caution in treating psychological classifications as predicates for excusing otherwise criminal conduct."[48]

Second, the Court observed that

> there is the potential of mental-disease evidence to mislead jurors (when they are the factfinders) through the power of this kind of evidence to suggest that a defendant suffering from a recognized mental disease lacks cognitive, moral, volitional, or other capacity, when that may not be a sound conclusion at all . . . [I]t is very easy to slide from evidence that an individual with a professionally recognized mental disease is very different, into doubting that he has the capacity to form *mens rea*, whereas that doubt may not be justified . . . Because allowing mental-disease evidence on *mens rea* can thus easily mislead, it is not unreasonable to address that tendency by confining consideration of this kind of evidence to insanity, on which a defendant may be assigned the burden of persuasion.[49]

Finally, the Court pointed out that

> [t]here are . . . particular risks inherent in the opinions of the experts who supplement the mental-disease classifications with opinions on incapacity: on whether the mental disease rendered a particular defendant incapable of the cognition necessary for moral judgment or *mens rea* or otherwise incapable of understanding the wrongfulness of the conduct charged. Unlike observational evidence bearing on *mens rea*, capacity evidence consists of judgment, and judgment fraught with multiple perils: a defendant's state of mind at the crucial moment can be elusive no matter how conscientious the enquiry, and the law's categories that set the terms of the capacity judgment are not the categories of psychology that govern the expert's professional thinking.[50]

10

Andrea Yates

In 1982, Andrea Kennedy graduated first in her high school class in Houston, Texas. Four years later, Kennedy, who had been captain of the school's swim team and an officer in its National Honor Society, graduated from the School of Nursing at the University of Texas. After becoming a registered nurse, she worked for the next 8 years at Houston's M.D. Anderson Cancer Center. While pursuing her nursing career, Kennedy met Russell "Rusty" Yates, an engineer at the National Aeronautical and Space Administration, and the two (both 25 years old) began dating. After a lengthy courtship, Kennedy married Yates in 1993. Taking her husband's surname, the 28-year-old Texan became Andrea Yates.

During the first 6 years of their marriage, Andrea Yates gave birth to four children: Noah in 1994, John in 1995, Paul in 1997, and Luke in 1999. Andrea left her nursing career in 1994 to care for the children. Although her husband was a professional with a good job with NASA, the couple lived first in a 38-foot mobile trailer and then in a 350-square-foot converted bus.

Four months after giving birth to Luke, in June 1999, Andrea attempted suicide, swallowing 40 to 50 prescription sleeping pills. She was hospitalized in a psychiatric unit for the first time, diagnosed with major depressive disorder (single episode, severe), and started on Zoloft, a common antidepressant medication. Efforts to engage her therapeutically were largely unsuccessful, and she was discharged after a week "because of insurance restrictions."[1] According to her hospital record, "the family contracted to keep a close eye on the patient."[2]

Less than a month later, in July 1999, Andrea was again hospitalized for psychiatric care. In the month after her discharge, Andrea lost 13 pounds, had little energy, was sleeping too much, and was having problems with memory and concentration. Rusty came home one day to find her holding a steak knife to her neck. He took the knife away from Andrea and, the next day, took her to the hospital, where was admitted with a diagnosis of postpartum depression with psychosis.

Often referred to as the "baby blues," postpartum depression is neither uncommon nor new. Symptoms, from sadness to depression to psychosis, occur frequently during the first year after giving birth and are generally short-lived. Fifty to 80 percent of all women experience some form of depressed mood after giving birth. Among those who do, about a sixth will suffer serious depressive symptoms such as insomnia, mood swings, anorexia, and suicidal ideation; approximately two in a thousand will become psychotic—in other words, lose touch with reality and demonstrate hallucinations, delusions, and/or thought disorder—as a result of postpartum depression.[3]

When psychotic symptoms occur in postpartum depression, they often focus on the child and have a violent or homicidal quality. As the American psychiatric Association's seminal *Diagnostic and Statistical Manual of Mental Disorders,* Fourth Edition (*DSM-IV*) indicates,

> When delusions are present, they often concern the newborn infant (e.g., the newborn is possessed by the devil, has special powers, or is destined for a terrible fate). In both the psychotic and non-psychotic presentations, there may be suicidal ideation [and] obsessional thoughts regarding violence to the child . . . Infanticide is most often associated with postpartum psychotic episodes that are characterized by command hallucinations to kill the infant or delusions that the infant is possessed, but it can also occur in severe postpartum mood episodes without such specific delusions or hallucinations.[4]

Andrea's second psychiatric hospitalization, though also short, resulted in a somewhat better understanding of her depression and its severity. For instance, Andrea told her attending psychiatrist why she had put the knife to her neck. Andrea said, "I had a fear I would hurt somebody . . . I thought it better to end my own life and prevent it . . . there was a voice, then an image of the knife . . . I had a vision in my mind, get a knife, get a knife . . . I had a vision of this person being stabbed . . . the aftereffects."[5] She added that she had initially experienced this violent vision when her first child was born.

After about 10 days of treatment with an antipsychotic medication, Haldol, Andrea's mental state improved significantly and she was discharged. But not before being warned of the risks of future pregnancies. Her psychiatrist told Andrea that giving birth again might well trigger another psychotic postpartum depression. That warning was likely based upon data cited in the *DSM-IV* indicating that "[o]nce a woman has had a postpartum episode with psychotic features, the risk of recurrence with each subsequent delivery is between 30% and 50%."[6] Though the warning to Andrea and Rusty was dire, the psychiatrist was not hopeful that it would be heeded. In her record, she wrote, "Apparently patient and husband plan to have as many babies as nature will allow! This will surely guarantee future psychotic depression."[7]

At Rusty's urging, Andrea decided to ignore that warning and within 8 months of her discharge she was again pregnant and had stopped taking Haldol. On November 30, 2000, Andrea and Rusty's fifth child, Mary, was born. The family had moved to a new and larger home and Andrea was homeschooling the children. Things were going reasonably well until the following March, 4 months after Mary's birth, when Andrea's father died and she began to decompensate. She started engaging in self-mutilation, refused to eat or drink, lost 5 pounds in less than a month, stopped feeding her baby, and read the Bible compulsively before falling into an almost catatonic state.

On March 31, 2001, Andrea was again hospitalized, this time until April 12, 2001. Hospital records indicate that she was minimally verbal if not mute, demonstrated psychomotor retardation, assumed a rigid, "almost catatonic" posture, and appeared to be responding to internal stimuli—in other words, hallucinations.[8] Although doctors certified Andrea for involuntary commitment to a nearby state hospital, they withdrew that certification when she agreed to remain hospitalized on a voluntary basis. By April 11, her mental state had improved substantially and she was requesting discharge. The next day she was discharged after agreeing to attend an outpatient partial hospitalization program. Andrea entered that program on April 13, 2001, with a diagnosis of postpartum depression and was discharged on April 18, 2001. At that time she was taking two antidepressant medications and a single antipsychotic.

Three weeks later, on May 4, 2001, Andrea was again virtually catatonic. Rusty returned home from work, found the bathtub filled with water for no apparent purpose, and was unable to get a response from Andrea. Again Andrea was hospitalized with a diagnostic impression of "severely depressed mood and semi-catatonic state."[9] Hospital staff believed that Andrea was selectively mute because although she would not speak with them, she was heard at times yelling and screaming in her room. After a week to 10 days in the hospital, Andrea's condition improved and she was again discharged to the partial hospitalization program.

After a week in the partial hospitalization program, on May 22, 2001, Andrea was discharged to the care of her family and psychiatrist. Over the next month Andrea had two visits with her psychiatrist. On June 4, 2001, the psychiatrist checked her medications and mental status and wrote the following note in her chart: "Patient seen and discussed with husband at length. Patient reports that she feels about the same as at the time of discharge. Husband says patient has been functioning at 65–70% of premorbid condition. No suicidal ideation at all. Patient denies any psychotic features, appears with masked facies [i.e., little facial expression] and akinesia [i.e., inability to initiate movement] so discussed tapering off of Haldol."[10]

Two weeks later, on June 18, 2001, Andrea again saw the psychiatrist. The doctor's notes of that visit indicate: "Patient seen with husband. Reports patient got better after discontinuing Haldol but in last 3–4 days seems to have declined some. They report her level of functioning has remained between 65–75%. Patient noted to be rather quiet—answered questions selectively. Denied any psychotic symptoms, suicidal ideation."[11]

Following that session on June 18, 2001, Andrea was given an appointment for a follow-up visit with the psychiatrist 8 days later. That appointment, however, was never kept because 2 days later, June 20, 2001, Andrea drowned all five of her children in the bathtub.

That morning, at around 9:00 A.M., shortly after Rusty left home for his engineering job at the Space Shuttle Program at NASA's Johnson Space Center, Andrea drew bath water to within 3 inches of the top of the tub and then, one by one, systematically drowned 3-year-old Paul, 2-year-old Luke, 5-year-old John, 6-month-old Mary, and 7-year-old Noah. Andrea then called 911 and spoke calmly but cryptically:

OPERATOR: What's your name?
Andrea Yates: Andrea Yates.
OPERATOR: What's the problem?
Andrea Yates: Um, I just need them to come.
OPERATOR: Is your husband there?
Andrea Yates: No.
OPERATOR: Well, what's the problem?
Andrea Yates: I need them to come.
OPERATOR: I need to know why they're coming, ma'am. Is he there standing next to you?
Andrea Yates: Pardon me.
OPERATOR: Are you having a disturbance? Are you ill? Or what?
Andrea Yates: Yes, I'm ill.
OPERATOR: Do you need an ambulance?
Andrea Yates: No, I need a police officer. Yeah, send an ambulance.
OPERATOR: What's the problem?
Andrea Yates: Um . . .
OPERATOR: Is someone burglarizing your house? I mean what is it?
Andrea Yates: [heavy breathing]
OPERATOR: What kind of medical problem do you have ma'am?

> *OPERATOR:* Hello?
> *Andrea Yates:* I just need a police officer.
> *OPERATOR:* Are you at [address], right?
> *Andrea Yates:* Yes.
> *OPERATOR:* Are you there alone?
> *Andrea Yates:* Yes.
> *OPERATOR:* Andrea Yates?
> *Andrea Yates:* Yes.
> *OPERATOR:* Is your husband there with you?
> *Andrea Yates:* No.
> *OPERATOR:* Okay, well why do you need the police ma'am?
> *Andrea Yates:* I just need them to be here.
> *OPERATOR:* For what?
> *Andrea Yates:* I just need them to come.
> *OPERATOR:* You sure you're alone?
> *Andrea Yates:* No, my sister's here.[12]

Once Andrea got off the phone with the 911 operator, she called Rusty at work and told him, "You need to come home," When Rusty asked, "Is anyone hurt?"[13] Andrea replied, "Yes, the children."[14] By the time Rusty made it home, the police had already arrived and discovered the bodies of his five children. Within hours, Andrea had given police a full, detailed confession:

> *Sgt. Mehl:* OK, an incident happened at your house this morning, right?
> *Andrea Yates:* Yes.
> . . .
> *Sgt. Mehl:* OK, and the incident we're about to discuss, um, resulted in the deaths of your five children, is that correct?
> *Andrea Yates:* Yes.
> . . .
> *Sgt. Mehl:* OK, and we also talked earlier, um, you've been treated for depression. Is that right?
> *Andrea Yates:* Yes.
> *Sgt. Mehl:* And who's your current doctor?
> *Andrea Yates:* Dr. Saeed.
> *Sgt. Mehl:* And the last time you saw him?
> *Andrea Yates:* Two, two days ago.
> *Sgt. Mehl:* OK, this morning, um, what time was it that you got out of bed this morning?

Andrea Yates: About 8:10.

Sgt. Mehl: OK, and who in your household was awake at that time?

Andrea Yates: Um, my husband, Mary, Luke and Paul.

Sgt. Mehl: OK, and what time does Rusty leave for work?

Andrea Yates: He left about nine.

Sgt. Mehl: And, by the time Rusty left, were all of your children awake at that time?

Andrea Yates: Yes.

. . .

Sgt. Mehl: Um, after Rusty left, you filled the bathtub with water, is that correct?

Andrea Yates: Yes.

. . .

Sgt. Mehl: How far did you fill it?

Andrea Yates: About three inches from the top.

Sgt. Mehl: About three inches from the top, um, after you drew the bath water, what was your intent? What were you about to do?

Andrea Yates: Drown the children.

Sgt. Mehl: OK. Why were you going to drown your children?

[15 seconds of silence]

Sgt. Mehl: Was it, was it in reference to, or was it because the children had done something?

Andrea Yates: No.

Sgt. Mehl: You were not mad at the children?

Andrea Yates: No.

Sgt. Mehl: OK, um, you had thought of this prior to this day?

Andrea Yates: Yes.

Sgt. Mehl: Um, how long have you been having thoughts about wanting, or not wanting to, but drowning your children?

Andrea Yates: Probably since I realized I have not been a good mother to them.

Sgt. Mehl: What makes you say that?

Andrea Yates: They weren't developing correctly.

Sgt. Mehl: Behavioral problems?

Andrea Yates: Yes.

Sgt. Mehl: Learning problems?

Andrea Yates: Yes.

Sgt. Mehl: So after you drew the bath water, what happened?

Andrea Yates: I put Paul in.

Sgt. Mehl: And how old is Paul?

Andrea Yates: Paul is 3.

Sgt. Mehl: OK, and when you put Paul in the bath water, was he face down or face up?

Andrea Yates: He was face down.

Sgt. Mehl: And he struggled with you?

Andrea Yates: Yes.

Sgt. Mehl: How long do you think that struggle happened?

Andrea Yates: A couple of minutes.

Sgt. Mehl: And you were able to forcibly hold him under the water?

Andrea Yates: Yes.

Sgt. Mehl: By the time you brought him out of the water, had he stopped struggling?

Andrea Yates: Yes.

Sgt. Mehl: There was no more movement?

Andrea Yates: No.

Sgt. Mehl: And, after you brought him out of the water, what did you do?

Andrea Yates: I laid him on the bed.

Sgt. Mehl: Face up or face down?

Andrea Yates: Face up.

Sgt. Mehl: Did you cover him?

Andrea Yates: Yes.

Sgt. Mehl: Did you cover his entire body?

Andrea Yates: Yes.

Sgt. Mehl: With what?

Andrea Yates: A sheet.

Sgt. Mehl: OK, so after you put Paul on the bed and covered him, then what happened?

Andrea Yates: I put Luke in.

Sgt. Mehl: OK, how old is Luke?

Andrea Yates: He's 2.

Sgt. Mehl: OK, and was he face down in the water or face up?

Andrea Yates: Face down.

Sgt. Mehl: Did he struggle?

Andrea Yates: Yes.

Sgt. Mehl: How long do you think that struggle lasted?

Andrea Yates: Just a couple minutes.

Sgt. Mehl: OK, and when you brought Luke out of the water, um, was he, any movement at all?

Andrea Yates: No.

Sgt. Mehl: What happened to Luke then?

Andrea Yates: I put him on the bed.

Sgt. Mehl: Um, did you cover him with the same sheet that you'd used to cover Paul?

Andrea Yates: Yes.

Sgt. Mehl: OK, so Paul and Luke are on the bed, then what happens?

Andrea Yates: I put John in.

Sgt. Mehl: OK, and how old is John.

Andrea Yates: John is 5.

Sgt. Mehl: OK. How did you get John to come into the bathroom?

Andrea Yates: I called him in.

Sgt. Mehl: OK, and, and he came in . . .

Andrea Yates: Yes.

Sgt. Mehl: Um, did you say anything to him?

Andrea Yates: I told him to get in the tub.

Sgt. Mehl: OK, and did he?

Andrea Yates: No.

Sgt. Mehl: Um, what did he do?

Andrea Yates: I put him in.

Sgt. Mehl: Did you pick him up, how? Under the arms?

Andrea Yates: Yes.

Sgt. Mehl: And did he go into the water face down or face up?

Andrea Yates: Face down.

Sgt. Mehl: OK. Did he struggle with you violently?

Andrea Yates: Yes.

Sgt. Mehl: Did that struggle last longer than with the younger children?

Andrea Yates: A little bit, yeah.

Sgt. Mehl: OK, but still you were able to hold John under the water?

Andrea Yates: Yes.

Sgt. Mehl: And eventually he stopped struggling?

Andrea Yates: Yes.

Sgt. Mehl: OK, when you brought John out of the water, was there any movement at all from him?

Andrea Yates: No.

Sgt. Mehl: What happened then?

Andrea Yates: I put him on the bed.

Sgt. Mehl: Did you then cover him along with Paul and Luke?

Andrea Yates: Yes.
Sgt. Mehl: OK, and then what happened?
Andrea Yates: I put Mary in.
Sgt. Mehl: Did you actually have to go out into the other room to get Mary?
Andrea Yates: No, she was in there already.
Sgt. Mehl: Was Mary in the bathroom with you when Paul, Luke and John all went in the water?
Andrea Yates: Yes.
Sgt. Mehl: OK, what was she doing?
Andrea Yates: She was crying.
Sgt. Mehl: OK, was she, was she sitting in a chair, one of those . . .
Andrea Yates: She was sitting down.
Sgt. Mehl: On the floor?
Andrea Yates: Um-hmm.
Sgt. Mehl: OK, um, so you picked Mary up?
Andrea Yates: Um-hmm.
Sgt. Mehl: She go into the water face down or face up?
Andrea Yates: Face down.
Sgt. Mehl: OK, she was able to struggle with you?
Andrea Yates: Yes.
Sgt. Mehl: Because she's only six months old, right?
Andrea Yates: Um-hmm.
Sgt. Mehl: But she struggled and how, how long do you think she was able to struggle for?
Andrea Yates: A couple of minutes.
Sgt. Mehl: OK, and after Mary had died, um, what did you do with her body?
Andrea Yates: I left it in there and called Noah in.
Sgt. Mehl: OK, did Noah come immediately?
Andrea Yates: Yes.
Sgt. Mehl: And, when Noah walked in the bathroom, did he see Mary in the tub?
Andrea Yates: Yes.
Sgt. Mehl: What did he say?
Andrea Yates: He said, 'What happened to Mary?'"
Sgt. Mehl: And what did you say?
Andrea Yates: I didn't say anything. I just put him in.
Sgt. Mehl: Did he try to run from you?
Andrea Yates: Yes.

Sgt. Mehl: Did he get out of the bathroom or were you able to catch him?
Andrea Yates: I got him.
Sgt. Mehl: OK, and Noah is 7, is that correct?
Andrea Yates: Yes.
Sgt. Mehl: Did Noah put up the biggest struggle of all?
Andrea Yates: Yes.
Sgt. Mehl: OK, did he go in the water face down or face up?
Andrea Yates: He was face down.
Sgt. Mehl: Um, when you were struggling with Noah, did you have to, did he try to flip over and come up for air at any time?
Andrea Yates: Yes.
Sgt. Mehl: Did he ever make it out of the water long enough to get a gasp of air or anything?
Andrea Yates: Yes.
Sgt. Mehl: How many times?
Andrea Yates: A couple times.
Sgt. Mehl: But you forced him back down into the water?
Andrea Yates: Yes.
Sgt. Mehl: How long do you think that struggle lasted?
Andrea Yates: Maybe three minutes.
Sgt. Mehl: OK, and after Noah was dead, when you brought him out of the water, was there any sign of life from him.
Andrea Yates: No.
Sgt. Mehl: What did you do with his body?
Andrea Yates: I left it there.
Sgt. Mehl: OK, so Mary and Noah were left in the bathtub?
Andrea Yates: I took Mary out.
Sgt. Mehl: After John, excuse me, after Noah was dead?
Andrea Yates: Yes.
Sgt. Mehl: OK, what did you do with Mary's body?
Andrea Yates: Put her on the bed.
Sgt. Mehl: Did you cover her?
Andrea Yates: Yes.
Sgt. Mehl: And you left Noah's body in the tub?
Andrea Yates: Yes.

. . .

Sgt. Mehl: OK, you had told me earlier that, that you'd been having these thoughts about hurting your children for up to two years. Is that, is that about right?

Andrea Yates: Yes.

Sgt. Mehl: OK, is there anything that happened two years ago that, that made you, that you believe led you to have these thoughts?

Andrea Yates: I realized that it was time to be punished.

Sgt. Mehl: And what do you need to be punished for?

Andrea Yates: For not being a good mother.

Sgt. Mehl: How did you see drowning your five children as a way to be punished? Did you want the criminal justice system to punish you or did you . . .

Andrea Yates: Yes.

Sgt. Mehl: OK, we were also talking earlier and there was one other time when you filled the tub with water and were going to do this and did not do it. Is that correct?

Andrea Yates: Yes.

Sgt. Mehl: How long ago was that?

Andrea Yates: It was two months ago.

Sgt. Mehl: OK, were all the children at home at that time?

Andrea Yates: Yes, Rusty was there too.

Sgt. Mehl: Rusty was there too? Do you think Rusty would have stopped you?

Andrea Yates: Yes.

Sgt. Mehl: So, you filled the tub with water that time. What is it within yourself that stopped you from, from doing it that time?

Andrea Yates: Just didn't do it that time.[15]

Based on her confession, Andrea was charged with multiple counts of murder. Given the nature of Andrea's crimes, the prosecutor may have felt he had no choice but to charge her with murder, despite her obvious mental illness. But Harris County, the Texas jurisdiction in which Andrea's crimes were committed, had long been known as the "death penalty capital of the world."[16] As one recent candidate for chief prosecutor there recently observed, "If Harris County were a state, it would rank third behind Texas and Virginia in the numbers of persons being sent to death row."[17] Thus, many were not surprised when the prosecutor decided not only to charge Andrea with murder but also to seek the death penalty in her case.

The prosecutorial decision to ask a jury to put Andrea Yates to death for the killings of her children may have been a function of the retributive political climate of Harris County and its history of sending so many killers to death row. But charging Andrea with capital murder may also have had a more practical motive. By making the death penalty an option for Andrea, the prosecutor assured that her jury would be "death qualified." That is, all potential jurors would be quizzed regarding their attitudes about capital punishment and would be excluded from serving on the jury if they had negative views of the death penalty so strong as to render them "unable to faithfully and impartially apply the law"—in other words, impose a death sentence if warranted.[18] Studies of "death qualified" juries have shown them to be more conviction-prone and less likely to adhere to criminal justice principles such as the presumption of innocence than juries that have not been "death qualified."[19]

Given her history of mental illness and faced with her own confession to charges that could result in her execution (or, at best, her imprisonment for life without parole) and a jury that would in all likelihood be predisposed to convict her, Andrea Yates had little choice but to plead not guilty by reason of insanity. But legally, to be tried at all, Andrea would first have to be found competent to stand trial. A determination that she was permanently incompetent to stand trial would take not only the death sentence but any prison sentence off the table. Such a determination would have much the same effect as an insanity acquittal: an indefinite (but in reality most probably a lifetime) commitment to a state psychiatric facility.

Seeking to avoid any possibility of capital punishment or even a life prison sentence, Andrea's lawyer's initially argued that she was not competent to stand trial—in other words, that as a result of her mental illness she did not have a rational or factual understanding of the charges against her and/or was unable to assist counsel in her own defense. Andrea's attorneys had good reason to anticipate that she would be unable to assist rationally in mounting a defense because she wanted to be found guilty and sentenced to die, believing delusionally that by being convicted and receiving the death penalty she would be able to kill Satan.

Under Texas law, a jury rather than a judge makes the competency determination. Thus, a jury trial was held in the matter approximately 4 months after the killings. Andrea's attorneys had the burden of proving that she was not competent because the law presumes that all defendants are competent until proven otherwise.

Expert witnesses for both sides agreed that Andrea had earlier been psychotic but that her condition had improved with treatment since the killings. Not surprisingly, however, those mental health professionals testifying for the defense found her competent to stand trial whereas those testifying for the prosecution disagreed.

Dr. Gerald Harris, a psychologist and professor at the University of Houston, testified that during the first two of four interviews with Andrea, "She told me she was talking to Satan and Satan was talking to her. She said she'd seen images of Satan on the walls."[20] Harris testified further that although Andrea's condition had improved by the time of the competency trial, he did not believe that she would be competent for at least another month: "She can't remember well and she can't think very well. I think it makes it hard to work with her attorney properly."[21] "When I asked her what this was about today, she wasn't able to tell me very well," Harris testified.[22] "About five minutes later, she'd forgotten what I told her."[23]

In a highly unusual move, one of Andrea's attorneys testified that he was having difficulties working with her because of limitations imposed by her mental condition.

Testifying for the prosecution, psychologist Dr. Steven Rubenzer told the jury that Andrea's psychosis was in remission and that "[s]he is competent to stand trial."[24] But Rubenzer, who also told the competency jury that Andrea had decided to kill her children the night before she did so, agreed with the defense experts that the stress of standing trial could cause Andrea's mental condition to deteriorate. On cross-examination, Rubenzer even conceded that with regard to competency to stand trial Andrea was "not quite there."[25]

In closing arguments to the jury, the prosecutor accused defense counsel of trying to confuse the issues. "The issue is whether she is presently competent, not whether she has a mental disease," he argued.[26] "She has to have a trial, and she's competent to have that trial today."[27] Andrea's lead defense attorney appeared to acknowledge that at some point Andrea would be competent to stand trial. "What's the rush?" he asked the jury.[28] "Give her the benefit of the ability to be cognizant of what she did [and] to be able to defend herself in a proper manner."[29]

The jury of 11 women and 1 man initially voted 8 to 4 in favor of finding Yates incompetent. Over the course of several more hours of deliberation, however, jurors' opinions shifted and Yates was found competent to stand trial. No appeal was allowed under Texas law, so the competency finding, however dubious, set the stage for another jury to weigh Andrea's claim of insanity against the prosecution's allegations that she killed her children in cold blood, knowing fully what she was doing.

At trial, Andrea bore the burden of proving by a preponderance of the evidence (i.e., more likely than not) that "at the time of the conduct charged . . . as a result of severe mental disease or defect, [she] did not know that this conduct was wrong."[30] This modern-day version of the archaic *M'Naghten* test of insanity is difficult for any defendant to meet, but undoubtedly even more so for a defendant such as Andrea Yates.

Not only would Andrea be tried by a "death qualified" jury that in all likelihood would be more prone to convict her than would an ordinary criminal jury, but the horrific nature of her crimes would surely work against her, despite her obvious history of mental illness. But beyond those disadvantages, the Andrea Yates the jury saw would not be the psychotic woman who killed her children. In order to restore Andrea to competence, and thus enable her to stand trial, psychiatrists had treated her for months with powerful antipsychotic medications. Thus, at the time of trial she was stable and, in most respects, appeared normal. Moreover, under Texas law, the jurors could not be told the consequences of an insanity conviction—that Andrea would be committed indefinitely to a state mental hospital—and thus might well believe that a verdict of insanity would free her. Finally, Andrea herself was an impediment to a successful insanity plea; she did not believe that she was mentally ill, opposed her attorney's efforts to portray her as insane, and felt that she deserved to die for her crimes.

Despite these disadvantages, however, Andrea had a compelling insanity defense. Her detailed psychiatric history ruled out any question of faking or malingering. There was no question that she was psychotic when she drowned her children, driven by delusions that Satan was speaking to her and that killing her children was the only way to save them from Hell. Also, many psychological and psychiatric experts had examined her and were willing to testify that she met the legal criteria for insanity, even under the very strict version of the *M'Naghten* rule applied in Texas.

A jury of eight women and four men was selected in January 2002, and the trial commenced on February 18. The prosecution's case-in-chief, which lasted a mere 3 days, was simple but designed to be persuasive, if not overtly prejudicial. The jury heard Andrea's 911 call, heard the testimony of the first officers to respond to the scene, heard Andrea's confession, learned of the autopsy findings, and were shown photographs and home videos of the children. The prosecutor even managed to convince the judge to allow the jury to see the children's pajamas on the theory that showed how small the children had been by comparison to Andrea.

The defense presentation was much longer, more complex, and driven largely by the testimony of psychiatric experts: nine psychiatrists and two psychologists. Five of the psychiatrists and one of the psychologists had treated Andrea on or immediately after the day of the killings.

Four of these psychiatrists and the psychologist testified that at the time she killed her children, Andrea either did not know wrong from right or believed that her homicidal acts were right. The fifth of these psychiatrists testified that she did not determine whether Andrea's knew wrong from right, but that Andrea had told her that drowning the children was the right thing to do. That psychiatrist, who worked for the prison system and treated Andrea while she was awaiting trial, testified that "of all the patients I've treated for major depression with psychotic features, she was one of the sickest."[31]

The key expert witness for the defense was Dr. Phillip Resnick, an internationally renowned forensic psychiatrist, professor of psychiatry and director of the Division of Forensic Psychiatry at Case Western Reserve University School of Medicine in Cleveland, lecturer in law and psychiatry at Case Western's School of Law, and probably the world's leading authority on mothers who kill their children.

According to Resnick, Andrea killed her children out of an altruistic, albeit irrational, motive. "There is no rational explanation to drown five children as a devoted mother unless you believe it's in their interest," he testified.[32] Andrea, Resnick told the jury, suffered from religious delusions and believed that she was saving her children from Satan by killing them: "Mrs. Yates had a choice to make: to allow her children to end up burning in hell for eternity or to take their lives on earth ... She would give up her life on earth ... and her afterlife for the purpose of eliminating Satan and protecting her children from the fate of eternal damnation."[33] Resnick also expressed the opinion that Yates laid her children on the bed and covered them out of respect, rather than in an effort to conceal the bodies.

The implication of Resnick's testimony was that even though Yates knew killing her children was *legally* wrong, she believed it was *morally* right because of her religious delusions. Indeed, on cross-examination, when asked by the prosecutor, "But she knew it was legally wrong?" Resnick replied, "That's correct ... I agree."[34] But, Resnick explained, Andrea believed she had no choice: "Because of her dilemma, what she perceived as right was to take her children's life on Earth to prevent them from eternal damnation."[35] "She did what she thought was right in the world she perceived through her psychotic eyes at the time," the psychiatrist added.[36]

Not surprisingly, of all the mental health experts who testified at Andrea's trial, only the one called by the prosecution concluded that when she drowned her children, the defendant knew that what she was doing was wrong. Dr. Park Dietz—one of America's most well-known forensic psychiatrists, who has worked and/or testified for the prosecution in countless high-profile cases including those of presidential assassin John W. Hinckley, Jr., serial killers Jeffrey Dahmer, Arthur Shawcross, Joel Rifkin, and serial bomber Theodore Kaczynski, to name but a few—never treated Andrea Yates. Indeed, by his own testimony, he had not treated patients in 2 decades. Hired by the prosecutors, Dietz examined Andrea and testified at her trial.

Dietz agreed with the defense experts that at the time Andrea killed her children, she was suffering symptoms of depression and psychosis. However, based on the legal standard for insanity—Andrea's understanding of the wrongfulness of her actions—Dietz testified, "My . . . opinion with reasonable medical certainty is that at the time of the drowning of each of the children, Mrs. Yates knew that her actions were wrong in the eyes of the law . . . in the eyes of society . . . in the eyes of God . . . Mrs. Yates may have believed the killings were in the best interest of the children and that the ends—saving the children—justified the means, which was to wrongly and illegally kill them."[37]

In support of his opinion, Dietz offered several examples of Yates's thinking and behavior he felt indicated that that she knew her homicidal actions were wrong. The first example offered by the psychiatrist was that Yates attributed her actions to Satan. As Dietz testified, "Mrs. Yates indicates that at that time before the homicide she had the idea of killing her children and she attributed the origin of that idea to Satan. So, of course, the idea comes from her mind, but she's mistakenly thinking Satan put it there. The fact that she regards it as coming from Satan is the first indication of her knowing that this is wrong. Because she recognizes even the idea of killing your children is an evil idea that comes from Satan. She doesn't think this is a good idea that comes from God."[38] Another example of Andrea's thinking and behavior that Dietz used to support his opinion was Andrea's concealing her homicidal thoughts from others because she knew they were wrong and that others would try to stop her.

On cross-examination, defense counsel raised the fact that Dietz had extremely limited experience dealing with postpartum depression and psychosis. In response to a question from Andrea's lead counsel, Dietz admitted, "I'm not sure that I have treated one but I have evaluated one."[39] Defense counsel also quizzed Dietz about his role in the production of the popular television series *Law & Order*.

When Dietz acknowledged being a consultant for the series, he was asked if any of the *Law & Order* shows dealt with postpartum depression. Dietz replied, "As a matter of fact, there was a show of a woman with postpartum depression who drowned her children in the bathtub and was found insane, and it was aired shortly before this crime occurred."[40]

Following Dietz's testimony, the defense recalled one of its expert witnesses, forensic psychiatrist Dr. Lucy Puryear, to rebut Dietz's testimony. During the cross-examination of Puryear, the prosecutor pressed her on the theory that Andrea may have gotten the idea to drown her children and claim insanity from the episode of *Law & Order* Dietz had mentioned during his testimony:

> Q. You know she watched "Law & Order" a lot; right?
>
> A. I didn't know. No.
>
> Q. Did you know that in the weeks before June 20th, there was a "Law & Order" episode where a woman killed her children by drowning them in a bathtub, was defended on the basis of whether she was sane or insane under the law, and the diagnosis was postpartum depression and in the program the person was found insane, not guilty by reason of insanity? Did you know that?
>
> A. No.
>
> Q. If you had known that and had known that Andrea Yates was subject to these delusions, not that she was the subject of a delusion of reference, but that she regularly watched "Law & Order" and may have seen that episode, would you have changed the way you went about interviewing her, would you have interviewed whether she got the idea somehow she could do this and not suffer hell or prison?
>
> A. I certainly wouldn't have asked her that question. No.
>
> Q. Would you have—you didn't have to ask her that question, but you could have explored that?
>
> A. If I had known she watched that show, I would have asked her about it, yes.[41]

Dietz's testimony regarding the *Law & Order* episode was also noted by both attorneys in their closing arguments to the jury in the guilt–innocence phase of Andrea's trial. Andrea's attorney alluded to it briefly, telling the jurors, "Or maybe even we heard some evidence that she saw some show on TV and knew she could drown her children and get away with it."[42] The prosecutor was much more direct, attempting to link the episode to Andrea's motive in killing her children: "She gets very depressed and goes into Devereux. And at times she says these thoughts came to her during that month. These thoughts came to her, and she watches 'Law & Order' regularly, she sees this program. There is a way out. She tells that to Dr. Dietz. A way out."[43]

Following these closing arguments, jurors, who had heard more than 3 weeks of testimony, took just 3 1/2 hours of deliberation to find Andrea guilty of capital murder.

On the same day the guilty verdict was rendered, Andrea's defense attorney learned that *Law & Order* had never aired an episode in which a mother drowned her children and claimed insanity. The show's director confirmed that an episode like the one Dietz described from the witness stand had never been written, produced, or televised. When Dietz learned that this portion of his testimony had been false, he wrote to prosecutors and explained that he had been mistaken and had confused the episode he described with infanticide cases featured in other episodes of *Law & Order*.

Andrea's attorneys argued that the false testimony by the prosecution's expert misled jurors into thinking that she had planned the drownings by watching a television show. The false testimony, they urged, was grounds for a mistrial. Although the judge denied the motion for a mistrial, later, during the penalty phase of the trial, she informed jurors that they had heard incorrect testimony from Dietz.

For whatever reason or reasons, the jury took little time in rejecting the death penalty and sentencing Andrea instead to life in prison. When later interviewed, jurors indicated that they had been persuaded by Dietz's coherent and detailed account of Yates's motives in drowning her children. Given the apparent weight the jury accorded Dietz's testimony, especially because it contradicted the testimony of the many psychiatric experts who testified for the defense, the defense appealed the jury's verdict. Among the many grounds they cited in the appeal was a violation of Andrea's due process rights because the prosecution had relied on "false or perjured testimony."[44]

Andrea's attorneys argued that Dietz's false testimony about the *Law & Order* episode provided critical support for the prosecution's theory that Yates knew her actions were wrong, that her crime was premeditated, and that she had relied upon a television program to deceptively create a defense of insanity.

Prosecutors argued that "there [was] no reasonable likelihood" that the testimony "could have affected the judgment of the jury."[45]

The appeals court disagreed and granted Andrea a new trial, holding that

> [f]ive mental health experts testified that appellant did not know right from wrong or that she thought what she did was right. Dr. Dietz was the only mental health expert who testified that appellant knew right from wrong. Therefore, his testimony was critical to establish the State's case. Although the record does not show that Dr. Dietz intentionally lied in his testimony, his false testimony undoubtedly gave greater weight to his opinion. On the other hand, had the jury known prior to their deliberations in the guilt-innocence phase of the trial, that Dr. Dietz's testimony

regarding the "Law & Order" episode was false, the jury would likely have considered him, the State's only mental health expert, to be less credible.

We conclude that there is a reasonable likelihood that Dr. Dietz's false testimony could have affected the judgment of the jury. We further conclude that Dr. Dietz's false testimony affected the substantial rights of appellant. Therefore, the trial court abused its discretion in denying appellant's motion for mistrial.[46]

Although the prosecutors had the discretion to accept an insanity judgment that would, in all likelihood, have resulted in a lifelong commitment to a state mental hospital for Andrea, they chose instead to try her again, hoping for at least another verdict of guilty and another sentence of life in prison. Because prosecutors had unsuccessfully pressed for a death sentence in her first trial, Andrea could not be tried for capital murder in her second trial. As a result, she was tried by a jury that was not "death qualified."

After hearing almost the same evidence that was heard by the first jury—except, of course, Dietz's false testimony—Andrea's second jury found her not guilty by reason of insanity. Subsequently she was committed to a secure state psychiatric facility, where she will remain under state custody and in treatment unless a court orders otherwise, quite likely for the rest of her life.

EPILOGUE

The 10 homicide cases described in this volume were all high-profile, notorious, and controversial. Yet, taken together they offer general insights into the way the insanity defense is used today.

First, as these 10 cases illustrate, contrary to public opinion, the insanity defense is rarely used and rarely successful when it is used. In only 2 of these cases—Torsney and Yates—did the defense succeed, and in 1 of those cases it took two trials before the defendant was finally acquitted by reason of insanity.

Second, as these cases also demonstrate, the insanity defense is often pled because the defendant really has no other defense. In a sense, the insanity defense is to criminal trials what the "Hail Mary" pass is to football. In all 10 of these cases, there was no question that the killings had been committed by the defendant. In virtually all of these cases, defense attorneys had little if any choice but to raise insanity as a defense for two reasons. First, the nature of the crimes raised serious doubts about the mental health of the defendants. Second, and perhaps more important, the evidence left no other viable alternative. Faced with the overwhelming probability of conviction followed by life imprisonment (or perhaps capital punishment) versus a remotely possible finding of insanity that would exonerate the defendant but probably result in a lifelong commitment to a mental hospital, these defendants—except for David Berkowitz—all made the calculated and rational decision to plead insanity and "roll the dice."

Third, these cases vividly illustrate what others have observed about the insanity defense for years. Often the facts of the case are so gruesome and unsympathetic to the defendant that they, rather than the defendant's mental illness, determine the outcome. It is hard to imagine, for example, that any jury anywhere would have found John Wayne Gacy, Arthur Shawcross, Andrew Goldstein, or Eric Clark not guilty by reason of insanity. In the cases of serial killers Gacy and Shawcross, there was certainly doubt as to whether they were even mentally ill, much less insane. But in Goldstein's case and that of Clark, there was abundant credible evidence, backed by a long-standing history of mental illness, diagnosis, and treatment, to support a finding of insanity. Still a jury found Goldstein guilty of murder for shoving a totally innocent, promising young woman to an instant and horrible death in front of a subway train for no apparent reason, whereas another convicted Clark in the utterly senseless murder of a uniformed police officer.

Fourth, as a number of these cases illustrate, psychologists and psychiatrists often see psychopathology where others would not, thereby making it possible for some rather dubious cases of alleged insanity to get before a jury. Jack Ruby and Robert Torsney are the most obvious examples considered here. Neither man had any history of mental illness prior to killing, and both appear to have been defended largely on the basis of extremely rare and, in their cases, probably nonexistent brain disorders. John Wayne Gacy had some limited history of psychiatric diagnosis before killing but had never been treated for any major mental disorder and appears, prior to the killings, to have been regarded as a nonpsychotic, personality disordered, sexual psychopath. Dr. Richard Rogers, who examined Gacy shortly before trial, found him to be an obsessive-compulsive personality with hypomanic features and evidence of sexual sadism, who tried to exaggerate his mental illness. Asked how—given the facts of the case—so many of his renowned mental health colleagues could have erroneously diagnosed Gacy as schizophrenic, Rogers theorized, charitably but probably correctly, that many psychologists and psychiatrists view all patients, including those seen in a forensic setting, through the lens of psychopathology.[1] Looked at through this professionally distorted lens, Rogers postulated, Gacy might well have appeared sicker than he was.[2]

Fifth, as these 10 cases all clearly show, for better or worse, insanity trials are almost always dominated by mental health experts, many of whom offer testimony that is clinically, legally, or factually suspect. The testimony of the defense experts who regarded Jack Ruby and Robert Torsney as suffering from a rare form of psychomotor epilepsy represent probably the clearest examples from among these cases. But there are others as well.

Consider, for example, the psychiatrist who, by her own admission in court, failed to use accepted professional standards when she hypnotized Arthur Shawcross and who accepted, without corroboration, Shawcross's implausible claims about being traumatized as a child and in Vietnam. Consider also the psychiatrist who, despite mountains of evidence that Andrew Goldstein had suffered from schizophrenia for years before killing, told the jury that he was a malingering antisocial personality, and admitted only on cross-examination that Goldstein was "probably schizophrenic" and not "making up his mental illness."[3] Recall that this is the same psychiatrist whose testimony led an appellate court to overturn Goldstein's murder conviction.

Finally, consider the expert witness who—in the case of Andrea Yates, a fan of the television program *Law and Order*—testified that "As a matter of fact, there was a [*Law & Order* episode] show of a woman with postpartum depression who drowned her children in the bathtub and was found insane, and it was aired shortly before this crime occurred."[4] That testimony, which was false, eventually resulted in a new trial for Yates, at which she was found not guilty by reason of insanity.

Sixth, it is not only the psychological and psychiatric experts, but also the attorneys, who ignore and/or distort evidence in insanity cases—often to the detriment of the defendant and/or society. For example, as the jurors made clear in the case of Jack Ruby, had defense attorney Melvin Belli not been so personally invested in proving Ruby insane, but instead had essentially thrown Ruby on the mercy of the court, Ruby would almost assuredly have escaped a capital murder conviction. Similarly, on the opposite side of the courtroom, the prosecutor in the Eric Smith case may have done a disservice to his client, the public, by failing to stipulate to the teenage boy's claim of insanity. If, as he claimed, the district attorney had been interested in making sure that Smith remained locked up for life as a means of protecting the public, it is clear that he would have done better not to oppose the insanity defense, thereby sending the youthful killer to a secure mental hospital from which he would likely never have been released. Ironically, by insisting that Smith was not insane, the prosecutor "won the battle" but may have "lost the war." Smith has been a model prison inmate, and there is good reason to believe that one day, perhaps sooner than later, he will be paroled.

Seventh, as a number of these cases suggest, even some judges appear to have particular difficulty dealing with insanity pleas. Recall, for example, the first judge in the David Berkowitz case, who apparently tried to get around the rule barring jurors from knowing the consequences of a verdict of insanity. Before he was removed from the case, that jurist told a newspaper reporter that in Berkowitz's case, speaking of the jury, "They'll know."[5] When asked how, the judge replied, "You're going to tell them."[6]

Consider also the judge in Scott Panetti's farcical capital murder trial who was required by law to allow the accused to serve as his own attorney. That jurist appeared to make every effort to exacerbate the problem of self-representation by holding the grossly mentally ill defendant to the same evidentiary standards as a qualified attorney, thereby excluding a good deal of relevant evidence that an attorney would probably have been able to get before the jury. Consider, too, the federal judge who later allowed a psychiatrist to testify against Panetti when the evidence suggested that, although she did not recall it, she had once examined Panetti at the behest of his defense attorney and thus what she learned from Panetti was privileged. Finally, recall that even after the prosecution's psychiatric expert admitted that a portion of his testimony against Andrea Yates had been false, the trial judge refused to grant a mistrial, a judgment a Texas appeals court later held was a clear abuse of discretion.

Eighth, these cases illustrate the problems that arise when lay jurors, unfamiliar with and unschooled in the discourse of psychology and psychiatry, are required, as they are in all insanity trials, to make sense of often highly technical, theoretical, and jargon-laden expert testimony. Consider, for instance, the expert testimony jurors in many of these 10 cases had to attempt to decipher: the testimony regarding the neuropsychology of seizure disorders in the Ruby, Torsney, and Shawcross cases; the psychoanalytically based testimony in the Gacy case, filled with Freudian concepts such as "representations of a block due to fear of castration which arose out of unresolved Oedipal feelings,"[7] "symbol for the penis which helps the individual deny the expectation of castration,"[8] "identifying with the aggressor,"[9] and "hostile threats and frightening figures that pervade his unconscious"[10]; and, of course, the experts' lengthy moral disquisitions about God, Satan, Hell, eternal damnation, and *Law and Order* in the Yates case.

How much of this testimony was intelligible and meaningful to the lay jurors who heard it? What, if any, impact did it have on the jury's verdict? If the jurors in the Ruby case are to be believed, even those who understood the expert testimony there gave it little credit. It requires little or no stretch to imagine that the jurors in many, perhaps most, of the other cases described here felt much the same way about the expert testimony they heard.

Of course, even when expert testimony on insanity is competent, truthful, and intelligible, jurors are still required to consider that testimony, as well as the other evidence, in light of an insanity standard that, though couched in legal jargon, many of them will see as inviting if not requiring an essentially moral rather than legal decision—in other words, whether the defendant's criminal conduct is to be regarded as blameworthy or excusable.

Moreover, as if that decision were not difficult enough, jurors are asked to render it while deliberately kept in the dark and left to their own imaginations as to the consequences of their decision. Recall, for example, what one of the jurors in the Jack Ruby case said about the defense attorney and his psychological and psychiatric experts: "[T]hey were saying, well, he did this and so what he needs to do is go to a shrink for a few months, and put him back out in society . . . [W]e didn't have much choice. It was either let him go to the shrink for a little bit, and turn him loose, or give him the death penalty."[11] This sort of false belief on the part of many jurors in insanity cases, of course, was the problem the recused judge in the David Berkowitz case tried to rectify extrajudicially by suggesting that a newspaper reporter inform potential jurors that the "Son of Sam" was "virtually certain to spend most, if not all of his life in a maximum-security mental institution—whether he was found guilty of murder or innocent by reason of insanity."[12]

Although defendants, attorneys, judges, experts, jurors, the media, and the general public continue to share misconceptions and biases regarding the legal concept of insanity, especially in homicide cases in which the stakes are often highest, the insanity defense seems likely to remain a fixture in American jurisprudence, at least in the foreseeable future. With that in mind, it is hoped that this volume will play at least some part in encouraging understanding of the insanity defense, the realities of its implementation, its limitations, and its need for further reform.

NOTES

PREFACE

1. Paul Heimel, *No Longer Any Danger: The Fitzsimmons Story* (Coudersport, PA: Enterprise Publishing, 1981), 14.
2. Ibid., 15.
3. Ibid.
4. Judgment, People v. Fitzsimmons, New York Supreme Court, Erie County, February 16, 1970, 1.
5. Ibid., 2.
6. Heimel, No Longer Any Danger, 20.
7. Ibid.
8. Ibid., 23.
9. Ibid.
10. Ibid., 33.
11. Ibid., 62–63.
12. Ibid., 94.
13. Gene Warner, "Insanity Plea on Life Support," Buffalo News, February 29, 2000, 1A.
14. Ibid.

INTRODUCTION

1. Michael Perlin, *Law and Mental Disability* (Charlottesville: Michie, 1994), 562.
2. Ibid., 563.
3. *M'Naghten's Case,* 8 Eng. Rep. 718, 722 (1843).
4. *Shirley v. State,* 149 Ga. App. 194, 202 (1979).
5. See, e.g., *Durham v. United States,* 214 F.2d. 862 (D.C. Cir. 1954).
6. American Law Institute, *Model Penal Code* (New York: American Law Institute, 1955), § 4.01(1).
7. *Ibid.*
8. 18 U.S.C. § 17.
9. *Ibid.* (emphasis added).
10. Federal Rule of Evidence 704(b).
11. Perlin, *Law and Mental Disability,* 574.
12. *Clark v. Arizona,* 126 S. Ct. 2709, 2720 (2006).

13. See, e.g., *Government of the Virgin Islands v. Fredericks*, 578 F.2d 927, 932 (3d Cir. 1978); *Wade v. United States*, 426 F.2d 64, 71 (9th Cir. 1970).
14. American Psychiatric Association, *Diagnostic and Statistical Manual of Mental Disorders, Fourth Edition* (Washington, D.C.: American Psychiatric Association, 1994).
15. Eric Silver, Carmen Cirincione, and Henry Steadman, "Demythologizing Inaccurate Perceptions of the Insanity Defense," *Law and Human Behavior* 18, no. 1 (1994), 65.
16. Eric Silver, "Punishment or Treatment?: Comparing the Lengths of Confinement of Successful and Unsuccessful Insanity Defendants," *Law and Human Behavior* (1995), 385–386.

CHAPTER 1, JACOB RUBENSTEIN

1. Warren Commission, *Report of the President's Commission on the Assassination of President Kennedy* (Appendix 16: A Biography of Jack Ruby), 781.
2. Ibid., 782.
3. Ibid.
4. Ibid.
5. Ibid.
6. Ibid., 783.
7. Ibid.
8. Ibid., 786.
9. Ibid.
10. Ibid., 799.
11. John Kaplan and Jon R. Waltz, *The Trial of Jack Ruby* (New York: MacMillan, 1965), 3.
12. Ibid., 17.
13. Melvin Belli, *Dallas Justice: The Real Story of Jack Ruby and His Trial* (New York: David McKay Company, 1964), 56.
14. Ibid.
15. Ibid., 66–67.
16. Ibid., 70.
17. Kaplan and Waltz, *The Trial of Jack Ruby*, 231.
18. Belli, *Dallas Justice*, 56.
19. Ibid., 57–58.
20. Ibid., 56.
21. Kaplan and Waltz, *The Trial of Jack Ruby*, 146.
22. Ibid., 173.
23. Ibid., 196.
24. Ibid., 197.
25. Ibid., 199.
26. Ibid.
27. Ibid., 204.
28. Ibid.

29. *Ibid.*, 213.
30. *Ibid.*, 212.
31. *Ibid.*, 214.
32. *Ibid.*
33. *Ibid.*, 215.
34. *Ibid.*, 219.
35. *Ibid.*, 220.
36. *Ibid.*, 223.
37. *Ibid.*, 226.
38. *Ibid.*, 227.
39. *Ibid.*, 236.
40. *Ibid.*, 237.
41. *Ibid.*
42. *Ibid.*, 239.
43. *Ibid.*, 239–240.
44. *Ibid.*, 240.
45. *Ibid.*
46. *Ibid.*, 249.
47. *Ibid.*, 250.
48. *Ibid.*, 251.
49. *Ibid.*, 253–254.
50. *Ibid.*, 254–255.
51. *Ibid.*, 255–256.
52. Belli, *Dallas Justice*, 59.
53. Kaplan and Waltz, *The Trial of Jack Ruby*, 256.
54. *Ibid.*, 268.
55. *Ibid.*
56. *Ibid.*, 270.
57. *Ibid.*, 285.
58. *Ibid.*
59. *Ibid.*, 295.
60. *Ibid.*, 300.
61. *Ibid.*, 302.
62. *Ibid.*, 340.
63. Belli, *Dallas Justice*, 56.
64. John Mark Dempsey, *The Jack Ruby Trial Revisited: The Diary of Jury Foreman Max Causey* (Denton TX: University of North Texas Press, 2000), 82–83.
65. *Ibid.*, 101–102.
66. *Ibid.*, 139.
67. *Ibid.*, 139.
68. *Ibid.*, 141.
69. *Ibid.*, 157.
70. *Ibid.*, 158–159.
71. *Ibid.*, 172.
72. *Ibid.*, 172–173.

73. *Ibid.*, 183.
74. *Ibid.*, 186.

CHAPTER 2, ROBERT TORSNEY

1. Richard Pollack, "The Epilepsy Defense," *The Atlantic,* May 1984, 20.
2. *Ibid.*
3. Psychiatric report of Dr. Daniel W. Schwartz re Robert Torsney (October 1977).
4. Psychological report of Dr. Joy B. Roy re Robert Torsney (September 1977).
5. Tom Goldstein, "The Problems of Insanity as Defense," *New York Times,* December 2, 1977, B4.
6. Jennifer Dunning, "Police Officer Tells How He Shot Youth," *New York Times,* November 19, 1977, 35.
7. William Winslade and Judith Wilson Ross, *The Insanity Plea* (New York: Charles Scribner's Sons, 1983), 135.
8. *Ibid.*
9. Psychiatric report of Dr. Daniel W. Schwartz re Robert Torsney (October 1977).
10. *Ibid.*
11. *Ibid.*
12. Thomas A. Johnson, "Guardians Association Asks Blacks in P.B.A. to Quit Union in Protest," *New York Times,* December 9, 1976, 41.
13. *Ibid.*
14. Selwyn Raab, "Officer Indicted on Murder Charge," *New York Times,* December 1, 1976, 49.
15. *Ibid.*
16. Psychiatric report of Dr. Daniel W. Schwartz re Robert Torsney (October 1977).
17. *Ibid.*
18. *Ibid.*
19. Psychological report of Dr. Joy B. Roy re Robert Torsney (September 1977).
20. *Ibid.*
21. Psychodiagnostic Report of Dr. Florence Schumer re Robert Torsney (October 1977).
22. *Ibid.*
23. *Ibid.*
24. *In the Matter of Robert Torsney,* 47 N.Y. 2d 667, 691 (1979).
25. Jennifer Dunning, "Police Officer Tells How He Shot Youth," *New York Times,* November 19, 1977, 35.
26. Jennifer Dunning, "Two Officers Testify Colleague Killed Boy Without Plain Cause," *New York Times,* November 15, 1977, 45.
27. Winslade and Ross, *The Insanity Plea,* 138.
28. *Ibid.*, 141.
29. Jennifer Dunning, "Psychiatrist Terms Officer Insane at Time He Killed Brooklyn Youth," *New York Times,* November 22, 1977, 28.
30. Jennifer Dunning, "Psychiatrist Says Torsney Shot Boy in a State of Panic," *New York Times,* November 24, 1977, 28.
31. Winslade and Ross, *The Insanity Plea,* 141.

32. Pollack, "The Epilepsy Defense," 20.
33. Jennifer Dunning, "Officer Torsney Acquitted as Jury Rules Him Insane in Killing of Boy," *New York Times,* December 1, 1977, 1.
34. Report of Psychological Evaluation by Dr. Alan S. Halpern re Robert Torsney (December 1977).
35. Ibid.
36. *In the Matter of Robert Torsney,* 47 N.Y. 2d 667, 678 (1979).
37. Ibid.
38. *In the Matter of Robert Torsney,* 66 A.D. 2d 281, 292 (New York, 1979).
39. *In the Matter of Robert Torsney,* 47 N.Y. 2d 667, 679 (1979).
40. Ibid.
41. Ibid., 680.
42. Ibid.
43. Ibid.
44. *In the Matter of Robert Torsney,* unpublished decision of Justice Leonard E. Yoswein, New York Supreme Court, Kings County, December 20, 1978.
45. *In the Matter of Robert Torsney,* 66 A.D. 2d 281, 295 (New York, 1979).
46. Ibid., 292.
47. Ibid., 247–248.
48. *In the Matter of Robert Torsney,* 47 N.Y. 2d 667, 682–683 (1979).
49. Ibid., 691.
50. Ibid.
51. Ibid.
52. Ibid., 693.
53. *Barefoot v.* Estelle, 463 U.S. 880, 901 (1983).

CHAPTER 3, DAVID BERKOWITZ
1. George Carpozi, Jr., *Son of Sam: The .44 Caliber Killer* (New York: Manor Books, 1977), 45.
2. Ibid., 48.
3. Ibid., 67.
4. Ibid., 90.
5. Ibid., 103–105.
6. Ibid., 121.
7. Ibid.
8. Ibid., 122.
9. Lawrence D. Klausner, *Son of Sam* (New York: McGraw-Hill, 1981), 140.
10. Carpozi, *Son of Sam,* 122.
11. Ibid.
12. Klausner, *Son of Sam,* 160.
13. Ibid.
14. Carpozi, *Son of Sam,* 134.
15. See Charles Patrick Ewing and Joseph T. McCann, *Minds on Trial* (New York: Oxford University Press, 2006).

NOTES TO CHAPTER 3

16. Klausner, *Son of Sam*, 150.
17. Ibid., 151.
18. Ibid., 172.
19. Ibid., 176.
20. Ibid.
21. Ibid., 177.
22. Carpozi, *Son of Sam*, 160.
23. Klausner, *Son of Sam*, 180.
24. Ibid., 181.
25. Carpozi, *Son of Sam*, 296.
26. Howard Blum, "Re-examination of Berkowitz Files Offers New Insights," *New York Times*, May 17, 1978, B1.
27. Ibid., B4.
28. Ibid.
29. Ibid.
30. Ibid.
31. Carpozi, *Son of Sam*, 297.
32. Ibid.
33. Ibid.
34. Klausner, *Son of Sam*, 373.
35. Marcia Chambers, "Berkowitz Termed 'Aware' but 'Emotionally Dead,'" *New York Times*, September 2, 1977, A1.
36. Max H. Siegel, "Berkowitz Asserts Demons Ruled Him," *New York Times*, October 21, 1977, 16.
37. Max H. Siegel, "Berkowitz Is Ruled Fit for Trial; Declares He'll Have a Lot to Say," *New York Times*, October 22, 1977, 1.
38. Ibid.
39. Ibid.
40. Klausner, *Son of Sam*, 374.
41. Max H. Siegel, "Berkowitz Is Ruled Fit for Trial," 1.
42. Joseph C. Fisher, *Killer Among Us* (New York: Praeger Publishers, 1997), 113–114.
43. Ibid.
44. Anna Quindlen, "Appeal on Berkowitz Planned by Lawyers," *New York Times*, May 10, 1978, A28.
45. Max H. Siegel, "Berkowitz Is Judged Competent; A Murder Trial Is Set for May 8," *New York Times*, April 25, 1978, 77.
46. Ibid.
47. "Son of Sam Pleads Guilty in Killings; Admits Starting 2,000 Fires in N.Y.," *Globe and Mail*, May 9, 1978, 1.
48. Lee Lescaze, "Berkowitz Pleads Guilty In 'Son of Sam' Murders," *Washington Post*, May 9, 1978, A1.
49. Ibid.
50. Ibid.
51. Ibid.

52. Max H. Siegel, "Berkowitz Outbursts Disrupt Court; Sentencing Put Off, Tests Ordered; Berkowitz Outbursts Delay His Sentencing," *New York Times*, May 23, 1978, A1.
53. Lee Lescaze, "Berkowitz Given Maximum 25-Years-to-Life Sentences; Berkowitz Given Maximum Sentences in 6 'Son of Sam' Murders," *Washington Post*, June 13, 1978, A1.
54. *Ibid.*
55. *Ibid.*
56. Max H. Siegel, "Upstate Judge Orders Berkowitz Committed to Psychiatric Center; 'Off the Wall,'" *New York Times*, July 7, 1978, A8.
57. *Ibid.*
58. *Ibid.*
59. Jerrold Footlick, "Insanity on Trial," *Newsweek*, May 8, 1978, 108.
60. David Abrahamsen, *Confessions of Son of Sam* (New York Columbia University Press, 1985), 156–157.
61. Frederick U. Dicker, "'Sam' Gets it Write: Killer's Parole Nixed—As He Asked in Letter to Gov," *New York Post*, July 10, 2002, 3.

CHAPTER 4, JOHN WAYNE GACY

1. Terry Sullivan, *Killer Clown: The John Wayne Gacy Murders* (New York: Pinnacle, 1983), 271.
2. Tim Cahill, *Buried Dreams* (New York: Bantam Books, 1986), 88.
3. Sullivan, *Killer Clown*, 271–272.
4. Clifford L. Linedecker, *The Man Who Killed Boys* (New York: St. Martin's Press, 1980), 37.
5. *Ibid.*
6. *Ibid.*, 40.
7. Sullivan, *Killer Clown*, 276.
8. Rachael Bell and Marilyn Bardsley, "John Wayne Gacy," http://www.crimelibrary.com/serial_killers/ notorious/gacy/gacy_1.html (accessed August 25, 2007).
9. See *People v. Gacy*, 468 N.E.2d 1171, 1193 (Ill., 1984).
10. *Ibid.* at 1191.
11. Cahill, *Buried Dreams*, 351.
12. *Ibid.*, 353.
13. Sullivan, *Killer Clown*, 330.
14. *Ibid.* at 329.
15. *Ibid.*
16. See *People v. Gacy*, 468 N.E.2d 1171, 1193 (Ill., 1984).
17. Cahill, *Buried Dreams*, 324–329.
18. *Ibid.*, 327.
19. *Ibid.*, 325.
20. *Ibid.*, 328.
21. *Ibid.*, 330.

22. *People v. Gacy*, 468 N.E.2d 1171, 1194 (Ill. 1984).
23. Sullivan, *Killer Clown*, 336–337.
24. Tim Cahill, *Buried Dreams*, 341.
25. *Ibid.*
26. *Ibid.*, 334.
27. *Ibid.*
28. *Ibid.*
29. *Ibid.*, 334–335.
30. *Ibid.*, 336.
31. *Ibid.*, 340.
32. Sullivan, *Killer Clown*, 343.
33 *Ibid.*
34. *Ibid.*, 344.
35. *Ibid.*
36. *Ibid.*, 345.
37. Cahill, *Buried Dreams*, 355.
38. *Ibid.*
39. *Ibid.*
40. *Ibid.*
41. *Ibid.*
42. *Ibid.*
43. Sullivan, *Killer Clown*, 348.
44. *People v. Gacy*, 468 N.E.2d 1171, 1205 (Ill., 1984).
45. *Ibid.*
46. Sullivan, *Killer Clown*, 348.
47. *Ibid.*
48. *Ibid.*, 349.
49. *Ibid.*
50. *People v. Gacy*, 468 N.E.2d 1171, 1198 (Ill., 1984).
51. *Ibid.*
52. Sullivan, *Killer Clown*, 352.
53. *People v. Gacy*, 468 N.E.2d 1171, 1199 (Ill., 1984).
54. Sullivan, *Killer Clown*, 354.
55. *Ibid.*
56. Sullivan, *Killer Clown*, 356.
57. *Ibid.*

CHAPTER 5, ARTHUR SHAWCROSS
1. Jack Olsen, *The Misbegotten Son* (New York: Island Books, 1993), 214.
2. *Ibid.*, 79.
3. *Ibid.*, 106.
4. N.Y. Penal Law § 125.20 (2).
5. *Ibid.*
6. Olsen, *Misbegotten Son*, 151.

7. *Ibid.*, 171.
8. *Ibid.*, 227.
9. *Ibid.*, 232.
10. *Ibid.*, 283–284.
11. Christopher Berry-Dee, *Talking With Serial Killers* (London: Blake Publishing, 2003), 75.
12. Transcribed Statement of Arthur J. Shawcross, January 4, 1980.
13. *Ibid.*
14. Olsen, *Misbegotten Son*, 505–506.
15. *Ibid.*, 530.
16. *Ibid.*, 531.
17. *Ibid.*, 513.
18. Trial transcript, *People v. Arthur Shawcross* (Monroe County Court, 1990, Ind. No. 90–0058), 5005, 5032. See also 4244–4247, 4810, 5101, 5135–5136.
19. *Ibid.*, 4244.
20. *Ibid.*, 5264.
21. *Ibid.*, 4021–4022.
22. Dorothy Otnow Lewis, *Guilty by Reason of Insanity* (New York: Ivy Books, 1998), 272.
23. *Ibid.* at 275–279.
24. Trial transcript, *People v. Arthur Shawcross* (Monroe County Court, 1990, Ind. No. 90–0058), 5404.
25. *Ibid.*, 4903.
26. *Ibid.*
27. *Ibid.*, 3925.
28. *Ibid.*
29. *Ibid.* at 5116.
30. *Ibid.*
31. *Ibid.*, 5253.
32. *Ibid.*, 5262.
33. *Ibid.*, 4689.
34. *Ibid.*, 5634.
35. *Ibid.*, 5636–5637.
36. *Ibid.*, 5638.
37. *Ibid.*
38. *Ibid.*, 5642.
39. *Ibid.*, 5644.
40. *Ibid.*, 5645–5647.
41. William Glaberson, "Defense Witness Assails Lawyers in Rochester Serial Murder Case," *New York Times*, December 15, 1990, 29.
42. Lewis, *Guilty by Reason of Insanity*, 280–281.
43. Associated Press, "Lawyers Seek Reversal," *Syracuse Post-Standard*, January 11, 1991, B1.
44. Affidavit of David A. Murante and Thomas J. Cocuzzi in Support of Motion, *People v. Arthur Shawcross*, January 9, 1991, 2.

NOTES TO CHAPTER 6

45. Associated Press, "Lawyers Seek Reversal," B1.
46. *Ibid.*
47. *People v. Shawcross,* 596 N.Y.S. 2d 622, 624 (1993).

CHAPTER 6, SCOTT PANETTI

1. Amnesty International, "'Where Is the Compassion?' The imminent execution of Scott Panetti, mentally ill offender," http://web.amnesty.org/library/Index/ENGAMR510112004 (accessed September 8, 2007), 4.
2. *Ibid.*
3. Meg Kissinger, "Madness, Murder and Shattered Lives," *Milwaukee Journal Sentinel* November 28, 1999), 1.
4. *Ibid.*
5. Initial Brief of Appellee-Respondent, *Panetti v. Quarterman,* Supreme Court of the United States (No. 06–6407), 2.
6. See Texas Criminal Procedure Article, 46.02 § 1(a).
7. *Panetti v. State of Texas,* unpublished decision, Fourth Court of Appeals, December 3, 1997 (No. 72,230), 23.
8. *Ibid.*
9. *Faretta v. California,* 422 U.S. 806, 819 (1975).
10. *Ibid.,* 834.
11. *Godinez v. Moran,* 509 U.S. 389, 399 (1993).
12. Kissinger, "Madness, Murder and Shattered Lives"; Ingrid Norton, "Victims Await Final Verdict in Decades Old Baylor U.-area Murder Case," *Daily Texan* via University Wire, April 17, 2007, http://www.highbeam.com/doc/1P1–137919674.html (accessed November 9, 2007).
13. Initial Brief for the Appellant-Petitioner, *Panetti v. Quarterman,* Supreme Court of the United States (No. 06–6407), 12; See also The Justice Project, "Scott Panetti Fact Sheet," http://www.thejusticeproject.org/press/releases/Panetti_Fact_sheet.pdf (accessed September 8, 2007).
14. *Ibid.*
15. *Panetti v. State of Texas,* unpublished decision, Fourth Court of Appeals, December 3, 1997 (No. 72,230), 32.
16. *Ibid.* at 8.
17. Amnesty International, "Where Is the Compassion?," 5.
18. *Ibid.*
19. *Ibid.*
20. Charles Patrick Ewing, "'Dr. Death' and the Case for an Ethical Ban on Psychiatric and Psychological Predictions of Dangerousness in Capital Sentencing Proceedings," *American Journal of Law and Medicine* 8, no. 4, 1983, 407.
21. Pat Gillespie, "James Grigson: Expert Psychiatric Witness Was Nicknamed Dr. Death," *Dallas Morning News,* June 14, 2004, 6B.
22. Texas Defender Service, "Scott Panetti Fact Sheet," http://www.texasdefender.org/panettifactsheet.asp (accessed September 9, 2007).
23. Amnesty International, "Where Is the Compassion?," 10–11.

24. *Ibid.*, 12.
25. *Ibid.*, 13.
26. *Ibid.*
27. *Panetti v. State of Texas,* unpublished decision, Fourth Court of Appeals, December 3, 1997 (No. 72,230), 27.
28. *Panetti v. Dretke,* 2004 U.S. Dist. LEXIS 27684 (January 30, 2004), 2.
29. Letter from Mark Cunningham, Ph.D., ABPP, to Michael C. Gross, Esq., February 3, 2004.
30. *Ford v. Wainwright,* 477 U.S. 399, 403–404 (1986).
31. *Ibid.*, 410.
32. *Ibid.*, 422.
33. *Ibid.*, 426–427.
34. *Panetti v. Dretke,* 401 F. Supp. 2d 702, 705 (2004).
35. Transcript, *Panetti v. Dretke,* U.S. District Court for the Western District of Texas (September 7, 2004), 32.
36. *Ibid.*, 89–90.
37. *Ibid.*, 109.
38. *Ibid.*, 109–110.
39. *Ibid.*, 110.
40. Transcript, *Panetti v. Dretke,* 69.
41. *Ibid.*, 70.
42. *Ibid.*, 69.
43. Transcript, *Panetti v. Dretke,* 167–168.
44. *Ibid.*, 137.
45. *Ibid.*, 139–140.
46. *Ibid.*, 149–150.
47. Transcript, *Panetti v. Dretke,* 23.
48. *Ibid.*, 30–31.
49. *Ford v. Wainwright,* 477 U.S. 399, 422 (1986).
50. *Panetti v. Quarterman,* 127 S. Ct. 2842, 2863 (2007).
51. *Ibid.*, 2860–2861.
52. *Ibid.*, 2861.
53. *Ibid.*, 2862.
54. *Ibid.*

CHAPTER 7, ERIC SMITH

1. Janice Bullard, "Police: Boy Lured to Death," *Rochester Times-Union,* August 19, 1993, 1A.
2. *Ibid.*
3. Steve Mills and Janice Bullard, "Teen's Arrest in Tot's Death Jolts Savona," *Rochester Democrat and Chronicle,* August 10, 1993, 1A.
4. Brief for Defendant-Appellant, *People v. Eric Smith* (N.Y.S. Appellate Division, Fourth Department, June 12, 1995), 3.
5. *Ibid.*, 4.

6. *Ibid.*
7. Meredith Vieira and Forrest Sawyer, "Eric Smith: Inside the Mind of a Child Killer," *ABC News Saturday Night*, transcript # 98070901-j18, July 9, 1998.
8. *Ibid.*
9. *Ibid.*
10. Brief for Defendant-Appellant, *People v. Eric Smith*, 5.
11. CBS News, "Why Did Eric Kill?," *48 Hours Mystery*, July 2, 2005.
12. Vieira and Sawyer, "Eric Smith: Inside the Mind of a Child Killer."
13. Brief for Defendant-Appellant, *People v. Eric Smith*, 6.
14. Signed Statement of Eric Smith, August 9, 1993 (Appendix A, Brief for Respondent, *People v. Eric Smith*, N.Y.S. Appellate Division, Fourth Department, September 7, 1995).
15. N.Y. Penal Law § 30.00 (2); see also N.Y. Penal Law § 60.10 and § 70.05.
16. Brief for Defendant-Appellant, *People v. Eric Smith*, 75.
17. "Eric Smith: Inside the Mind of a Child Killer," *ABC News Turning Point*, transcript # 97081401-j09, August 14, 1997.
18. Jeffrey Blackwell, "Stiff Penalty Urged for Young Killers," *Rochester Democrat and Chronicle*, May 24, 2002, 1B.
19. CBS News, "Why Did Eric Kill?"
20. *Ibid.*
21. CBS News, "Why Did Eric Kill?"
22. N.Y. Penal Law § 40.15.
23. N.Y. Penal Law § 125.25(1)(a).
24. Brief for Defendant-Appellant, *People v. Eric Smith*, 12.
25. See, e.g., Justice and Kraft, "Early Warning Signs of Violence: Is a Triad Enough?" *American Journal of Psychiatry* 131, no. 4, 1974, 457.
26. Vieira and Sawyer, "Eric Smith: Inside the Mind of a Child Killer."
27. *Ibid.*
28. Brief for Defendant-Appellant, *People v. Eric Smith*, 12–13.
29. CBS News, "Why Did Eric Kill?"
30. "Eric Smith: Inside the Mind of a Child Killer," *ABC News Turning Point*.
31. CBS News, "Why Did Eric Kill?"
32. Brief for Respondent, *People v. Eric Smith* (N.Y.S. Appellate Division, Fourth Department, September 7, 1995), 49.
33. CBS News, "Why Did Eric Kill?"
34. ABC News, *Turning Point*, Transcript # 143, December 14, 1994.
35. *Ibid.*
36. Brief for Defendant-Appellant, *People v. Eric Smith*, 14–15.
37. American Psychiatric Association, *Diagnostic and Statistical Manual of Mental Disorders, Fourth Edition* (Washington, DC: American Psychiatric Association, 1994), 612.
38. Brief for Defendant-Appellant, *People v. Eric Smith*, 14.
39. *People v. Smith*, 217 N.Y.S. 2d 824, 834 (1995).
40. Brief for Respondent, *People v. Eric Smith*, 42.
41. *Ibid.*, 50.

42. Brief for Defendant-Appellant, *People v. Eric Smith*, 20.
43. *Ibid.*, 20.
44. *Ibid.*
45. *Ibid.*
46. *Ibid.*
47. *Ibid.*
48. CBS News, "Why Did Eric Kill?"
49. Brief for Defendant-Appellant, *People v. Eric Smith*, 18.
50. *Ibid.*, 19.
51. *Ibid.*
52. *Ibid.*, 22–23.
53. Brief for Respondent, *People v. Eric Smith*, 51.
54. Brief for Defendant-Appellant, *People v. Eric Smith*, 54.
55. *Ibid.*, 55.
56. *Ibid.*, 54.
57. *Ibid.*, 25.
58. Brief for Respondent, *People v. Eric Smith*, 54.
59. Brief for Defendant-Appellant, *People v. Eric Smith*, 23.
60. *Ibid.*, 25.
61. Shirley Salemy, "Jury 'Didn't Feel He Had a Disease,'" *Rochester Democrat and Chronicle*, September 17, 1994, 1.
62. *Ibid.*
63. *People v. Smith*, 217 N.Y.S. 2d 824, 832 (1995).
64. *Ibid.*
65. Larry Wilson, "Eric Smith Denied Parole," *Elmira Star Gazette*, June 10, 2004, 1A.
66. Larry Wilson, "'I Have Remorse,' Eric Smith Says," *Elmira Star Gazette*, July 2, 2006, 1C.

CHAPTER 8, ANDREW GOLDSTEIN

1. Brief for Defendant-Appellant, *People v. Andrew Goldstein* (N.Y.S. Appellate Division, First Department, April 29, 2004), 26.
2. *Ibid.*
3. *Ibid.*
4. *Ibid.*, 27.
5. *Ibid.*, 28–29.
6. *Ibid.*, 29.
7. *Ibid.*
8. *Ibid.*
9. *Ibid.*, 30.
10. *Ibid.*, 17.
11. *Ibid.*, 18.
12. *Ibid.*
13. *Ibid.*
14. *Ibid.*

15. *Ibid.*, 22–23.
16. *Ibid.*, 23–24.
17. Patricia Hurtado, "A Descent Into Schizophrenia: Doc Describes Man's Illness in Subway Killing," *Newsday,* October 19, 1999, A31.
18. Laura Italiano, "Schizophrenia Splits Subway-Push Jury," *New York Post,* November 1, 1999, 18.
19. Barbara Ross, "Doc Tells of Suspect's Dark Past," *New York Daily News,* October 19, 1999, 32.
20. David Rohde, "Defense Rests Murder Case With a Video Confession," *New York Times,* October 22, 1999, B3.
21. Ellis Henican, "Case of Insanity in the Courtroom," *Newsday,* October 27, 1999, A8.
22. Laura Italiano, "Shrink: Sexy Victim Too Much for Subway-Push Fiend," *New York Post,* October 27, 1999, 22.
23. *Ibid.*
24. Ellis Henican, "Case of Insanity in the Courtroom," *Newsday,* October 27, 1999, A8.
25. *Ibid.*
26. *Ibid.*
27. David Rohde, "Expert Disputes Schizophrenia Defense," *New York Times,* October 23, 1999, B3.
28. *Ibid.*
29. *Ibid.*
30. Brief for Defendant-Appellant, *People v. Andrew Goldstein,* 14.
31. *People v. Goldstein,* 810 NYS 100, 102 (2005).
32. Brief for Defendant-Appellant, *People v. Andrew Goldstein,* 14.
33. *Ibid.*, 33.
34. *Ibid.*, 14.
35. *Ibid.*, 37–38.
36. David L. Shapiro, "Insanity and Assessment of Criminal Responsibility," in Charles Patrick Ewing (Ed.), *Psychology, Psychiatry and the Law: A Clinical and Forensic Handbook* (Sarasota FL: Professional Resource Press, 1985), 75.
37. *People v. Goldstein,* 810 NYS 100, 102–103 (2005).
38. *Crawford v. Washington,* 541 U.S. 36 (2004).
39. People v. Goldstein, 786 N.Y.S. 2d 428, 432 (2004).
40. *People v. Goldstein,* 810 NYS 100, 129 (2005).

CHAPTER 9, ERIC MICHAEL CLARK

1. Respondent's Brief on the Merits, *Clark v. Arizona,* March 6, 2006, Supreme Court of the United States (No. 05–5966), 3.
2. *Ibid.*, 4.
3. *Ibid.*
4. *Ibid.*
5. *Ibid.*

6. Ibid.
7. Ibid., 5.
8. Ibid.
9. Petitioner's Opening Brief, *Clark v. Arizona*, February 2, 2006, Supreme Court of the United States (No. 05–5966), 8.
10. Arizona Revised Statutes § 13–502.
11. Respondent's Brief on the Merits, *Clark v. Arizona*, 3.
12. Ibid.
13. Ibid.
14. Ibid.
15. Joint Appendix, v. I, Petition for Certiorari, filed August 17, 2005, *Clark v. Arizona*, Supreme Court of the United States (No. 05–5966), 14–15.
16. Ibid., 17.
17. Ibid.
18. Ibid.
19. Ibid., 38–39.
20. Joint Appendix, v. II, Petition for Certiorari, filed August 17, 2005, *Clark v. Arizona*, Supreme Court of the United States (No. 05–5966), 158.
21. Ibid.
22. Ibid., 223.
23. Ibid., 168.
24. Ibid., 173.
25. Ibid., 175.
26. Ibid., 178.
27. Brief *Amicus Curiae* for the American Psychiatric Association, American Psychological Association, and American Academy of Psychiatry and the Law, *Clark v. Arizona*, January 30, 2006, Supreme Court of the United States (No. 05–5966), 4.
28. Ibid.
29. *Arizona v. Clark*, unpublished memorandum decision, Arizona Court of Appeals, January 15, 2005, 12.
30. Ibid., 12–13.
31. Ibid., 13–14.
32. Ibid., 15–16.
33. Ibid., 16.
34. Ibid., 19.
35. Ibid.
36. *Clark v. Arizona*, 126 S. Ct. 2709, 2719 (2006).
37. Ibid., 2709.
38. Ibid.
39. Ibid., 2722.
40. Ibid.
41. Ibid., 2723.
42. Ibid., 2718.
43. Ibid., 2731.

NOTES TO CHAPTER 10

44. *Ibid.*
45. *Ibid.*
46. *Ibid.*, 2731–32.
47. *Ibid.*, 2734.
48. *Ibid.*
49. *Ibid.*, 2735.
50. *Ibid.*

CHAPTER 10, ANDREA YATES

1. Discharge Summary re Andrea Yates, June 24, 1999, http://www.courttv.com/trials/yates/docs/discharge1.html?page = 12 (accessed August 27, 2007).
2. *Ibid.*
3. See Charles Patrick Ewing, *Fatal Families: The Dynamics of Intrafamilial Homicide* (Thousand Oaks CA: Sage Publications, 1997), 61–62.
4. American Psychiatric Association, *Diagnostic and Statistical Manual of Mental Disorder, Fourth Edition* (Washington DC: American Psychiatric Association, 1994), 386.
5. Psychiatric Assessment re Andrea Yates, July 21,1999 http://www.courttv.com/trials/yates/docs/psychiatric1.html?page = 6 (accessed August 27, 2007).
6. American Psychiatric Association, *Diagnostic and Statistical Manual of Mental Disorder, Fourth Edition.*
7. "Release of Yates' Records a Legal Maneuver; Medical History Could Aid Either Side of Case," *Houston Chronicle*, September 2, 2001, A37.
8. Lee Hancock, "Yates Long Had Visions of Violence; Medical Records Outline Mother's Mental Decline; Troubles Started After the Birth of the First of Her Five Children," *Dallas Morning News*, September 2, 2001, 1A.
9. Report of Park E. Dietz, M.D. re *State of Texas v. Andrea Pia Yates*, February 25, 2002, http://parkdietzassociates.com/files/Report_of_Dr._Park_Dietz_re._Andrea_Yates__2002.pdf (accessed on August 30, 2007), 38.
10. *Ibid.*, 42.
11. *Ibid.*
12. CNN, "911 Tape Reveals Unemotional Andrea Yates," January 6, 2002, http://archives.cnn.com/2001/US/12/10/yates.911/ (accessed on August 30, 2007).
13. "Killing Justice?" *The Irish Times*, January 30, 2002, 13.
14. *Ibid.*
15. Transcript of Andrea Yates' confession, February 21, 2002, http://www.chron.com/disp/story.mpl/special/drownings/1266294.html (accessed August 30, 2007).
16. Kris Axtman, "Growing Introspection in Death-Penalty Capital," *Christian Science Monitor*, November 16, 2004, 2.
17. Cindy Horswell, "Hopefuls Clash on Approach to Office; Incumbent Says Challenger Lacks Experience and in Turn Is Called an 'Embarrassment,'" *Houston Chronicle*, October 25, 2004, B1.
18. See *Witherspoon v. Illinois*, 391 U.S. 510 (1968); *Lockhart v. McCree*, 476 U.S. 162 (1986); and *Wainwright v. Witt*, 469 U.S. 412 (1985).

19. Mike Allen, Edward Mabry, and Drue-Marie McKelton, "Impact of Juror Attitudes about the Death Penalty on Juror Evaluations of Guilt and Punishment: A Meta-analysis," *Law and Human Behavior* 22, no. 6, 1998, 715.
20. Michelle McCalope, "Doctor: Texas Mother Saw 'Satan'; Hearing Held for Woman Charged in Children's Drowning," *Washington Post,* September 20, 2001, A28.
21. Ibid.
22. Ibid.
23. Ibid.
24. Bruce Nichols, "Expert Says Yates Ill but Fit for Trial; Psychiatrist for the Prosecution Contradicts Defense Witness," *Dallas Morning News,* September 21, 2001, 35A.
25. Lisa Teachey, "Expert: Yates Contemplated Killing Children for Months," *Houston Chronicle,* September 21, 2001, A1.
26. Pam Easton, "Mom to Stand Trial in Kids' Killings," *Newark Star-Ledger,* September 23, 2001, 55.
27. Ibid.
28. Ibid.
29. Ibid.
30. Texas Penal Code Ann. § 8.01.
31. Anne Belli Gesalman, "A Dark State of Mind," *Newsweek,* March 4, 2002, 32.
32. "Psychiatrist: Yates Thought She Was Saving Kids," *New York Newsday,* March 6, 2002, A15.
33. Suzanne O'Malley, "Death Waits at Home; 'Hurry,' He Told His Mother. 'Something's Wrong at the House,'" *Toronto Sun,* March 7, 2004, 30.
34. "Psychiatrist: Yates Thought She Was Saving Kids," *New York Newsday,* March 6, 2002, A15.
35. Steven Long and Brad Hunter, "Killer Mom Drowned Kids to 'Save' Them from Satan," *New York Post,* March 6, 2002, 21.
36. "Jury Views Psychiatrist Interview of Yates in Jail," *Los Angeles Times,* March 2, 2002, 20.
37. Trial transcript, testimony of Park Dietz, *State of Texas v. Andrea Pia Yates,* March 7, 2002, 117–118.
38. Ibid., 86.
39. Ibid., 139.
40. *Yates v. State of Texas,* 171 S.W.3d 215, 218 (2005).
41. Ibid., 219.
42. Ibid.
43. Ibid.
44. Ibid., 216.
45. Ibid., 222.
46. Ibid.

EPILOGUE

1. Richard Rogers, Ph.D., personal communication, September 10, 2007.
2. Ibid.

3. Ellis Henican, "Case of Insanity in the Courtroom," *Newsday*, October 27, 1999, A8.
4. *Yates v. State of Texas*, 171 S.W.3d 215, 218 (2005).
5. Joseph C. Fisher, *Killer Among Us* (New York: Praeger Publishers, 1997), 113–114.
6. *Ibid*.
7. Tim Cahill, *Buried Dreams* (New York: Bantam Books, 1986), 334.
8. *Ibid*.
9. *Ibid.*, 340.
10. *Ibid*.
11. John Mark Dempsey, *The Jack Ruby Trial Revisited: The Diary of Jury Foreman Max Causey* (Denton TX: University of North Texas Press), 172–173.
12. Joseph C. Fisher, *Killer Among Us*, 113–114.

INDEX

Abrahamsen, David
   report on David Berkowitz, 45–46
Alexander, Bill
   prosecutor of Jack Ruby, 10, 15
American Law Institute
   insanity standard, xviii–xix, xx–xxi
Anderson, Mary
   testimony of, in *Panetti v. Dretke*, 96–97

Bailey, F. Lee
   attorney for George Fitzsimmons, xiii–xiv
Barry, David
   report on Arthur Shawcross by, 70
Belli, Melvin
   assessment of Jack Ruby by, 7–10
   hired as Jack Ruby's attorney, 7
Berkowitz, David
   background of, 42–43
   crimes of, 3–39, 41–42
   guilty plea entered by, 47–48
   psychological and psychiatric evaluations of, 45–46
   sentencing of, 48
   see also "Son of Sam"
Brocher, Tobias
   testimony of, in *People v. Gacy*, 62
Bromberg, Walter
   report on Jack Ruby by, 8
   testimony of, in *State v. Jack Ruby*, 16

Causey, Max
   jury foreman in *State v. Jack Ruby*, 17–19
Cavanaugh, James
   testimony of, in *People v. John Wayne Gacy*, 61–62
Clark, Eric Michael
   appeals, 135–140
   background of, 128–129
   capacity to form mens rea, 130, 136–140
   competence to stand trial, 130
   conviction, 135
   crime, 129–130
   sentencing of, 135
Clark, Frank J., xv
Competency for execution
   see Ford v. Wainwright
Conroy, Mary Alice
   testimony of, in *Panetti v. Dretke*, 91–93
Cormack, Peter
   report on Eric Smith by, 106
Crawford v. Washington, 124–126
Cunningham, Mark
   report on Scott Panetti by, 91–92
   testimony of, in *Panetti v. Dretke*, 94

Dietz, Park E.
   false testimony as grounds for new trial in *State v. Andrea Yates*, 158, 163
   testimony of, in *People v. Arthur Shawcross*, 75–78
   testimony of, in *State v. Andrea Yates*, 155–156

Elisio, Thomas
   testimony of, in *People v. John Wayne Gacy*, 57–58
Eth, Spencer
   testimony of, in *People v. Andrew Goldstein*, 118, 121
Extreme emotional disturbance defense, 66, 103

Fawcett, Jan
   testimony of, in *People v. John Wayne Gacy*, 63
Federal Insanity Defense Reform Act, xix–xxi
Federal Rule of Evidence 704, xx, xxii
Fitzsimmons, George, xi–xvi
Flechner, Robert
   juror in *State v. Jack Ruby*, 20
Ford v. Wainwright, 92–93

INDEX

Freedman, Lawrence Z.
　testimony of, in *People v. John Wayne Gacy*, 58

Gacy, John Wayne
　background of, 51
　conviction, 63
　crimes, 51–52, 55–57
　execution of, 63
　intelligence, 52
　psychological and psychiatric evaluations of, 58–63
　sentencing, 63
Gaughan, Charles
　judge in *People v. George Fitzsimmons*, xi–xii
Gibbs, Frederic
　testimony of, in *State v. Jack Ruby*, 16–17
Goldstein, Andrew
　appeals, 125–126
　background of, 114–115
　confession, 116–117
　conviction, 124
　crime, 116
　plea bargain, 127
　sentencing, 124, 127
　see also Crawford v. Washington
Grigson, James P.
　testimony of, in *State v. Scott Panetti*, 89, 91
Guttmacher, Manfred
　report on Jack Ruby by, 8
　testimony of, in *State v. Jack Ruby*, 12–14

Harris, Gerald
　testimony of, in *State v. Andrea Yates*, 152–153
Hartman, Arthur
　testimony of, in *People v. John Wayne Gacy*, 60
Hegarty, Angela
　testimony of, in *People v. Andrew Goldstein*, 119, 121–124
Herman, Stephen
　report on Eric Smith by, 106–107
　testimony of, in *People v. Eric Smith*, 109–111
Heston, Leonard
　testimony of, in *People v. John Wayne Gacy*, 60
Hinckley, John W. Jr., xix
Holbrook, John
　testimony of, in *State v. Jack Ruby*, 15

Holton, J. G.
　juror in *State v. Jack Ruby*, 20
Howard, Tom
　first attorney for Jack Ruby, 6–7, 20–21

Insanity defense
　burden of proof, xx
　practical effect of, xxii–xxiii
　state laws summarized, xx
　tests of
　　see American Law Institute
　　see Federal Insanity Defense Reform Act
　　see M'Naghten rule
　　see Irresistible impulse standard
　　see Product test
Irresistible impulse standard, xviii

Kelleway, Pere
　testimony of, in *State v. Jack Ruby*, 15
Kraus, Richard
　report on Arthur Shawcross by, 69–70

Lewis, Dorothy
　report on Arthur Shawcross by, 70–73
　testimony in *People v. Shawcross*, 70–73

Model Penal Code
　see American Law Institute
M'Naghten rule, xiv, xviii, xx–xxi, 9, 11, 103, 118, 136–138, 154
Moran, John
　testimony of, in *State v. Eric Clark*, 133–135
Morenz, Barry
　testimony of, in *State v. Eric Clark*, 131–133
Morrison, Helen
　testimony of, in *People v. John Wayne Gacy*, 62–63

Nevins, Joseph
　judge in *People v. George Fitzsimmons*, xii
Nuchereno, John R., xv

Olinger, Shef
　testimony of, in *State v. Jack Ruby*, 14
Oswald, Lee Harvey, 5–6

Panetti, Scott
　background of, 81–82
　competence for execution, 90–98
　competence to stand trial, 83–84

186

conviction, 88
crime, 82–83
self-representation, 84–88
sentencing, 89
Parker, George,
testimony of, in *Panetti v. Dretke*, 94–95
Product test, xviii, xx

Quinn, Kathleen
report on Eric Smith by, 108
testimony of, in *People v. Eric Smith*, 111–112

Ramsay, John
testimony of, in *State v. Scott Panetti*, 87
Rappaport, Richard
testimony of, in *People v. John Wayne Gacy*, 59–60
Reifman, Robert
testimony of, in *People v. John Wayne Gacy*, 59–60
Resnick, Phillip
testimony of, in *State v. Andrea Yates*, 155
Rogers, Richard
quoted regarding John Wayne Gacy, 162
testimony of, in *People v. John Wayne Gacy*, 61
Rosin, Susana
testimony of, in *Panetti v. Dretke*, 93
Roy, Joy B.
report on Robert Torsney by, 26–27
testimony of, in *State v. Robert Torsney*, 28
Rubenstein, Jacob
see Ruby, Jack
Rubenzer, Steven
testimony of, in *State v. Andrea Yates*, 153
Ruby, Jack
appeal, 21
background of, 3–5
conviction, 17
death sentence, 17
psychological testing, 10–11

Schumer, Florence
report on Robert Torsney by, 27
Schwab, Robert
testimony of, in *State v. Jack Ruby*, 16
Schwartz, Daniel
report on David Berkowitz by, 44–45
report on Robert Torsney by, 25–26
testimony of, in *People v. David Berkowitz*, 46

testimony of, in *People v. Robert Torsney*, 28
Seale, F. E.
testimony of, in *State v. Scott Panetti*, 87
Selck, Wolfgang
testimony in *State v. Scott Panetti*, 87
Shafer, Roy,
report on Jack Ruby by, 7–8
testimony of, in *State v. Jack Ruby*, 10–11
Shawcross, Arthur
appeal, 80
confession, 68
conviction, 79
crimes, 64–65, 67
psychological and psychiatric evaluations of, 69–78
sentencing, 79
Siegel, Herbert
attorney for George Fitzsimmons, xiii–xiv
Silverman, Seth
testimony of, in *Panetti v. Dretke*, 93–94
Smith, Eric
appeal, 112–113
background of, 104–105
confession, 101–102
conviction, 112
crime, 99–100
parole denied, 113
sentencing, 112
"Son of Sam"
letter to police from, 38–39
psychological profile of, 39–40, 42
see also Berkowitz, David
Sowell, Douglas
juror in *State v. Ruby*, 19–20
Speigel, Herbert
report on Robert Torsney by, 27–28
testimony of, in *State v. Robert Torsney*, 28
Stubblefield, Robert
testimony of, in *State v. Jack Ruby*, 14–15

Towler, Martin
testimony of, in *State v. Jack Ruby*, 11–12
Torsney, Robert
appeals, 31–33
background of, 22–23
bail, 25
commitment and hospitalization, 29–31
crime, 22–24
insanity acquittal, 29
psychological evaluations of, 26–28

INDEX

Torsney, Robert (*continued*)
    release from commitment and hospitalization, 31–33

Traismen, Robert
    testimony of, in *People v. John Wayne Gacy*, 58–59

Van Gorp, Wilfred
    testimony of, in *People v. Andrew Goldstein*, 118

Wade, Henry,
    prosecutor of Jack Ruby, 10

Walker, Earl
    testimony of, in *State v. Jack Ruby*, 14–15

Waters, Eugene
    testimony of, in *State v. Scott Panetti*, 87

Weidenbacher, Richard
    report on David Berkowitz by, 44–45

Yates, Andrea
    background of, 141–144
    competence to stand trial, 152–153
    confession, 145–151
    conviction, 157
    death-qualification of jurors, 151–152
    insanity acquittal, 159
    police (911) call, 144–145
    sentencing, 158

Printed and bound by CPI Group (UK) Ltd, Croydon, CR0 4YY